Laurence D. Hebb

from his affectionate
and admiring father –
Andrew

Management
by Majority

**The early days of
co-operative insurance
in Ontario**

Andrew O. Hebb

Published by The Co-operators Group Limited

Guelph, Ontario, Canada

1993

Canadian Cataloguing in Publication Data

Hebb, Andrew O. (Andrew Olding), 1905-

Management by majority: the early days of co-operative
insurance in Ontario
Includes Index.
ISBN 0-96 96 804-0-6
1. Insurance, Cooperative—Ontario—History.
2. Co-operators' Fidelity and Guarantee Association—
History. I. Title.
HG8550.Z9C66 1992   334'.683'09713   C93-090026-X

Controversial story of a co-operative insurance beginning
—includes glimpses into the board rooms and minute-books
of four corporate sponsors.

Revised, updated 1993 Edition

Managing Editor: Zahid Qureshi
Editor: Marian D. Hebb
Copy Editor: Bonnie Clarke
Production: Sue Hodgins
Word Processing: Barbara Allen, Barbara Cunningham, Dawn Sibbilin

The Co-operators Group Limited
Priory Square
Guelph, Ontario
Canada N1H 6P8
Telephone (519)824-4400. Telefax (519)824-0599

Printed and bound in Canada.

*Printed on 10% Post Consumer,
50% Recycled, Acid Free paper*

Table of Contents

Management by Majority

The early days of co-operative insurance in Ontario

Foreword

Pooling funds to provide for insurance against adversity is a natural, spontaneous co-operative activity. The Greeks and the Phoenicians insured their ships at sea. Since the days of the Roman empire, groups of people, usually merchants or bankers, have utilized insurance programs. Insurance permitted the accumulation of wealth and the rise of Europe. Fire insurance was born in England after the Great Fire of London in 1666. In the eighteenth and the nineteenth centuries, insurance companies were an essential ingredient of industrialization. It was, in fact, an instinctive, common way to protect one's self from adversity, one that could be adapted by various groups in society, including those with few financial resources as well as those with great wealth — the farmer and the wage-earner as well as the banker and the merchant.

Broadly speaking, there have been two ways to organize insurance companies. The first, and most common, was simply an extension of capitalist forms of ownership and control: companies would be owned by families or, more commonly, by share-owners. Control would lie with a few major investors, and profits would be distributed on the basis of investment. The second method attempted to vest ownership in policy-owners or members; ownership would be widely distributed, control would often be less secure, and profits or surpluses would be

I

distributed on the basis of use. This latter form, with more "mutuality" than the former, was called "mutual" insurance. Sometimes efforts have been made to seek out more explicitly co-operative forms of organization, based on innovative democratic techniques and, most importantly, a close affinity with the established co-operative movement. In Ontario, Co-operators' Fidelity and Guarantee Association (CF&GA), formed in 1946 and transformed to become Co-operators Insurance Association in 1951, was one such attempt.

Although initially an urban credit union project, farmers took CF&GA into livestock transit insurance in 1947 and into automobile insurance in 1949. Canadian farmers had experimented with insurance since the 1830s, and the reasons were clear enough. Farming has always been a hazardous vocation, and farm families have always struggled to find ways to survive a disaster, a bad harvest or even a series of bad years. The need to do so became even more pressing as farm families moved to commercial agriculture, with the resultant dependence on one or two crops or one kind of livestock.

As an economy and to help each other, farmers have embraced their own insurance programs. In the 1940s there were more than 60 farm fire mutuals in Ontario. The idea had crossed the border from the United States in the latter half of the previous century. The United Grain Growers and particularly the Wheat Pools created their own insurance programs during the 1920s, and several of the co-operatives in the fruit and dairying sectors sponsored special insurance programs for their members.

The Grange, a militant farmers' educational organization, open to both men and women, which came into Ontario from the United States in 1874 and petered out in the nineties, sponsored a mutual fire insurance company and a life insurance company. The Dominion Grange Mutual Fire Insurance Company transferred its loyalty to the Patrons of Industry (also originating in the United States), when the Patrons succeeded the Grange in Ontario farmer favor, but went into voluntary liquidation in 1899. A life insurance company founded by the Dominion Grange in 1880 enjoyed some success but went downhill with the Grange and was taken over by a benefit association in Boston, Massachusetts.

Thus, it was not without precedents when, at the end of World War II, the leaders of the Ontario farm movement turned seriously to the idea of creating insurance companies; they were simply continuing an interest that had been evident for over a century. Moreover, as the men and women of the province returned from the armed forces and wartime work to more traditional kinds of economic activity, the pace of rural change picked up momentum. There were pressures on the countryside to absorb more workers and young families; there was an increasing demand for consumer goods, forcing farm families to specialize in fewer crops or in one type of livestock; there were immense financial benefits if farm families could prudently add new tractors and equipment.

At the same time, there was an outburst of agrarian confidence. There had been five continuous years of relative prosperity. Not available since 1941, new passenger cars in limited numbers were offered for sale in 1947. Tractors, milking machines, cold storage facilities, multiple plows and better disc harrows were fast becoming necessities if families were to earn reasonable incomes. Farm kitchens increasingly possessed faucets and the outdoor toilet was disappearing slowly. The modernization of the countryside, a process that had started generations earlier, was proceeding at an unheralded pace.

Institutionally, the symbols of this rapid rural development as the forties opened were the United Farmers' Co-operative and its educational companion, the Ontario Federation of Agriculture (OFA), whose membership included all the province's farmers. Unobtrusively but effectively, H. H. Hannam, by the power of ideas, dominated both organizations. Secretary of the United Farmers' Co-operative Company, he was a former president of the OFA and, as president of the Canadian Federation of Agriculture since 1940, an honorary and voting member of the OFA executive. Hannam's faithful OFA lieutenant was secretary-manager Vivian S. Milburn, a former United Farmers' Co-operative director, who in turn was surrounded by such able advisers as OFA president Alex McKinney, Whole Milk League secretary Roy Lick, OFA hog section assistant secretary Wilfred L. Bishop and OFA executive member Mrs. O. G. Anderson of Wingham. McKinney was followed as president in 1944 by K. M. Betzner and in 1947 by R. A. Stewart - a succession of co-operative and innovative presidents.

Working with Hannam, in his other fief, to reorganize the co-operative company, were W. C. Good, who for many years had held tenaciously to his concept of a central co-operative owned by local co-operatives, and company president R. J. Scott, with other directors supportive. When Hannam moved to Ottawa in 1944, president Scott, company secretary Leonard Harman and company director Ralph Staples carried the reorganization torch. In January 1945 Scott became the first president of the newly organized Ontario Co-operative Union, and newcomer A. C. Savage, first world war veteran and former civil servant, became secretary.

The new generation of leadership had all been hardened by the Depression, and, in diverse ways, they were all in touch with the basic changes sweeping the rural areas. The two organizations maintained good relations with the local rural communities, through a growing number of UCO member co-operatives, county Federations of Agriculture, and increasingly through Farm Radio Forum. Farm Radio Forum, in fact, was a powerful medium for communication and mobilization in the early 1940s and it became an important vehicle for the insurance company. So too did the United Co-operatives of Ontario which became, in 1948, the successor of the United Farmers' Co-operative. This restructuring arguably gave more control to 150 local co-operatives, and was, therefore, more democratic, but above all, it unleashed considerable enthusiasm that made it possible for CF&GA to survive some of its early difficulties.

The study that follows, written with great care by one of the central figures who brought CF&GA to life, examines the formation of the company and its development until it was restructured into Co-operators Insurance Association in 1951. As one reads its pages one can glimpse the kinds of problems that inevitably perplex a new insurance company, especially one that defiantly attempts to find its own ways of doing business. Reviewing such a history can be a salutary exercise, particularly if, for example, one tends to look a little critically at similar efforts within co-operative groups in African or Asian countries today. The problems the organizers of CF&GA faced were not unusual but they were not easily resolved even though they might have been predictable. How to meet the reserve requirements of the Ontario superintendent of insurance? How to devise workable remuneration plans for agents? How to obtain agreement on a novel six-month premium plan? How to co-operate in a sales program with a national co-operative life insurance company? How to retain urban credit union participation when farmers put their strong shoulders to the wheel? These problems were not easily resolved, and they feature prominently in the account that Andrew Hebb has prepared. Perhaps more importantly, though, the major challenge confronting those who developed CF&GA was working out how the new company would reflect co-operative values and adhere to co-operative organizational principles. These were difficult problems because, even though insurance is a naturally attractive business for co-operators and co-operatives, it is not easily adapted to co-operative structures. One of the problems is that, although insurance is important to those who purchase it, it tends to be an annual chore, a cost to be borne but not an activity — such as marketing one's produce or purchasing one's groceries — that elicits much continuing interest from the purchaser. Thus, creating a structure that can be continuously controlled and effectively led by members is difficult. Even the mutual form of organization, while theoretically controlled by individual members, can often in fact become dominated by management groups or handfuls of people who happen to be able to attend annual meetings readily.

One possible solution to this problem within co-operative circles is to invest control with larger co-operatives — consumer, banking, marketing — which often also contribute much of the start-up or sustaining capital. The most complete example of this type of organization was the Co-operative Insurance Society, Manchester, owned by the English Co-operative Wholesale Society and the Scottish Co-operative Wholesale and, in the 1940s, one of the largest insurance companies in Great Britain. The dilemma of these two alternatives — on the one hand, vesting control in only occasionally interested individuals or a management clique or, on the other hand, tying the company to a large co-operative — came on CF&GA as an early-life crisis, demanding quick decision. Implicitly and explicitly, it is what caused much of the discussion and the tension described by Andrew Hebb.

Another essentially co-operative issue that perplexed the company's founders was finding appropriate roles for those who were associated intimately with CF&GA. The issue has several layers. One obvious one was establishing an appropriate role for the board of directors. Some of the directors came from the United Farmers' Co-op/United Co-operatives of Ontario connection; others from the Ontario Federation of Agriculture and the Ontario Credit Union League. In their own *milieux* they were knowledgeable and informed; they were also functioning in an environment where clear and meaningful roles for boards and management had evolved over time. In contrast, the new insurance company was started with direct assistance by directors, while the commissioned and salaried employees were largely learning their tasks on the job. The result was a difficult period — indicated by some of the struggles Hebb describes — as the two stakeholder groups gradually and sometimes painfully learned their appropriate roles.

Another distinct set of co-operative problems emerged from the unique features of the Ontario co-operative movement in the late 1940s. At that time, the provincial movement was dominated by the United Co-operatives of Ontario, a multi-purpose general co-operative different from the specialized grain co-operatives of the West. The all-inclusive Ontario Federation of Agriculture, publisher of the Rural Co-operator, was committed to co-operative education. There was also the more recently organized Ontario Co-operative Union. There was a small but growing credit union movement largely influenced by American precedents and therefore concentrated among employees of sympathetic companies or government departments. This particular mixture of co-operative enthusiasms was unlike any other grouping in the other Canadian provinces, and those differences help to explain some of the attitudes which characterized the company's early leaders.

Following in the footsteps of the leadership of the United Farmers' Co-op and UCO, the leaders of the CF&GA never hesitated to look south for inspiration and models. As Andrew Hebb so carefully documents, many of the leaders of Ontario's co-operatives were deeply impressed by the agrarian/co-operative systems in Indiana and Ohio. They found a similar rural base, congenial socio-political views, and an admirable entrepreneurial spirit. The UCO leaders who played such an important role in the development of CF&GA naturally brought their American influences with them to their new co-operatives, and thus CF&GA owed much to the model of farmer-owned insurance programs in Indiana and Ohio.

While these ties between Canadian and American co-operative leaders were natural and generally beneficial, the associations between Canadian and American credit unionists were far more problematic. The emergence of CF&GA coincided with a nation-wide struggle among some English-Canadian co-operators to create an integrated, national co-operative financial system that would embrace credit unions, insurance companies, and ultimately, a trust company. This project, complex enough in itself, was beset with controversy because it tended to conflict with the accelerating ambitions, the tried formulas, and the business interests of the Credit Union National Association (CUNA) and CUNA Mutual, the driving force behind credit unions in the United States and Canada. Located in Madison, Wisconsin, the CUNA companies had created an integrated operation based largely on closed bond credit unions and cost-effective insurance programs for the members of those credit unions. H. A. Crofford, Regina, president of Co-operative Life, A. B. MacDonald, Ottawa, general secretary, Co-operative Union of Canada, Alex Laidlaw, Antigonish, Nova Scotia, associate director of extension, St. Francis Xavier University, and H. L. Fowler, Regina, secretary of Federated Co-operatives, were the architects of the Canadian co-operative financial system. Unlike the leaders of CUNA in the 1940s and 1950s, they were deeply involved in the broad co-operative movement, particularly agricultural marketing and consumer co-operatives. In fact, they saw the contemplated national financial system as the major source of funds for the entire co-operative movement. They were also strong nationalists and frequently argued vigorously that Canadians should develop their own co-operative structures to meet their own needs. In understanding how national structures could be built, they thought, reflecting many of the national trends of the day, that the best way to organize was through creating as strong as possible national insurance companies. For that reason, they resisted the idea, championed by some in Ontario and other provinces, that the best way to create a national program was through a series of regional other-than-life insurance companies.

The emerging national Canadian financial vision had some of its most complex and debilitating struggles with the established American vision in Ontario. Some of the resultant tensions are evident even in the early days of the province's credit union history, the period covered by Andrew Hebb's study. In one sense, the struggle among contending co-operative groups might be surprising since co-operators are supposed to co-operate with each other. But, on the other hand, the issues were significant, there were good arguments on both sides, and despite the differences, accommodations were ultimately made, albeit in a period long after that chronicled by Andrew Hebb.

This history, then, is a glimpse into the lives and activities of a group of co-operative pioneers. They were ambitious, determined, and visionary; sometimes they were quarrelsome and poorly organized. Nevertheless, they demonstrated considerable idealism and they showed remarkable pragmatism. Above all, although amateurs in the insurance business, they managed to launch a successful insurance company through determination and faithful adherence to a Farm Bureau model. At the same time, they dealt with issues that transcended many of the passing problems in the company's formative years. Indeed, in somewhat different forms, many of the fundamental issues remain alive to this day.

Andrew Hebb is to be congratulated for the painstaking care he has taken — in the best journalist traditions in which he was originally trained — to present the story in an honest and straightforward way. This is not easy to do when one is among the more important figures in what happened.

Ian MacPherson
Victoria, B.C.
November, 1992

Chapter 1

Before the Beginning

Ten years before this story of a co-operative insurance company begins, five "United Farmers" and secretary Herbert H. Hannam "discovered" the Farm Bureau co-operatives and insurance companies in Indiana and Ohio. They had gone to Columbus, Ohio, to attend a general congress of the Co-operative League of the United States. On a honeymoon motor-trip, Leonard Harman, Hannam's part-time assistant editor of the newly founded Rural Co-operator, and his bride, were also there. Earlier in the same miraculous year, 1936, the United Farmers had played a leading role in the founding of Ontario Chamber (later Federation) of Agriculture, and Hannam became the first president.

From the time of that USA visit on, Farm Bureau leaders spoke at United Farmers and Ontario Federation of Agriculture (OFA) conventions in Toronto, and Ontarians, eager visitors to Indianapolis and Columbus, became enviously aware of Farm Bureau co-operatives, insurance companies and credit unions. At United Farmers' Co-operative Company annual meeting in 1938, Ohio Farm Bureau secretary Murray Lincoln said:

> *The farmers of Ohio got tired paying high rates to insurance companies which invested their savings in the very corporations which grew fat at the expense of*

1

agriculture.

After his return from the 1936 congress in Columbus, United
Farmers secretary Hannam wrote (as part of a United Farmers of
Ontario "Charter"):

> *Every purchase we make of farm supplies or family*
> *needs, every insurance premium we pay, every payment*
> *of interest on loans - these are the weapons we may use*
> *to rebuild our economic system from the bottom up in*
> *such a way that it is controlled by and in the interests of*
> *the people themselves.*

Inspired by Antigonish, and the credit unions of Nova Scotia,
Hannam and his assistant, Harvey MacDougall, helped their fellow
employees organize a United Farmers credit union, but, for lack of
permissive legislation, they could not incorporate it, to limit the legal
liability of members. MacDougall then organized Ontario's first rural
credit union at Park Head in Bruce county, near Owen Sound.
Hannam's friend, Hon. P. M. Dewan, minister of agriculture and a
former co-operative manager at Woodstock, did not have easy access
to the Ontario premier, but through the intervention of radical
employer, J. J. Harpell, of Garden City Press, Hannam received a
telephone call - "This is Mitch Hepburn - what can I do for you?" The
outcome, in 1939 and 1940, was the amendment of legislation enacted
in 1922 but not proclaimed until 1928, and finally suspended in 1936
for fear of speculators and swindlers in co-operators' clothing. The
new law required a credit union officer handling money to "furnish a
bond for the due accounting of moneys received by him and the
faithful performance of his duties..." and, as Shakespeare liked to say,
"thereby hangs a tale."

By request of Hannam and urban credit unions, the friendly and
co-operative minister of agriculture would administer the new credit
union law. The first inspector was Frank Perkin, who had studied
economics at the University of Toronto, and as a civil servant had
helped to draft the new law.

Early in 1940 "Herb" Hannam, who had just been elected president
of the Canadian Chamber (later Federation) of Agriculture, presided
over the formation of the Toronto chapter of credit unions. In wartime
May 1941 he was too busy to attend a meeting in Hamilton to form a
"league", as provided for in the new legislation. His assistant,
Leonard Harman, who had taken over from MacDougall in 1940,

attended and became a director. Gordon Smith of Hamilton Municipal Employees Credit Union was elected president.

Beginning in January 1941, a CBC once-a-week evening radio program, sponsored by the Canadian Association for Adult Education (CAAE) and the Canadian Federation of Agriculture (CFA), lit a fire in rural Ontario. The program became known as "Farm Radio Forum" and farm listening-discussion groups as "forums". Farm neighbors listened together to a national broadcast on a topic of farm concern, and tried to agree on answers to questions provided by mail in advance. If there were too many people gathered in one home for comfortable discussion and debate, they divided themselves into two or more groups to meet in parlor, dining-room and kitchen, each with a chairman and secretary. Finally they came together again to reconcile and consolidate their answers. These "findings" the forum secretary mailed to an Ontario secretary, who summarized and reported them in a provincial broadcast immediately following the next week's national broadcast.

The United Farmers and the Ontario Federation of Agriculture organized the first forums. Forums and forum members mobilized more forums. They multiplied! His services contributed by United Farmers' Co-operative, Leonard Harman was Farm Radio Forum's first Ontario secretary. He continued as secretary during the 1941-42 winter season, and, although appointed Rural Co-operator editor in January 1942, served the next winter as both Ontario secretary and national secretary! He had been appointed editor of the four-page monthly Rural Co-operator to ease the pressure on Hannam as United Farmers secretary and Canadian Federation of Agriculture (CFA) president. After re-election as CFA president in January 1943, Hannam spent most of his time on CFA wartime problems, from his Toronto office at 28 Duke Street, United Farmers headquarters, and in June the co-operative company board granted him leave of absence, and appointed Harman acting secretary.

Ralph S. Staples of Cavan in Peterborough county, who had been elected in November, 1940, vice-president of the United Farmers of Ontario, and unexpectedly the very next day a co-operative company director, and re-elected in 1941 and in 1942 to both posts, succeeded Harman as both Ontario and national secretary of Farm Radio Forum. Staples was widely known as a leader in Alan Plaunt's short-lived New Canada Movement of winter 1933-34.

In Ontario, Farm Radio Forum was growing, growing, growing! Thousands of farm men and women participated in the forums, and other thousands listened in their own homes. Forum discussions ranged from broadcast topics to local problems, and "action projects" often followed. Hannam, MacDougall and Harman had tried over a period of years, in the name of the United Farmers of Ontario, to establish Antigonish-style study groups, with limited success, but they had developed, through a program called "Neighbor Nights", a group discussion "technique", and they had tilled the soil for Farm Radio Forum.

The "United Farmers" consisted of the United Farmers of Ontario, based on farmers' clubs, and the United Farmers' Co-operative Company, commonly and incorrectly called "the UFO Co-operative Company" or just "the UFO", but sometimes in this story to be called "U. F. Co-op". The United Farmers of Ontario (UFO) had strayed into politics during the first world war, and recently had tried to climb out again - in politics it had made enemies for itself and for the co-operative company. In November 1943, after several years of planning and negotiation, the UFO turned its co-operative education chores over to Ontario Federation of Agriculture (OFA) and to United Farmers' Co-operative Company (U. F. Co-op), and, together with its affiliates, UFWO (women) and UFYPO (young people), ceased operation. More than fifty UFO clubs were or became business "affiliates" of the co-operative company, and others became "forums" or joined county Federations of Agriculture.

U. F. Co-op had pressured the UFO to stop collecting dues and to retire, to distance U. F. Co-op business from long memories of party politics, and to make more room for the Ontario Federation of Agriculture. OFA took up the co-operative cause. At the OFA annual meeting in January 1944 president Alex McKinney said:

> ...*our ability to solve our problems in the years that lie ahead will depend upon...the degree to which we support the co-operative movement.*

As a gesture of good will, the Federation elected the three retiring UFO presidents to the OFA executive: D. E. Stauffer (UFO), Mrs. O. G. Anderson (UFWO) and Clifford Allen (UFYPO). And the meeting re-elected to the executive U. F. Co-op president R. J. Scott and retiring U. F. Co-op secretary Hannam, who was about to move to Ottawa to be both president and managing director of the Canadian

Federation of Agriculture (CFA).

In February Hannam, liked and admired by OFA colleagues and idolized at U. F. Co-op, resigned as company secretary and was invited to attend future board meetings at his convenience, with his expenses to be paid by U. F. Co-op. In March the board appointed 33-year-old Leonard Harman "general secretary," a new title for a position that was to be "co-ordinate with that of general manager," that is, of equal rank.

With encouragement and $1,000 a year from U. F. Co-op, Ontario Federation of Agriculture (OFA) had become effectively sponsor-manager of Ontario's flourishing Farm Radio Forum, and in September, with U. F. Co-op's advertising and financial underwriting, became nominal publisher of the Rural Co-operator, which now had its own staff and published two eight-page issues a month instead of one four-page issue. With the help of 25 cents group subscriptions from county Federations of Agriculture, circulation had soared to over 25,000 copies. Hannam's dream of "Farm Bureau" integration of farmer membership organization and central farm co-operative seemed to be coming true.

Now, sadly, two events cast shadows over the alliance between OFA and U. F. Co-op. Recruited as "national organizer" of a renewed and stronger Co-operative Union of Canada, powerful A. B. MacDonald, of Antigonish, persuaded U. F. Co-op directors to form a provincial Co-operative Union, following a Saskatchewan model. At the first and only joint OFA/U. F. Co-op convention, in December 1944, MacDonald told the OFA annual meeting that co-operatives were not the business of the Federation! An Ontario Co-operative Union came into being in January 1945, with U. F. Co-op president R. J. Scott as president. The new Union established itself at 28 Duke Street, and seemed to take the place, in the heart of U. F. Co-op, which the UFO had vacated in favor of OFA.

On top of that rejection of OFA as chief co-operative educator, popular R. J. Scott resigned as U. F. Co-op president, at the request of his fellow directors, as soon became common knowledge, followed by speculation and rumors. In apparent good health, playing an active role at an OFA executive meeting the very next day, Scott suggested bringing Farm Radio Forum leaders to a conference where "the technique of conducting radio forums could be outlined to them." An announcement in the next issue of the Rural Co-operator said that shareholders and patrons would "learn with surprise" that Scott had resigned as president because of his "health" and family and farm responsibilities. In the months that followed Scott recruited OFA and local co-operative leaders in an unsuccessful attempt to win control of the co-operative company's board of directors in December 1945.

Upon these troubled co-operative seas an ambitious new insurance company was launched in 1946.

Chapter 2

Honesty is the Best Policy

Working closely together, two credit unionists were principally responsible for the birth of Co-operators' Fidelity and Guarantee Association. At an executive meeting of the Ontario Credit Union League, in February 1945, A. C. Savage, a first world war veteran, and Leonard W. Mitchell, a young lawyer, moved that a committee consisting of Robert A. Macdonald, the League president, and themselves, investigate "bonding credit union officers and other relative insurance features, and in co-operation with the inspector of credit unions draft a report" for the League board of directors.

The other executive members present, treasurer Alan R. Morgan, Hamilton, and volunteer general manager George W. Scott, saw no reason for dissent. The only executive member absent, vice-president Cy J. Watson, Windsor, incensed by a short notice for the meeting, had telegraphed angrily that Windsor district credit unions would not recognize any business transacted at this meeting.

Savage had left the civil service almost a year earlier to join United Farmers' Co-operative Company, at the invitation of Leonard Harman, both founding directors of the League, and at the beginning of 1945 Savage, Harman and Mitchell had participated in the organization of the Ontario Co-operative Union, which later changed its name to Co-operative Union of Ontario.

In April the Union was setting up an "employee security" committee, and Mitchell reported that the League directors had considered the subject of bonding co-operative employees, and invited the Union to co-operate with the League committee. This would be easy, for Savage was secretary-treasurer of the new Union, Mitchell was vice-president, and Robert Macdonald would become a Union board member in June.

Later in April, at a Sunday board meeting of the League in London, Mitchell reported on the bonding of credit union officers.

In June the new board of the Union confirmed Savage as secretary-treasurer and instructed him to obtain a $1,000 fidelity bond. Such a bond would cost the Union $10, and Savage reported to an executive meeting in July that he had not arranged this insurance as yet. Savage and Mitchell and perhaps some other people were beginning to think that it might be possible to avoid payment of seemingly fat premiums to commercial insurers to guarantee the honesty of co-operators. The Union executive apparently wished to speed up the investigation of fidelity bonding, and appointed two members of its employee security committee, Mitchell and Savage, to investigate "bonding and insurance."

When the League executive, at a weekend meeting in Hamilton late in August, on the motion of Watson and Savage, instructed the League's committee on bonding to co-operate with the Union's committee, and report to the next League board meeting, it was telling president Macdonald, Savage and Mitchell of the League to co-operate with Mitchell and Savage of the Union. There is no record that Savage and Mitchell reported their radical proposals to this League executive meeting - probably they did - or of opposition, although C. Gordon Smith, who would disagree at the next board meeting, was present. Two days later, Mitchell presented a written committee report to the Union executive. There are no minutes of whatever discussion took place, but it was agreed to provide each director with a copy of the report and to "advise the provincial department of insurance of our contemplated action in applying for incorporation."

Meeting in September at the Co-operative Training School in Toronto, the Union board of directors enlarged the project by striking from the insurance report the words "and for the present the only class (of insurance) in which we are interested is bonding." The nine directors and Savage were to act as incorporators, with the proviso that the president and secretary could make any necessary changes or additions to these names. The Union would pay the cost of incorporation. Savage and Mitchell were pushing ahead although as yet they lacked the approval of the League. When the League board met at Niagara Falls on a Saturday and Sunday in mid-October, Savage and Mitchell moved "that the report of the bonding committee of the Ontario Credit Union League be adopted." There is no record of the discussion or whether the directors had received copies of the report in advance of the meeting. The resolution carried, but with the League's former and first president, Gordon Smith, opposed. A second resolution, moved by Mitchell and A. E. Borland, Peterborough, "That the Central Credit department be given authority to purchase $2,500 stock in the proposed co-operative insurance company, such stock to be only 50% paid up," was also carried, with Smith's opposition again recorded.

At that time Gordon Smith was an employee of the city of Hamilton and founder and treasurer of Hamilton Municipal Employees Credit Union. He was also chief agent in Canada of CUNA Mutual Insurance Society and the representative of CUNA and CUNA Supply Co-operative. He and his wife had done a great deal of voluntary work for CUNA Mutual and CUNA; and made their home available as the Canadian office; in 1945 Smith was receiving only $25 a month as remuneration. CUNA was promoting the bonding insurance of a United States mutual insurer, and he saw the proposed Ontario co-operative insurance company either as unnecessary competition or credit union bonding as an impractical venture for a brand-new provincial company. If he thought it impractical, time would prove him largely right (for eventually the Ontario co-operative insurance company turned over to CUNA its credit union bonding operations).

Savage and Mitchell were discussing the projected company with Ontario government officials - F. V. Johns, deputy provincial secretary, with control over the organization of companies, R. B. Whitehead, K. C., superintendent of insurance, and Cecil Richards, chief insurance inspector and himself an active credit unionist. It was simple to obtain a company charter from Mr. Johns; it was more difficult to obtain an insurance licence (or licences) from Mr. Whitehead. With Mr. Johns the only difficulty was the name. The requested name was: Co-operative Union Mutual Insurance Company.

A provision in the Companies Act forbade a provincial corporation, other than a company organized under the co-operatives part of the Act or a credit union, to include in its corporate name "the word 'co-operative' or any abbreviation or derivative thereof." Not even a mutual insurance company could call itself co-operative. Eventually there was some compromising, and some co-operative interpretation of the law, and agreement on the use of "Co-operators." The agreed name, "Co-operators' Fidelity and Guarantee Association," indicated that Savage and Mitchell were still thinking primarily of fidelity insurance.

They faced the fact that Ontario legislation made no provision for a truly co-operative insurance company. A so-called mutual company looked like a co-operative but effective control usually slipped into the hands of the management. A joint stock company lent itself to management control too, unless the owners were democratic organizations rather than individuals.

Savage, as a "national" director of CUNA, and Mitchell, as a candidate for election as a director of CUNA Mutual, were enthusiastic supporters of CUNA Mutual, partly because of its emphasis on term life insurance. They were aware of the unsuccessful proposals to turn CUNA Mutual into a joint stock company owned by CUNA, but they were satisfied that the change in 1944 from mail balloting to policyholder area meetings, permitted by the Wisconsin state legislature, would secure co-operative control. CUNA managing-director Roy Bergengren had written enthusiastically of area voting as "putting mutuality into a mutual insurance company" and as "truly co-operative and democratic." Ontario legislation permitted Ontario companies neither mail balloting nor area meetings, but in the beginning Savage and Mitchell thought of the proposed Ontario insurer as a provincial company with a limited number of policyholders, principally credit unions and co-operatives. They chose a hybrid form of organization provided for in the Companies Act - intended as a way of getting a mutual company on its feet - a mutual insurance company with guarantee capital stock. Such a company seemed to fit nicely into the co-operative community - each policyholder would have one vote and each shareholder would have only one vote. There would be a large measure of democracy and also a way to raise capital. The Companies Act provided for the retirement of the share capital when earnings made that possible!

In this choice they had the guidance and approval of the Ontario superintendent of insurance and his chief examiner. Granting an insurance licence was largely within the superintendent's discretion. The Act provided for "an authorized guarantee capital stock of not less than $300,000 and not more than $500,000," but actual paid-in capital was for the superintendent to decide. It was his responsibility to see that any insurance company he licensed was able to fulfil its commitments. This was more than solvency - it was even more than ability to meet probable liabilities, it was more like ability to meet possible liabilities. Whitehead and Richards were fair, friendly and helpful, but, with their knowledge of the problems of the insurance companies under their supervision, they were dubious about the proposed fidelity insurance company. They were not impressed by the argument that credit unionists, co-operators and co-operative employees were less likely to be dishonest than other people. They wanted to know how much risk the company proposed to assume, what reinsurance arrangements it would make, who was going to manage the company, and who the directors were.

Savage, the former civil servant and former vice-president of the Civil Service Federation of Canada, and Mitchell, an incisive-mannered solicitor, impressed the superintendent with their capability and knowledge of insurance. Applicants for incorporation, who would become the provisional directors of Co-operators' Fidelity and Guarantee Association (CF&GA), were to be Savage and the nine directors of the Ontario Co-operative Union. Savage dropped one Union director from this list because there was no statutory provision for ten directors, and then another Union director to make room for Andrew Hebb, then editor of the *Rural Co-operator*, who had been employed for less than two years in the early thirties by United States Fidelity and Guaranty Company. Savage felt that this background on the part of one of the applicants would be helpful with the superintendent. Of the other applicants, four were directors of United Farmers' Co-operative Company - Ralph S. Staples, R. J. Scott, Wm. G. Nicholson, and W. J. Wood, an Alliston farmer and former businessman. Three were directors of Ontario Credit Union League - Savage, Mitchell and Robert A. Macdonald, League president. The other applicant, Chas. M. Haapanen, was the manager of a big and successful Finnish consumer co-operative in Timmins. Formerly he had managed another Timmins chain of stores, which had been captured by Communists.

Chapter 3

Securing a Licence

The province granted letters patent January 31, 1946, but the superintendent of insurance required $50,000 in subscribed capital, and $25,000 cash paid in, before he would license the company to write bonding insurance. Shares were by statute $100 each, and to meet these two requirements simultaneously the board decided to accept only $50 on each $100 share.

Each of the provisional directors except R. J. Scott, who became ill and never attended a meeting, bought a share on February 26 in the United Farmers board room at 28 Duke Street, Toronto. Meeting under the guidance of Mitchell, shareholders Wood, Savage, Nicholson, Hebb and Mitchell elected the nine applicants as directors; meeting as directors they adopted by-laws prepared by Mitchell, and elected Wood president, Macdonald vice-president, Savage secretary-treasurer, and Hebb assistant secretary; meeting again as shareholders they confirmed the by-laws and authorized the board to delegate its powers to an executive committee. The by-laws limited dividends on shares to four percent per annum and provided for "patronage returns" and "deferred patronage returns" to policyholders.

In an article published in the Rural Co-operator and the Credit Union News in March, Savage wrote optimistically: "The surplus earnings of the new insurance co-operative after taking care of necessary reserves, etc., will be declared to the members on a patronage dividend basis." He wrote confidently that "shares will qualify to earn four percent per annum." While for the present the Association would "concentrate on fidelity bonds ... in the near future it is hoped that arrangements will be completed to write other insurance." It was not the intention of the new Association "to compete with CUNA Mutual Insurance Society," but it would later on "be interested in the program of Co-operative Life Insurance Company of Saskatchewan," then considering entry into Ontario, "with special attention to business which is not covered by CUNA Mutual." Before the Association could commence business, the article said, it was necessary to obtain subscriptions for $50,000 of guarantee capital stock.

When the board met in April, Savage had obtained 18 applications for shares, most of them for substantial amounts. United Farmers' Co-operative Company and Ontario Credit Union League each purchased 25 shares, and First Co-operative Packers (COPACO), Barrie, bought 20 shares.

Buying 10 each were four credit unions and a caisse populaire: Hepcoe, Holy Rosary Parish (Toronto), Co-operative Service (Toronto), St. Peter's Parish (Toronto) and la Caisse Co-opérative de Notre Dame d'Ottawa. CUMBA Co-operative Health Services, serving Toronto credit union members, subscribed for 10 shares, and two credit unions, West Fort William and Terminal of Toronto, five shares each. Farmers' co-operatives did not have money available for substantial investment - Brockville and Shelburne co-operatives each bought one share. Other purchasers included a League director, George Selkirk, Fort William, who bought one share.

Practically all subscriptions resulted from contacts which Savage made in the course of his money-raising and organizational work for United Farmers'. Without his persuasive enthusiasm the company could not have gathered up enough money to obtain a fidelity insurance licence. The board at this meeting asked Savage and Hebb to organize the sale of stock, through the other directors if necessary, but Savage continued to raise the money himself. The board authorized Savage and Hebb to continue reinsurance negotiations with "Ohio Farm Bureau Mutual Insurance Company and any other mutual insurance company," and asked Mitchell, as solicitor, to prepare application and policy forms.

The directors did not meet again until the middle of August, but by that time Savage had secured applications for another 138 shares, bringing paid-in capital up to $17,250 (including 31 fully paid shares). Some people wanted to pay for their shares in full, but the board would accept only 50 percent, and insisted on leaving the liability for the other 50 percent with the shareholders. The subscription list reflected again Savage's activities and travels for United Farmers'. CUMBA subscribed for an additional 15 shares - for a total of 25; two other hospital co-operatives, Dufferin, one share, and Simcoe county, 10 shares, were subscribers. Dundalk Farmers Co-operative and Consumers Co-operative Society, Timmins, of which CF&GA director Haapanen was manager, with five shares each, were the larger subscribers among 11 other co-operatives. Taking 10 shares each, Rochdale Credit Union, Woodstock, and St. Peter's Parish (Toronto) Credit Union, bringing its total shares to 20, were leaders among 10 credit union subscribers. Society St. John the Evangelist subscribed for 10 shares, and Rev. L. E. C. Frith, as an individual, subscribed for 20 shares - 25 years later he still held 20 common shares (in the successor company), more than any other individual.

There were 316 shares sold, and the board planned special approaches to co-operative organizations to sell another 184 to attain the objective of $50,000 subscribed and $25,000 paid-in capital. The directors removed a limit, which they had agreed on earlier, of 25 shares to be held by any organization or individual.

Before adjourning, the board instructed Hebb, Mitchell and Savage to report on the possibility of writing various kinds of insurance through an agency, and to review the forms and policies prepared by Mitchell and to recommend fidelity insurance premiums. Savage reported that parliament had approved a bill incorporating Co-operative Life Insurance Company, Regina, as a federal company, and that R. H. Milliken, K. C., Co-operative Life's solicitor, would come to Toronto to resume discussions about Ontario licensing.

It was two and a half months later when the board met again, at the end of October. Applications for 214 shares were awaiting allotment by the board, and Mitchell, as solicitor, had applied on behalf of the company for a licence to write fidelity insurance. United Farmers' Co-operative Company had agreed to buy 100 additional shares, on the understanding that the insurance company would try to find other persons or organizations to buy these shares back from the co-operative company. St. Peter's Parish (Toronto) Credit Union increased its subscription to 25 shares; Toronto Municipal Employees' Credit Union, of which CF&GA director Robert Macdonald was president and unpaid secretary-treasurer, applied for 25 shares; COPACO, Barrie, increased its subscription to 30 shares; Consumers Co-operative Society and Dufferin Co-operative Medical Services increased their subscriptions to 10 shares; Beaver Credit Union (CPR employees at Toronto "Junction"), an employee credit union in a big company which did not wish its name used as part of the credit union's name, bought 10 shares; St. Joseph's Parish (Toronto) Credit Union eight shares, Hamilton Dominion Civil Servants' Credit Union six shares, and several credit unions and co-operatives five shares each. Of 24 applications, 12 were from credit unions, eight from co-operatives and four from individuals, who included CF&GA president W. J. Wood, increasing his shares to 10, Austin McQuarrie, Shelburne, buying five, and the national organizer of the Co-operative Union of Canada, A. B. MacDonald, buying one. Secretary-treasurer Savage reported purchase of $5,000 of 2-3/4% province of New Brunswick bonds due 1965 at 97.75 and $5,000 of 2-3/4% province of British Columbia bonds due 1959 at 99.50.

Perhaps the superintendent of insurance and the chief inspector had hoped that the new company would not be able to raise $25,000, but, if so, they had reckoned without Savage. Now that the company was asking for a licence, the superintendent was imposing various conditions - undoubtedly suggested to him by his chief inspector, Cecil Richards, who had primary responsibility for the companies under their supervision. Most insurance companies operating in Ontario were federally licensed and supervised, although they had to obtain an Ontario licence for each class of insurance they wished to write within the province. They paid the province the same premium taxes as provincially licensed companies, and they were a lot less trouble. Provincially licensed companies tended to be smaller companies, and Ontario supervision was stricter than federal supervision. To meet the superintendent's requirements, the board enacted a by-law to limit the organizations for which the company could write bonds to co-operatives, credit unions and farm and educational organizations. This limitation would help to avert criticism of the department of insurance by other insurance companies and by Ontario insurance agents, and it might reduce the possibility of unsuccessful operation. The company also undertook not to retain, for its own risk, more than $5,000 per person, or $3,000 per position, or $25,000 under one schedule (of several or more persons or positions), until its capital and surplus exceeded $100,000.

Chapter 4

First Employee

Ohio Farm Bureau Insurance Companies were unable to offer
reinsurance but the board was happy to learn that Co-operative
Insurance Society, Manchester, England, would provide reinsurance
"not to exceed $100,000 any one position or name." CIS (not a
mutual but owned by the English and Scottish co-operative wholesale
societies) was one of Britain's largest insurance companies, writing all
classes of insurance, including life. CF&GA would now secure office
space and begin operations. Hebb, Mitchell and Savage would be an
underwriting committee. One of the graduates of the Ontario
Co-operative Union's co-operative school for Second World War
servicemen, Bernard Shea, would transfer from the Union staff to
become the first employee of Co-operators' Fidelity and Guarantee
Association. He would succeed Hebb as assistant secretary, and
would also operate an insurance agency to place insurance with other
companies. His salary, including agency commissions, would be $40
a week.

Shea was a good choice as the Association's first employee. An
Alberta high school commercial graduate, with an inquiring,
questioning outlook, he had left home rebelliously during the
Depression to fend for himself. He had widened his education on the
road as a salesman, in the air force, in the Co-operative Union school

and through reading. He proved capable and resourceful and was, for a little while, the company's entire staff - typing policies, keeping records, writing letters. He contributed to committee and board discussions, and made many friends for CF&GA among credit unionists and farmers.

The Association got its fidelity bonding licence and was able to issue its first policies, probably retroactively, as of Monday, November 4, 1946. With brief and hurried instructions from Savage, on the run most of the time, and advice from Hebb, Mitchell and sometimes chief inspector Richards, Shea made his own way in insurance. United Farmers' Co-operative Company provided desk space in the Rural Co-operator office, and someone contributed a battered and discarded wooden desk and kitchen chair. If the insurance company bought furniture or equipment, the full purchase price, not just depreciation, would be an expense of operation - and eat up income or capital. Someone, perhaps the Rural Co-operator, lent a typewriter. The Rural Co-operator, with Hebb as editor-manager, and the Credit Union News, with Savage as manager, were providing free publicity and advertising.

Still raising share capital, and investing it, and now selling the Association's bonding services, the secretary-treasurer was paid nothing by CF&GA. Savage had been driving himself hard in the two years since he left the civil service. Fighting unfair proposals to tax patronage dividends paid by co-operatives in reduction of the cost of goods, organizing co-operatives, making speeches to rapt audiences, squeezing in visits to credit unions, raising capital for United Farmers' Co-operative Company, managing the insurance company and the Ontario Co-operative Union, he began to feel the strain. At a December board meeting he reported medical advice to take things easy and asked for a month's leave of absence from his unpaid insurance duties. This, of course, the board granted but didn't hesitate to instruct him, on the motion of Nicholson and Staples, who were also on the Union and United Farmers' boards, "to conduct a vigorous campaign" to re-sell the 100 shares of CF&GA stock which United Farmers' had agreed to buy and hold temporarily. He was also to "embark upon an educational campaign ... to explain fidelity insurance to co-operative people." Hebb, Mitchell and Shea were to carry on day-to-day operations in Savage's absence.

The company was now in the insurance business, with over $28,000 capital paid in, less incorporation, licence and incidental expenses of $1,247, a licence to write fidelity bonds, a reinsurance agreement with CIS, Manchester, and, Shea reported, considerable fidelity insurance in force. One of the first insurance lessons the board had to learn was the big difference between written and earned premium - particularly when policies were for a three-year term. A quaint Canadian insurance custom permitted fire and casualty companies to claim 20 percent of a premium as immediately earned - the 20 percent presumed to have been paid to an agent - but the remaining 80 percent was unearned, and was earned only gradually over the term of the policy. If CF&GA received $150 in three-year premiums in November 1946, $30 plus one-half of one thirty-sixth of the balance was earned at the end of November, or $30 plus one and a half thirty-sixths at the end of December. Only earned premium qualified as current income; unearned premium was future income and a current liability. Visiting the office, and sitting down at Shea's desk, chief inspector Richards opened journal and ledger accounts to show Shea how he wanted the records kept. Richards came to the office several times to help with or check up on the accounting, and on one occasion went with Shea to call on a bonded defaulter - and successfully persuaded him to reimburse his employer.

Shea reported to the December meeting that he had obtained a personal insurance licence. A broker had agreed to accept applications from Shea for insurance which CF&GA was not licensed to write. The objective was to increase CF&GA revenues and incidentally its insurance knowledge. This was the beginning of a long struggle with the treasurer of United Farmers' Co-operative Company to obtain the commission on the co-operative company's fire and other insurance. United Farmers' switched its fidelity business promptly but treasurer S. R. Newland felt that the company's agents had obtained some good fire insurance settlements for United Farmers' and he did not want to ask them to share their commissions with a sub-agent. United Farmers' board supported the CF&GA request for the company's insurance but did not order the treasurer to transfer it.

Chapter 5

Annual Meeting

The CF&GA board did not meet again until February 11, 1947, the day of the first annual meeting. The underwriting committee of Hebb, Mitchell and Savage had exceeded instructions, received in December, to investigate credit union blanket bonds. They had secured an amendment to the CIS, Manchester, reinsurance treaty to cover blanket bonds, and obtained a similar amendment to the company's insurance licence. The only other directors at the meeting were president Wood, in the chair, and Staples, and the board approved ratifying resolutions and a schedule of premium rates which were similar to those of CUNA. Through Lumbermen's Mutual, CUNA was pioneering this blanket bond coverage which protected a credit union against the dishonesty of its own officers and employees and against burglary and theft by outsiders.

Savage had found purchasers for the extra 100 shares bought by United Farmers' to permit the Association to obtain an insurance licence. Garden City Press Employees Credit Union took 50 shares (and held them until 1970) - the biggest single sale up to this time; and CUMBA Co-operative Health Services took an additional 25 shares - to hold a total of 50 shares. Hepcoe Credit Union (Ontario Hydro employees) bought 15. Among the remaining transferees was United Farmers' secretary Leonard Harman, purchaser of one share, who was to play a major role in the Association's affairs in troubled times ahead.

Director Robert A. Macdonald had joined the board meeting in mid-afternoon, and A. H. K. Musgrave, an Ontario Co-operative Union employee, was present as a visitor. The board considered letters from co-operators in Manitoba and the Maritime provinces concerning possible joint action in the provision of bonding services, and discussed fire and automobile insurance. In an optimistic mood, directors discussed the relative merits of direct provincial licensing in other provinces and prior federal incorporation and licensing.

The annual meeting took place in the evening (urban credit unionists usually could not attend daytime Monday to Friday meetings, as preferred by farmers), in the same room at the Royal York Hotel, with about 30 people present. President Wood felt that fidelity insurance had been a wise choice as an initial venture, and compared the founders with the Rochdale co-operative pioneers. The president read a directors' report, prepared by Savage and approved by the board, and Savage presented a financial report for two months of 1946 - November and December - and a personal report as secretary-treasurer. With earned premium of perhaps $225 and possibly $400 investment income, the company had expenses of about $1,500 after deducting commissions retained on reinsurance ceded and an operating loss of $893.96. The company was "an acorn" which would "grow into one of the greatest oak trees in the co-operative movement in the Dominion of Canada," Savage declared. "In my opinion your Association, properly developed and expanding into other fields of insurance, will assist greatly in supplying capital for the co-operative movement." The secretary-treasurer recommended that the Association write automobile insurance and fire insurance on first-class urban risks. He felt that the Association could raise the additional capital that would be needed. In the meantime, to secure the additional bonding business needed for successful operation the "directors should consider proper office accommodation and sufficient staff to carry on the business efficiently."

Despite his own optimism, Savage dutifully recorded in the annual meeting minutes Hebb's foreboding that 1947 earned premium in bonding might not be more than $2,500, and his agreement on the need for expansion into other classes of insurance.

The terms of all directors expired at this meeting, but the directors elected would serve for varying terms. One of the first directors, R. J. Scott, had died in 1946. Hebb, Macdonald and Savage did not stand for re-election - Macdonald, president of the League, because of inability to attend the weekday meetings apparently preferred by farmers, Hebb and Savage to make room for other people to participate. Hebb was trying to involve the Ontario Federation of Agriculture and its secretary-manager, Vivian S. Milburn, who was a former U. F. Co-op director and a former president of Ontario Whole Milk Producers League.

Directors were elected to serve for three, two or one-year terms on the basis of the number of votes received: three years, K. N. M. Morrison, M.B.E., general manager of COPACO, W. J. Wood, U. F. Co-op director (elected 1945 and 1946) and Ontario Co-operative Union vice-president, and Leonard Harman; two years, Leonard W. Mitchell, V. S. Milburn and U. F. Co-op director R. S. Staples, now Ontario Co-operative Union president; one year, C. M. Haapanen, manager, Consumers Co-operative Society Ltd., Timmins, and an Ontario Co-operative Union director, Wm. G. Nicholson, Port Elgin, a director of U. F. Co-op and Ontario Co-operative Union, and John M. Hallinan, later in 1947 appointed general manager of Ontario Credit Union League.

Morrison, Harman, Milburn and Hallinan were new directors. Morrison had become general manager of heavily indebted First Co-operative Packers (COPACO) in 1934 at the request of the Ontario government, and, with Hugh Bailey as president, had pulled it out of the mud. Harman and his directors were reorganizing United Farmers' Co-operative Company, of which Bailey was now general manager. Milburn was building the Ontario Federation of Agriculture. A former president of Toronto Credit Union Chapter, Hallinan had caught fire co-operatively in student days at Regis College, Toronto.

Meeting the same evening, the new board elected Wood president, Mitchell vice-president and Harman executive member. Savage became secretary-treasurer again, and Hebb, Mitchell and Savage the underwriting committee. In his seventies, and almost 20 years older than Savage or any board member, Wood had been a generous contributor to company capital with his purchase of 10 shares. Like many Ontario farmers of his time, his schooling had ended at Grade 8. Married to a sister of Mrs. T. P. Loblaw, and one-time operator of a grocery store in Alliston, he helped Loblaw, although not as first lieutenant, launch his self-service groceterias, following Loblaw's resignation as general manager of United Farmers' Co-operative Company. In 1935 he purchased from the Loblaw estate the farm home and 200 acres of the Loblaw farm near Alliston, and became a farmer. Ten years later he was an Ontario Federation of Agriculture director, first president of the Ontario Cream Producers Association, and, as the only person on two rival slates of candidates in December 1945, each seeking control of United Farmers' Co-operative Company, he led the poll and became executive member. As president of CF&GA, however, he presided acceptably over board meetings, but did not play an active role in development of the new company. He visited the office faithfully, to ask Shea, "Is everything all right, Barney?" and then, reassured, departed without sitting down.

Shea was struggling with his unaccustomed tasks, and trying to pass along what he learned to his associates and employers. Fidelity underwriting required investigation of the employment histories of persons to be bonded, and resulted in occasional refusals. The bonding company found it easier than the employer to obtain unfavorable information. Since the co-operative or credit union usually employed first, and then joined with the employee in applying for a bond, a refusal caused trouble.

Chapter 6

Unlicensed Reinsurance

Insurance accounting was difficult too. Following the guidelines of chief examiner Richards, Shea and the company's auditors, also beginners in insurance, had produced a financial statement for the annual meeting, and had made a return to the superintendent of insurance. When the chief examiner reviewed the return, he realized that Co-operative Insurance Society, Manchester, the reinsurer, was not licensed in Canada, and that he would have to require a reserve for unlicensed reinsurance.

The amount required for 1946 was only $55, and would not have appreciably worsened the reported operating loss, but the company was writing more insurance now, and the cumulative reserve requirement to the end of February was $607, and according to a statement presented by Shea, pushed the company into a loss of $2.28 for the two months!

A company auditor, T. C. Pawlett of Millar, MacDonald & Co., Winnipeg chartered accountants, who were auditors for a number of western co-operatives, explained this setback to a board meeting in March 1947. Even if CF&GA ceded no more reinsurance in 1947 - which, of course, was not possible - the reserve requirement at the end of the year would have grown to $1,890, with only $660 received in commissions from the reinsurer. Suppose, he said, that the company ceded reinsurance premiums of $1,100 a month for 12 months, the unlicensed reinsurance requirement at the end of 1947 would be $11,000, but commission received on reinsurance only $3,960. It seemed to the directors that the more insurance they wrote the deeper they would sink into the mire, and, after discussion, decided to inquire if CIS, Manchester, would seek a Canadian licence.

Listening to the auditor's recital of the unlicensed reinsurance problem was K. N. M. Morrison, the shrewd general manager of First Co-operative Packers (COPACO), Barrie, attending his first regular board meeting. A New Brunswick boy, Morrison had pulled COPACO out of a much deeper mire. Enlisted by Savage, he played a major role on the board for the next three years. Convinced that the company's funds, all in government and municipal bonds, at a return of less than three percent, could be invested more advantageously, Morrison proposed, and the board agreed, to invest $8,000 in mortgages on real estate if "available on a reasonable and safe basis," and that Savage, Harman and Hallinan be an investment committee.

After lunch Savage presented a report on possible entry into automobile insurance: insurance adjusters charged $4 an hour; insurance agents received 30 percent of written premiums; claims were about 50 percent of premiums. Co-operative insurance companies in the United States did not as a rule pay standard commissions, and Savage thought that it might be possible to secure the help of local co-operatives in selling automobile insurance and in settling claims.

"Possibly we could handle automobile insurance on a group basis," suggested Milburn. [Over 20 years later the board of CF&GA's successor company, Co-operators Insurance Association (CIA), would discuss a trend to group automobile insurance in the United States, and some group experiments in Ontario - but the Ontario Insurance Act did not permit a lower automobile insurance premium for members of a group than for individuals.]

Savage reported that automobile premiums for the entire Dominion in 1946 amounted to $33 million, a 39 percent increase over 1945. (CIA alone, writing only in Ontario, had $35 million in automobile premiums in 1971.)

Morrison and Milburn moved that the president and secretary push ahead with automobile insurance plans. They were to obtain information from Farm Bureau Automobile Insurance Company ("Nationwide" in later years), Columbus, Ohio, and to advise the

Ontario Federation of Agriculture at an impending meeting of the proposed development. Milburn was OFA secretary, and he could have carried the news himself, but, an experienced manager of farm people, he catered to their cherished delusion that an employee was not telling them what to do. The Federation soon became a sponsor, and, as the automobile insurance program progressed, the most important sponsor: first, because interested farmers could find $50 to invest, and, second, because farmers had motor vehicles to insure, while at that time comparatively few urban credit unionists could spare $50 or owned an automobile.

In addition, there were at that time far more farmers. Nearly 700,000 people or about 15 percent of Ontario's population lived on farms. Ontario Credit Union League included over two hundred credit unions with probably more than 30,000 individual members, including a small proportion of rural credit unions and some farmer members.

Chapter 7

Buying a Filing Cabinet

Credit unions and co-operatives, under the spell of Savage's charm and confidence, had put up a lot of capital, but individuals would have to put up the money for automobile insurance. Savage was more confident of success than his colleagues but he respected their caution. When he reported, at a CF&GA board meeting in May 1947, that the Ontario Co-operative Union had been able to buy a filing cabinet - a post-wartime scarcity - he said that he would lend it to the company until such time as the board wished to buy it. After discussion, however, the board by formal motion agreed to purchase the cabinet - its first equipment purchase - for $60. At this time the directors were probably not aware that a $60 expenditure for equipment was a $60 operating expense in the current year - and not just a $12 depreciation expense. They themselves received no remuneration for attendance at board meetings, and travel expense only if they had no other organization source of reimbursement.

Shea had been drumming up fidelity business through personal contacts, letters, circulars and publicity, and sought the directors' suggestions. In addition to faithful performance and fidelity bonds, there were now 10 credit union blanket bonds, a coverage developed by CUNA, which insured against robbery, burglary and theft in addition to internal dishonesty. The more business the company wrote, however, the more it would lose, because of the reserve required for unlicensed reinsurance. Shea reported to the board that chief examiner Richards said there were two ways to avoid this reserve: remitting premiums annually after the year-end, or the deposit of securities in Canada by Co-operative Insurance Society. Secretary-treasurer Savage was asked to discuss these suggestions with CIS, Manchester: first, he was to ask approval to pay reinsurance premiums annually, and then, if the answer was unfavorable, he was to ask about depositing securities in Canada.

At this day-long meeting in May the board functioned, as usual, as a management committee, with Mitchell playing a leading part. On this occasion he moved 19 of 23 resolutions. Incisive and dynamic, Mitchell was more at home at an insurance board than the others. Like many Ontario lawyers at that time, he was himself licensed as an agent. Generously, at this meeting, he offered to obtain mortgages for the company without commission or finder's fee, and subsequently arranged an $8,000 mortgage loan to Campus Co-operative.

At this May meeting the board spent more time on automobile insurance and determined to go ahead if the money could be raised. Rather inconsistently, and for reasons not recorded, the board decided not to accept any more subscriptions for capital stock for the present.

The insurance adviser idea, which was to become of major importance, was born at this meeting. Mitchell proposed, and the board agreed, to ask the Ontario Credit Union League to endorse the Association as its official agency for credit union insurance other than life and to try to appoint an insurance adviser in each credit union, to handle fidelity, fire and automobile insurance. (The board addressed a similar request to the Ontario Co-operative Union and proposed to appoint an insurance adviser in each co-operative.)

Mitchell felt that the company should enter home fire insurance rather than automobile insurance. But Farm Bureau insurance companies in the United States had found fire insurance more difficult than automobile insurance, and advised against a start in fire insurance. Their companies were mutuals and not subject to income tax, but nevertheless it was difficult to earn enough to finance growth. The agent's commission on a new three-year premium used up in the first year the earned portion of the premium. The Farm Bureau companies did not use a policy fee as in automobile insurance. Home fire insurance would have been an urban project, because Milburn at least thought competition with the local farm fire mutuals would be unwise and unco-operative. (CIA's late start in fire insurance - 1956 - enabled CUNA-sponsored CUMIS Insurance in the 1960s to gain League approval to write home fire insurance on the ground that CIA had only about 20,000 policies in force on the homes of credit union members - out of a potential 175,000.)

A number of forces seemed to be taking Co-operators' Fidelity toward the country at this time, although in the first five months 90 fidelity and blanket bonds had been purchased by 38 credit unions, 26 co-operatives and six farm and other organizations. But there were only 300 or so credit unions in Ontario at that time - the League had not engaged its first employee, and did not have an office. Most of the Co-operators' Fidelity directors were farmers or employed by farm organizations and farm co-operatives. Automobile insurance would be easier to sell in the country, partly because part-time agents were permissible by law in municipalities of less than 10,000 population and easily recruited, and partly because of Federation of Agriculture and co-operative sponsorship, and a thousand Farm Radio Forums.

Chapter 8

Co-operative Life, Regina

An impending and fruitful alliance with Co-operative Life Insurance Company was also taking Co-operators' Fidelity out to the country. The name "Co-operators' Fidelity", and later "Co-op Fidelity", gradually replaced "CF&GA" as the company moved toward automobile insurance. Co-operative Life Insurance Company had grown out of a mutual benefit association and had been incorporated as a Saskatchewan mutual company in the spring of 1945. The farmer president, H. A. Crofford, met with an Ontario farm group at the time of the annual meeting of the Canadian Federation of Agriculture at London the following winter (January 1946). His story was that Co-operative Life wrote policies for a maximum of $4,000 so that it would not over-sell anyone. The company was democratic - each policyholder had one vote. The commission paid to agents did not vary with the type of policy - so the agent would not sell an ordinary life policy if a term policy would be better for the client. When a premium was unpaid there was an automatic policy extension for a reduced amount of insurance rather than the usual automatic policy loan which at six percent would soon eat up the policy. With these seemingly plausible points, Crofford won a sympathetic hearing.

In February 1946 Ontario Co-operative Union invited Co-operative Life Insurance Company to apply for an Ontario licence. The company now had a Dominion charter (by act of parliament) and was already licensed in the four western provinces. Savage became secretary to an Ontario advisory committee, with W. G. Nicholson, as chairman. Nicholson, a quiet and well-liked Bruce county farmer, was at this time a director of Co-operators' Fidelity, a director of United Farmers' Co-operative, a director of the Ontario Co-operative Union, and also a director of a local farm supply co-operative at Port Elgin and of the Bruce county hospital insurance co-operative. The committee agreed to raise a $5,000 guarantee fund, for use if necessary to strengthen Co-operative Life reserves. Staples became a candidate for appointment as Ontario manager of Co-operative Life. The other principal applicant was an urban resident, with labor background, active in the Co-operative Commonwealth Federation (CCF), forerunner of the New Democratic Party (NDP). Selection of Staples, on the recommendation of the primarily rural advisory committee, strengthened the likelihood that Co-operative Life would seek rural policyholders in Ontario, as in Saskatchewan. Staples became secretary of the advisory committee in March 1947, and in April Co-operative Life secured an Ontario licence and Staples began work as Ontario manager.

For the next year and a half a number of the same persons, either as members or guests, attended the meetings of both the Co-operative Life advisory committee and Co-operators' Fidelity board. Both groups were proceeding cautiously in this unaccustomed business of insurance. Participants in 1947 advisory committee meetings included Ontario Federation of Agriculture representatives Mrs. C. A. Campbell, Pakenham, K. M. Betzner, Waterloo, R. A. Stewart, Almonte, Robert Morrison, Alvinston, and V. S. Milburn. W. C. Good, a director of United Farmers' Co-operative, of which he had been the first president in 1914, was one of the most faithful attendants, and W. A. Amos succeeded W. J. Wood as a committee member. Leonard Mitchell represented the Ontario Co-operative Union. President Crofford, whose brother C. H. Crofford was general manager of Co-operative Life, attended most meetings.

At the first meeting after Staples' appointment, Crofford suggested that substantially lower agents' commissions than in Saskatchewan might be appropriate in Ontario. Mitchell, who had been writing articles on insurance in the Credit Union News, did not think there should be any agents. To meet another Ontario criticism Crofford suggested omission of children from co-operative members' group insurance. He expressed concern about the $5,000 which Ontario was to raise, and at the next meeting, in May 1947, said that the company had already spent $2,300 in Ontario without any income in return. Staples suggested that distribution of life insurance through local co-operatives, county Federations of Agriculture and like organizations might be the most economical in the long run.

At the following meeting a letter from general manager C. H. Crofford said that Co-operative Life directors were unhappy about Ontario, with expenditures of $3,158 and receipts of $212. Staples was able to report that premiums collected had reached $1,089, principally from extensive member group insurance (life insurance equal to the member's annual purchases) sold to Ontario co-operatives. Staples also reported that the superintendent of insurance had not approved any of four applications by employees of local co-operatives for life insurance licences.

The advisory committee discussed co-operation with Co-operators' Fidelity in its proposed automobile insurance program. Milburn suggested that county Federations of Agriculture and the Ontario Federation of Agriculture would participate actively in an automobile insurance program, and that they and the Farm Forums might undertake an extensive insurance promotion program during the coming winter. The committee had written to 400 people asking each to contribute $50 to the Co-operative Life guarantee fund, but had received only $1,650. The fund had now reached $1,950. W. C. Good wrote his cheque for $50 to bring the total to $2,000.

The committee asked for French-language life insurance application forms and literature. Co-operators' Fidelity board had decided against sharing an office with Co-operative Life at 134 Bloor Street East, but Ontario Credit Union League was going to do so. The life company had been paying $30 a month rent and would now pay only $20 a month. (Co-operators' Fidelity was still enjoying free space at 28 Duke Street.) Savage proposed a protest to the superintendent of insurance against his department's refusal to issue a life insurance licence to a part-time employee of Kempenfeldt credit union. The superintendent's office was holding applications from several co-operative employees. President Crofford would see the superintendent.

The special expense fund reached $3,150 in October. President

Crofford said it would be necessary to have the full $5,000 before the year-end. In December 1947 the advisory committee became concerned that Co-operative Life proposed to write credit union savings and loan insurance similar to insurance offered by CUNA Mutual. Staples informed the committee of this decision by Co-operative Life. Savage said he had not known of this decision until he attended a CUNA meeting in Florida. He said the Ontario committee should have been consulted in advance of action. He added that this program would hurt the Ontario Credit Union League and that the League had requested its discontinuance. The committee asked Co-operative Life not to write such insurance in Ontario. Staples also reported appointment of 10 district representatives and 16 part-time representatives. (This was the beginning of the sales organization which would launch the Co-operators' Fidelity automobile program in 1949.) The special expense fund had reached $3,500.

Harman proposed a Co-operative Life conference in Brockville at the time of the annual meeting of the Canadian Federation of Agriculture, that head office give advisory committees more information on company policy, and that the committee consider organizing a tour of western Canada to coincide with the annual meeting of Co-operative Life in Regina. These discussions on how to sell individual life insurance, and experimental appointment of agents, under the auspices of the Co-operative Life advisory committee, produced only modest life sales but were to prove important to Co-operators' Fidelity in 1949.

Chapter 9

Broadening Out

In the summer of 1947 Co-operators' Fidelity was making new commitments and large plans. Representatives of Ontario Hog Producers Association, president Charles W. McInnis, Clayton Frey and Wilfred Bishop (the latter two farmers were Ontario Agricultural College graduates), attended a July board meeting. The board decided to write livestock transit insurance and instructed the secretary to try to raise an additional $10,000 capital. The board was to approve the rates, and Milburn was to attempt to enlist the support of the Ontario Beef Producers Association.

Financial statements showed a six-month company loss of $1,873, and an eight-month agency profit of $362. Agency business included 39 automobile policies and 22 fire policies. To write automobile insurance would require subscription of $50,000 additional capital ($25,000 paid in), Savage reported. He proposed to employ a canvasser to sell 500 shares to 500 automobile owners ($100 subscribed, $50 paid) recommended as prospects by local farm co-operatives, but a preliminary two-week experiment would precede employment of a canvasser. A motion by Milburn and Harman authorized the executive committee to initiate such a plan and if necessary to employ a canvasser.

The board allotted 20 shares to Toronto Police Employees Credit

Union. A member of this credit union, Harold Anthony, was bringing to "the Shea agency" automobile insurance applications from his fellow credit union members.

Following this meeting, to carry out the experimental part of the Savage plan, Hebb, who was then editor of the Rural Co-operator, canvassed some farmer leaders of Stouffville District Co-operative. Eight persons bought a $100 share ($50 paid) to help the company enter automobile insurance. A brief canvass of a few members of Malton District Co-operative brought one or two more shareholders. Encouraged by this reaction, by additional subscriptions by United Farmers for 50 shares, and by COPACO for 25 shares, and a promise of extensive help by the Ontario Federation of Agriculture, the executive apparently concluded that the company could raise an additional $25,000 without a paid canvasser.

Beginning in 1947, United Farmers' Co-operative arranged a series of low-cost bus tours to visit farm co-operatives in Indiana, Ohio, New York and Pennsylvania for farm men and women. Ontario Federation of Agriculture and Ontario Co-operative Union encouraged participation. An incidental purpose of these tours, which brought people together from across the province and fostered friendships, tour organizer Leonard Harman (looking back) said, was to heal the rift between U. F. Co-op and OFA arising out of the forced resignation in 1945 of R. J. Scott as co-operative company president. Usually a U. F. Co-op director, perhaps accompanied by his wife, was tour director. Insurance was a special interest, particularly in Indiana, where the Farm Bureau sold its automobile insurance to members only.

In September 1947, Savage reported an encouraging meeting with the board of directors of the Ontario Federation of Agriculture and received approval to write to Ontario credit unions asking for share subscriptions and help in obtaining automobile insurance applications. Robert Dinnage, assistant general manager, CIS, Manchester, together with the chairman of the CIS board and another director, was coming to Canada to discuss reinsurance. Morrison invited the CF&GA board to bring the visitors to Barrie for a meeting in the COPACO board room and dinner as guests of COPACO.

The Ontario Credit Union League (OCUL) board regretted that it was unable to sponsor Co-operators' Fidelity as its official other-than-life insurance organization, Savage reported. This was Mitchell's proposal. His resolution at a Co-operators' Fidelity board meeting in May 1947 asked for endorsation of the company as "the official agency for credit union insurance (other than life)." At an OCUL executive meeting in June at the summer cottage of Earle Reed, London's "Mr. Credit Union," Mitchell modified his proposal in fairness to CUNA. His motion recommended to the OCUL directors recognition of Co-operators' Fidelity as "an official agency of this League" for "insurance other than life" and was adopted by the executive. At an OCUL board meeting in August Mitchell tried to make his request even more acceptable by changing "insurance other than life" to "insurance other than fidelity and life" but apparently the board majority saw recognition of Co-operators' Fidelity as somehow a threat to CUNA.

While CUNA Mutual, Madison, Wisconsin, did not write casualty and property insurance, Credit Union National Association (CUNA) was an agent for other insurance companies for the sale of such coverages, and the two organizations, CUNA Mutual and CUNA, were under integrated management, with Roy F. Bergengren as managing director, and Gordon Smith, Hamilton, as Canadian manager of both operations. Smith was a guest at the OCUL board meeting in August. At the same meeting Co-op Fidelity director John M. Hallinan was appointed general manager of the League.

Ontario Co-operative Union, on the other hand, with Savage as secretary, had named Co-operators' Fidelity as its official insurance organization. Savage also reported to the September meeting of the insurance board that he had raised some capital for livestock transit insurance.

Since livestock transit insurance policyholders were truckers, not livestock producers, how could CF&GA help the producers? Staples suggested that it might be possible to write a master policy for the Ontario Hog Producers Association, and pay patronage dividends to the Association. Mitchell moved a comprehensive motion, to study the Staples idea, to consider insuring cattle under a similar policy, to apply for a licence, to write an experimental policy with COPACO and other packing-houses, to charge prevailing premium rates, with the ultimate objective of reducing the cost of marketing livestock.

Of 16 motions adopted at this all-day meeting in September 1947 Mitchell initiated eight. His record was even more pronounced for the two preceding meetings; in July nine of 15 resolutions; in May he had

initiated 18 of 23 resolutions. Mitchell was not impatient but his
knowledge of insurance and business as a practising lawyer enabled
him to follow safely a natural inclination to reach conclusions quickly.
Other board members, including the president, W. J. Wood, were
finding their way more slowly.

Savage reported that he had arranged to have CF&GA share office
space with Co-operative Life Insurance Company at 134 Bloor Street
East in Toronto, and to pay half the monthly rent of $60. (The
landlord, Dr. H. A. Bruce, former lieutenant-governor of Ontario, told
Staples he was not sure his colleagues on an insurance company board
on which he served would be happy about his tenants.) Subsequently
the Ontario Credit Union League had arranged to share the space, and
each organization would have to pay only $20 a month. Nevertheless,
Co-operators' Fidelity board decided to pay the share of the rent for
which it was committed and to terminate the arrangement. The
proposed location had no expansion possibilities and offered little if
any advantage over rent-free 28 Duke Street.

Shea reported an eight-month operating loss of $1,975, with 151
fidelity bonds in force, and ten-month agency income of $467. The
board increased Shea's salary to $50 a week, and approved a purchase
by Savage of a $2,000 25-year 2-3/4% province of Ontario bond at a
price of 101-1/2.

The November visit of Aneurin Davies, chairman of CIS,
Manchester, and Robert Dinnage, recently appointed general manager,
brought encouragement. This was the first of many Canadian visits by
Dinnage, and for the Ontario insurance co-operative the beginning of a
long and helpful association. Davies stood on his dignity, expecting
his general manager to help him on and off with his coat.

Guests at the Co-operators' Fidelity board meeting in Barrie
included, in addition to Davies and Dinnage, H. A. Crofford, president
of Co-operative Life Insurance Company, Hugh Bailey, general
manager of United Farmers' Co-operative since December 1945, and
Hebb.

The board accepted a proposal from Dinnage to reinsure 75 percent
of automobile standard limits (liability for $5,000 injury to one
person, $10,000 injury to more than one person, and $1,000 damage to
property - known as "five, ten and one"), and all risk above standard
limits. (This "quota share" arrangement never went into effect, as a
result of later and contrary advice from O. C. Griffith, Farm Bureau

Insurance, Columbus, Ohio.) The reinsurer would allow a commission on the reinsurance premium to cover the cost of writing the business. Co-operators' Fidelity would expect to get applications free of cost in the early stages. Premiums might be 10 percent below tariff rates. (Even if lower rates were possible, they might frighten the reinsurer and the superintendent of insurance.)

Chapter 10

Musical Chairs

The year 1948 was a time of learning and struggle - in democratic control of an insurance company, in livestock transit insurance, in bonding insurance - and a time of preparation for automobile insurance - raising capital, reaching some major decisions about automobile insurance, and in deciding to co-operate with Co-operative Life in the sale of automobile and life insurance in Ontario. The first board meeting in February appointed Harman, Mitchell and Savage to prepare a statement for the annual meeting on the difficulties and possibilities of a delegate system of control, and enacted a by-law, which met defeat at the annual meeting, to change the name of the company to "Co-operators Insurance Association, or some other suitable name."

Guests at a second board meeting in February were Roy Bergengren, managing director of CUNA Mutual and CUNA, from Madison, Wisconsin, and W. A. Amos of United Farmers' Co-operative. A letter from V. S. Milburn recommended that the company change its name and devise a system of representative control.

At the annual meeting two days later, Harman discussed the problem of providing consistent and stable elected leadership, as well as good management under democratic control, in a mutual insurance company. If annual meetings were held in Toronto, Toronto policyholders would dominate the company.

There were three directors to be elected for three-year terms. Four were nominated, Haapanen, Hallinan and Nicholson, whose terms had expired, and L. J. Billy, manager of La Caisse Co-opérative de Notre Dame d'Ottawa. Hallinan, Nicholson and Billy were elected. (The defeated Haapanen wrote insurance for the company without cost for many years.) The meeting expressed approval of plans to write automobile insurance as soon as $50,000 capital could be raised.

Meeting a week later, the board received with regret the resignation of Savage as secretary-treasurer because of poor health. He was also secretary of the Ontario Co-operative Union. As he said in his letter of resignation, "CF&GA came into being at my suggestion," and he had raised most of the capital. Mitchell, whose contribution was second only to Savage's, resigned as a director "in view of my position as solicitor," although he had given his professional services without remuneration. Some board members felt that his legal knowledge made him too dominant a member of the board, and had suggested to him that he should resign as a board member but carry on as solicitor with remuneration. Voting by ballot without nomination, the board elected Harman president, Morrison vice-president, and Milburn executive member. The executive and Billy became the investment committee.

At this meeting there was "considerable discussion" of proposals by the Ontario Federation of Agriculture for delegate representation at annual meetings, and "some understandings for the future were arrived at." (When the notice for the next annual meeting went out in 1949, an attached, unsigned memorandum entitled "A Plan for Representation" proposed that credit unions and caisses populaires in Ontario should nominate three of the directors, the Ontario Co-operative Union one, and a provincial insurance association, representative of the county Federation insurance committees and of farm policyholders and shareholders, the other five directors.)

In April 1948 the executive recommended that the directors most actively associated with credit unions nominate someone to fill the board vacancy (resulting from Mitchell's resignation), and that one of these directors become an executive member. Accordingly, the board elected Savage, nominated by Billy and Hallinan, as a director, and added Hallinan to the executive. As also recommended by the executive, Andrew Hebb, editor of the Rural Co-operator, became secretary-treasurer "without pay" as of April 5, and Shea assistant secretary-treasurer at a salary of $50 a week.

Chapter 11

Life Advisory Committee 1948

The Co-operative Life advisory committee was also discussing insurance progress and problems. In February 1948 the committee consisted of Wm. G. Nicholson, chairman, W. C. Good, Mitchell, R. A. Stewart (president of OFA) of Almonte in Lanark county, W. A. Amos and K. M. Betzner (past president of OFA). Also attending the February meeting were Co-operative Life president Crofford, R. H. Milliken, K. C., a director of Co-operative Life and also of the Bank of Canada, Milburn, Savage, Hebb and Staples, who was Ontario manager and committee secretary.

Staples reported appointment of nine "district representatives", two other full-time and 19 part-time representatives. The district representative, following U.S. Farm Bureau insurance companies, was supposed to select, train and supervise other representatives, and receive an over-ride commission on their sales.

Stating that the committee's role had not been defined, Nicholson said the committee felt it might have been consulted in advance on such matters as the announcements that Co-operative Life would write credit union loan and savings life insurance in Ontario and that the company would write endowment insurance. Crofford shrewdly questioned whether a provincial advisory committee could advise intelligently on broad company policy. The company had been "pushed into" credit union insurance by a demand in other provinces, and the board had decided that agents needed endowment insurance to be in a strong bargaining position.

"Nobody likes it, not even the Co-op Life board, and not much of it will be sold," he said.

The committee agreed by resolution with Milliken's suggestions that Co-operative Life should provide the Ontario committee with a monthly report of sales by province and a summary of business before the board, and to consult the Ontario committee with regard to any changes made before these are applied to Ontario.

Control of the company by individual policyholders appears unworkable, Crofford said, and Alberta had proposed reorganization as a joint stock company with shares held by co-operative organizations. The committee endorsed reorganization as a federal joint-stock company.

Venturing on ground where angels might "fear to tread", Crofford then proposed that Co-operative Life should also write fire and casualty insurance. There was possibility of strong support from CIS, Manchester. Alberta and Manitoba had already given their approval and British Columbia was going to meet to consider the proposal.

When he had recovered his breath, Milburn, who at one time had represented a local fire mutual in Peterborough county, said an attempt to compete with the 67 locally owned and controlled farm fire mutuals in Ontario would be ill-advised. (Moreover, Co-operative Life would be in competition with Co-operators' Fidelity.) The advisory committee, Milburn said, had been trying to develop greater co-ordination between Co-operators' Fidelity, now planning entry into automobile insurance, and Co-operative Life.

"It has been possible to make folks feel that CF&GA is their own," but Milburn doubted if they would feel the same way if the Ontario company were merged with a Dominion company. Good felt that Co-operative Life expansion into casualty insurance might be best done under a separate charter. Savage proposed a co-operative casualty company in each of five regions, Maritimes, Quebec, Ontario, Prairies and British Columbia.

"We may find ourselves saddled with a number of insurance

companies which, set in their ways, work together less and less as time goes on," Crofford replied. "There is no good reason why we cannot set up a pattern of government in one company which will give policyholders effective, democratic control. Financially it is much easier to do it in one company."

Stewart attributed the success of county co-operative medical services associations in Ontario to local ownership and control and suggested that a Dominion co-operative insurance company wouldn't be much different from any other company.

Crofford asked whether the Ontario special expense fund should be used to offset the Ontario operating loss, although the company as a whole was in a strong year-end position. "Should the other provinces help to carry Ontario?" he asked. Milliken intervened to say that the only intention was to consider the over-all position of the company.

Meeting in March 1948, after consultation with the organizations represented, United Farmers', Ontario Co-operative Union and Ontario Federation of Agriculture, the advisory committee was of the opinion "that Co-op Life can meet the needs of its members for life insurance more effectively if efforts are confined to life insurance alone," but, if at the request of other provinces, the company undertakes other insurance, "under no circumstances should Co-op Life extend operations in Ontario without the approval of the Ontario life insurance advisory committee."

The committee did not object to the introduction of children's and endowment policies into Ontario provided that the representative received no more for selling these types of insurance. There should be a continuing effort to tell prospective policyholders of the disadvantages of endowment insurance.

Sales representatives were not receiving enough help, Staples said, reporting sales since the beginning, of $175,000 in individual life insurance, with premiums of $3,018, and group premiums of about $7,900.

It would be desirable to have a committee member attend Co-operative Life's annual meeting in Regina but there was no way to provide the travelling expenses. At its next meeting the committee asked head office to present to the annual meeting the Ontario committee's opinion on extension into other lines of insurance. Savage reported that Co-op Life had purchased $10,000 United Farmers' 4% debentures. Nine full-time representatives had sold

$48,000 life insurance in four months of 1948, and 20 part-timers had sold $50,000, in individual life insurance. Ten of the 1947 representatives had not applied for licence renewal. Harman urged greater effort in the sale of group insurance.

The committee thought its secretary should not be an employee of Co-operative Life, and Harman (president of Co-operators' Fidelity) replaced Staples in this capacity. Harold Ghent, manager of a farmers' co-operative at Newmarket, replaced Mitchell as an Ontario Co-operative Union representative on the committee.

The May meeting, attended by Crofford, asked Nicholson to attend the annual meeting of Co-operative Life, and nominated him to be a director (Co-operative Life would pay his expenses). Harman, Staples, Milburn and Hebb reported on a visit to Farm Bureau insurance companies in Ohio and Indiana, and their (multiple-line) unified promotion and distribution of life and other kinds of insurance. The committee also discussed integration of life insurance sales with the sale of automobile insurance to be offered by Co-operators' Fidelity.

Crofford had told the committee earlier that no additional capital would be needed to turn Co-operative Life into a joint-stock company. He now reported that the company would need to have $250,000 subscribed and $100,000 paid in, in contrast with only $50,000 now lent to the company by various co-operative organizations. He proposed that each participating province would provide one director, and Saskatchewan the balance, to facilitate meetings. The advisory committee approved the proposal for selection of directors and left to Co-operative Life board the decision between nine and eleven board members.

When the committee met in August, Crofford reported that there was interest in the Maritimes in co-operative insurance. Harman put forward a proposal from Co-operators' Fidelity executive:

1. That Co-operative Life select, train and supervise agents to distribute the automobile insurance Co-operators' Fidelity expects to have available January 1, 1949. ["Distribute" equalled "sell." This was a co-operative idea; co-operators were buyers rather than being "sold to."]
2. That during the first year of co-ordinated distribution, Co-operators' Fidelity pay Co-operative Life a sum equal to 10 percent of policy fees on all business written in rural Ontario.

3. That the Co-operative Life advisory committee and the board of Co-operators' Fidelity be composed of the same persons.

The committee expressed approval of life and automobile insurance co-ordination and asked Harman to take up the combined committee-and-board suggestion with the three organizations represented on the committee. (This appears from the records to have been the final meeting of the separate committee.)

Chapter 12

Responsibilities as Democratic Surety

To advise a distant life board was easy enough - to operate an insurance company and a casualty company at that - was more onerous.

Co-operators' Fidelity board was trying to keep three balls in the air - bonding, livestock transit and automobile insurance. In February 1948 Shea reported requests from caisses populaires for bonds to be issued in the French language. The board approved a motion by Hallinan and Mitchell stating readiness of the company to issue French-language contracts, with the translation of policies to be approved by our solicitor (Mitchell). An unsuccessful experiment in employment of a bilingual secretary followed.

Shea reported several requests by labor unions for fidelity bonds. He was told that the unions usually paid their own claims rather than submit them to a bonding company. Mitchell pointed out that the CF&GA by-laws prohibited such bonds.

In May, on Billy's suggestion, the board decided that printing of French-language application forms only would be satisfactory for the present, and to defer printing policies in French. At the same time, the board decided to prepare a policy in French (typed, not printed) for Billy's caisse populaire - the second such policy issued.

Fidelity bonding was a rough business when claims began to develop. The first claim was for a defalcation by a truck driver. The employee was dismissed, and became elusive. When the board decided eventually to ask for prosecution, Mitchell said it was too late.

In May the board faced a second claim. The company had bonded the same person as an employee of both a local farm supply co-operative and a medical co-operative. The supply co-operative had an operating loss, possibly contributed to by dishonesty, of $12,000. The supply co-operative did not make an insurance claim, but in his capacity as manager of the county medical co-operative, the principal (of the two surety bonds) had transferred without authorization $1,500 from the medical co-operative to the supply co-operative. The cheque was not co-signed, as it was supposed to be. In addition, there was another $700 missing, and the medical co-operative might have a claim for $1,000.

Staples and Nicholson proposed to give the executive "full authority to deal with the possible claim, with a recommendation that they should not seek to avoid the claim on the basis of a technicality." An amendment by Savage and Hallinan, which was adopted, eliminated the recommendation and told the executive to report back for further instructions "if they deem it necessary." Savage explained that he was not recommending non-payment but that too many co-operatives were lax in business matters and that Co-operators' Fidelity should consider "the salutary effect of non-payment on other co-operatives."

At the next meeting Shea read letters from the medical co-operative, and Nicholson and Savage reported they had been in touch with the medical co-operative. Savage said that a just claim should be paid promptly, and advised prompt legal action against the defaulter.

The board then agreed by resolution to authorize the staff to handle and settle fidelity claims. Following settlement of the claim under discussion, the defaulter agreed to repay the amount of the claim, and Billy patiently collected the instalments over an extended period of months.

Now the board had to wrestle with the question whether the company would write a bond for another medical co-operative on an individual it had already bonded for a credit union. Before issuing a second bond, the board decided, the company would require agreement that someone would co-sign cheques signed by the insured person. The application was still outstanding at the next meeting, and the board requested thorough investigation. Morrison thought perhaps the company should require an audit of the credit union.

At a third meeting Hallinan and Milburn brought favorable reports on the individual, and after extensive debate the board decided against a proposal to require co-signing of cheques in the credit union as well as in the co-operative. Following lunch with Hallinan and Billy, Morrison said that CUNA bond rates were really lower, the credit union loss record extremely good, and no new requirements should be made of credit unions. Billy still favored co-signing of cheques in both organizations.

Timmins Consumers Co-operative had transferred its fidelity insurance to Co-operators' Fidelity, but Co-operators' had not issued the usual "superseded suretyship rider." The co-operative had discovered a pre-existing loss of $700, for which the former insurer was no longer liable. Co-operators' was not legally liable, but, Shea said, perhaps was under a moral obligation. The Consumers manager and former Co-operators' Fidelity director, C. M. Haapanen, said that the co-operative would not make a claim, but that Co-operators might take care of the amount at some future time when it was stronger. The board decided to take no action. (Paid later? Maybe, but probably not.)

The staff was having difficulty with another claim. A parish credit union, and important shareholder, had a loss of $399 but was refusing to lay a charge against the credit union member who said he had lost the money while visiting a beverage room on his way home from "banking night" at the credit union. The board disagreed over this claim, a majority at first supporting the secretary and assistant secretary in demanding that the credit union lay a charge, but eventually ordering the claim paid, and turning over negotiation of the credit union's obligations to a committee headed by the president.

At a meeting in November 1948 the president reported that the credit union had laid a charge. The board had discussed this claim at each of five successive board meetings. This was the last claim of any kind that the board of directors of Co-operators' Fidelity, or its successor, Co-operators Insurance Association, ever dealt with or received a report on prior to settlement (even years later when individual claims exceeded $200,000).

Chapter 13

Livestock Transit Insurance and Much, Much More

Preparation for automobile insurance was the big business of 1948, but the board also put a great deal of energy and time into the promotion of bonding and livestock transit insurance. Harman presided over the many board meetings, and executive meetings, co-ordinated the careful planning for entry into automobile insurance, and refereed the accompanying debate, but Morrison, vice-president, and Milburn, an executive member, were the leaders in the development of livestock transit insurance.

Attending a Co-operators' Fidelity board meeting in early May, W. E. Tummon, secretary of the Ontario Hog Producers Association, said that Hartford Fire, the only insurance company writing livestock transit insurance in Ontario, insured only about half the province's hogs. Tummon was a former Conservative member of parliament with friends at Queen's Park. He said that the meat processors had agreed to collect premiums for Co-operators' Fidelity, suggested a master policy to be held by the Hog Producers Association, and proposed organization by county, beginning with Oxford and Norfolk. Milburn reported that the Ontario Beef Cattle Producers Association had agreed to participate in a co-operative livestock transit insurance program. With independent First Co-operative Packers, at Barrie, it was possible to move more quickly. Present at this same meeting, Frank J. Servais, COPACO office manager, said that a policy with COPACO (which he and Co-operators' Fidelity staff had prepared), covering livestock brought to the plant by PCV trucks (that is, licensed as public commercial vehicles), would become effective as soon as signed. The board asked for extension of the policy to cover rail shipments to COPACO. The policy was in effect later in the month when Servais attended another board meeting. He said it would cover 65 percent of the hogs processed at Barrie.

Savage suggested investigation of the risk in insuring livestock brought in by farmers in their own trucks. Savage also discussed insurance on livestock shipments to United Farmers' at the Ontario Stockyards, West Toronto. Charles Zeagman, United Farmers' manager, was personally indebted to the Hartford Fire manager for a blood transfusion for a member of his family. Harman reported that Zeagman was ready to co-operate with Co-operators' Fidelity in the deduction of premiums.

A letter from Servais, read to the board by Shea in June, suggested extension of the COPACO policy to cover non-PCV truckers, but Servais' boss, "Ken" Morrison, COPACO general manager and Co-operators' vice-president, suggested caution and further discussion. Present at this meeting, Chas. W. McInnis, president of Ontario Hog Producers Association, proposed that the company begin livestock transit insurance in a few counties. Morrison proposed co-operative trucking of livestock - he said PCV licensing would not be necessary.

In July the assistant secretary, Shea, reported inclusion of a non-PCV trucker under the COPACO policy. The board approved covering such truckers, on their merits, each such risk accepted to be reported to the board for approval. In September the executive recommended that individual livestock transit policies be issued to truckers, and favored opening an office at the Ontario Stockyards and appointment of a full-time representative to work from the office. Harman felt there was no need for concern about truckers (as policyholders) having a vote at shareholder/policyholder meetings.

Co-operators' Fidelity directors were pinning their hopes for break-even operations on automobile insurance. Their discussions of democratic control grew out of confidence that the Association would soon have hundreds and then thousands of automobile policyholders. Their arguments over the payment of fidelity claims, with no company objectives or predetermined policies to guide them, were self-education in insurance. Livestock transit insurance, taking time and energy, was contributing, too, to their schooling, and to staff knowledge of insurance, but automobile insurance plans were the major activity of 1948.

Members of the joint publications and publicity committee (publishing the Rural Co-operator), U. F. Co-op executive member Staples and Harman, on behalf of the co-operative company, and Alex McKinney and OFA vice-president Robert W. Morrison, on behalf of the Ontario Federation of Agriculture, were individually involved in co-operative insurance efforts, and encouraged the Rural Co-operator editor, Hebb, to give as much help as he could as secretary-treasurer of Co-operators' Fidelity. Hebb spent a good deal of time at the Ontario Federation of Agriculture office, at 409 Huron Street in Toronto, helping secretary-manager Milburn with Federation resolutions and publicity.

At the beginning of 1948, Milburn was making automobile insurance a major OFA program, as Shea reported to a Co-operators' Fidelity board meeting early in February. The next meeting had Milburn's letter on the change of name and democratic control.

In April, Milburn initiated a board resolution to sell at least 600, rather than 500, additional shares as automobile insurance capital. The board asked Milburn to accept the responsibility for selling shares through rural organizations and Savage and Billy through credit unions and caisses populaires respectively.

Milburn, who had participated in a United Farmers' Co-operative tour of Indiana Farm Bureau co-operatives in October 1947, initiated a motion to authorize the president to spend up to $200 to take a board and staff group to the United States to study automobile insurance. As a result, following the first board meeting in May, Harman, Hebb, Milburn, Shea and Staples spent a week in Indiana and Ohio.

This was a first visit to Indianapolis and Columbus for Hebb and Shea, and perhaps for Staples, but Harman had been visiting the Farm Bureau co-operatives of these states ever since his honeymoon in 1936. Employed on the home farm in York county, he had been president of the UFYPO (United Farm Young People of Ontario) earlier, and later became vice-president of the UFO (United Farmers of

Ontario), while his wife Violet, a former school teacher, was secretary of the United Farm Women of Ontario. In 1940 he became an employee of United Farmers' Co-operative Company and educational secretary of the UFO, resuming the role of assistant editor of the Rural Co-operator, responsible to Herbert Hannam. In 1943 he became United Farmers acting secretary in succession to Hannam, and in 1944 general secretary.

While Harman was the Indiana and Ohio insurance tour conductor, Staples, already immersed in the problems of selling insurance, and convinced of the desirability of multiple-line selling, asked many of the questions which enabled the five Ontario visitors to agree on the secrets of Farm Bureau insurance success.

In the county towns of Indiana they found thriving Farm Bureau farm supply co-operatives and, usually on the same premises, a combined Farm Bureau membership organization and Farm Bureau Insurance office. A district agent was in charge of the office and of local agents. The district agent was required to meet both life and casualty (automobile, fire and family liability) sales quotas.

The district agent's contract required him to pay the county Farm Bureau a share of the office rent and secretarial costs. His contribution varied with his sales - a percentage of the automobile and family liability policy fees, and of the first premium on other insurance (with no policy fee), and a small payment for each renewal. Agents did not collect premium renewals. A policy fee was an extra payment which the policyholder made when he purchased an automobile or family liability insurance coverage. Acceptable to the policyholder because of a six-month premium, and the lower renewal cost, it was a variation from pioneering State Farm Mutual's "membership fee" (payable only once in a lifetime for each policy or coverage) and lapsed two years after a policy lapsed (or was cancelled).

This was important because Indiana Farm Bureau Insurance Company was required to cancel a policyholder's automobile insurance if he did not pay his annual Farm Bureau membership fee (doubled from $5 to $10 in 1948). The district agent was responsible for the annual canvass for Farm Bureau membership fees, but policyholders were expected to pay their insurance premiums by mail or in person. The company billed them from Indianapolis, and they could mail their payments to head office as requested, or take them to the county office. The county office was conveniently located in the county town at the centre of each of Indiana's 80 neatly rectangular counties.

Because of the policy fee, the direct billing which permitted an agent renewal commission of only three percent, the support of the county Farm Bureau and the county Farm Bureau co-operative, and a county Farm Bureau credit union in 45 of 80 counties, and multiple-line insurance selling (with life insurance making an important contribution to agent income), Farm Bureau automobile insurance premiums were far enough below competitive premiums that the policyholder could pay a Farm Bureau membership fee as well and still save money. Even with the policy fee to pay, as well as the Farm Bureau membership fee (associate membership for persons who did not live on a farm), a new policyholder would either save money immediately, or anticipate savings at renewal.

In Indianapolis the group met Harvey Hull, president of Indiana Farm Bureau Co-operative, Hassil Schenck, full-time president of the Farm Bureau and of the Farm Bureau insurance companies, and the insurance managers, Jack J. Rosebrough, manager of the automobile and fire insurance companies, Morley Ringer, manager of Hoosier Life Insurance Company, and Ed Stevens, manager of the joint sales agency. Although there was some dissatisfaction with this triumvirate management arrangement, the visitors were encouraged to think that a similar arrangement for Co-operators' Fidelity, Toronto, and Co-operative Life, Regina, would be practical in Ontario. The fact was, however, that the three Indiana Farm Bureau managers were in the same office, and all three responsible to president Schenck. Subsequently, Rosebrough became general manager of all operations of the automobile, fire and life companies.

After a day and a half in Indianapolis the group spent two days with officers of Farm Bureau Insurance Companies, Columbus, Ohio: C. W. Leftwich, vice-president and secretary, Murray Lincoln, president and general manager, Ray Rausch, agency service, R. W. Griffith, casualty statistician, O. C. Griffith, reinsurance underwriter, C. W. Eberhard, casualty underwriting manager, and E. A. Rule, assistant treasurer and office manager. While Indiana Farm Bureau insurance companies were confining their operations to rural Indiana, and selling automobile insurance only to Farm Bureau members, Ohio Farm Bureau companies were selling 70 percent of their insurance in urban areas and had extended operations into Pennsylvania and a number of other eastern states. Ohio Farm Bureau automobile insurance got an early start in the twenties, under dynamic Murray Lincoln, with some help and advice from State Farm Mutual of Bloomington, Illinois - inventor of the formula involving policy fee, low renewal commission, six-month premium and direct billing - a formula which was to take State Farm to first place in the United States in automobile insurance written.

The Indiana Farm Bureau had been an agent for State Farm Mutual automobile insurance for 10 years before starting its own company in February 1935. The Ohio Farm Bureau set up its own company in 1926 when the state department of insurance refused to approve working with State Farm.

These visits to Indiana and Ohio were the beginning of never ending help from these companies (Farm Bureau, Columbus, Ohio, became Nationwide Insurance). Indiana's intensive operations were producing lower-cost insurance than Ohio's extensive operations, and as far as possible Co-operators' Fidelity tried to follow Indiana. However, it was Farm Bureau, Columbus, through O. C. Griffith, which provided continuous advice in the next few years and probably enabled inexperienced Co-operators' Fidelity and staff to pull through the first crucial years in automobile insurance.

Both Indiana and Ohio were integrated multiple-line organizations selling their insurance through multiple-line agents, and Staples had no difficulty in convincing his companions that this was the right co-operative insurance program. His employers in Regina, however, had not acquainted themselves with co-operative insurance programs in the United States and had launched a conventional life insurance sales plan.

Staples was also clear that the six-month premium was highly desirable (in fact, an essential part of the policy fee and direct billing formula), although someone - perhaps cautious Milburn - had doubts and the tour group reserved judgment on this point, but formulated a long list of other recommendations which the Co-operators' Fidelity board adopted with few changes. A central office in each county for credit union, local co-operative, insurance and Federation of Agriculture services was to be a long-term objective. There was to be immediate discussion with Co-operative Life to arrange distribution of co-operative automobile and co-operative life insurance under unified direction. The board said such discussions should include CUNA Mutual Insurance Society too.

In the early stages co-operative automobile insurance would be offered to members of participating organizations only. Co-operators' Fidelity would pay urban credit union chapters and county Federations 20 percent of the policy fees and 25 cents per annum per renewal for satisfactory office facilities and services for the company's agents, the board also decided. Use of tabulating equipment from the beginning, if available economically, could effect great savings. Use of "continuous" policies would effect an important economy - at that time most companies issued a new policy annually, often delivered personally to the policyholder.

Two reinsurance recommendations came from O. C. Griffith of Ohio Farm Bureau. The board approved both. One was to try to reduce the fidelity insurance retention on named individuals from $5,000 to $3,000. The other was to ask the reinsurer, CIS, Manchester, for an excess reinsurance treaty in automobile insurance, in place of the quota arrangement already agreed on.

"With a quota treaty you are just an agent," said Griffith. "With an excess treaty you will be in the insurance business, with a chance to make or lose money."

The tour group felt that there would be some advantages in having automobile reinsurance with Ohio Farm Bureau, but recommended asking CIS, Manchester, for automobile liability reinsurance for losses in excess of $2,500 in any one accident. The board agreed.

The board interrupted a meeting in June 1948 at 28 Duke Street to hold a five-hour insurance conference with the Ontario Federation of Agriculture executive. Milburn explained plans made to overcome difficulties in the way of democratic representation. There was discussion of the duties of the new county Federation insurance committees.

Milburn and Staples reported on the sale of automobile and life insurance in Indiana and Ohio. Milburn said that in Indiana low-cost automobile insurance was building the Farm Bureau, enabling the Farm Bureau to collect a substantial membership fee. Staples said that both Indiana and Ohio found that it was not until they got into life insurance, providing full-time jobs for agents, that they got really substantial volume in automobile insurance.

Co-operators' Fidelity directors agreed with suggestions by OFA executive members that it would be necessary to provide truck insurance. Shea said that the Indiana and Ohio co-operative companies found it to their advantage to pay automobile claims promptly and generously, but that strict underwriting was also necessary. Staples explained 80/20 collision insurance, popular in Indiana. Mrs. C. A. Campbell saw a need for more satisfactory forms of collision insurance.

OFA president R. A. Stewart, the chairman, thought the meeting favored a combination of 80/20 with $25 deductible. Staples thought the combination undesirable.

It was not important. Really important and encouraging was the fact that the influential Ontario Federation of Agriculture was adopting automobile insurance as a major project.

Chapter 14

Deadline January

There could be no automobile insurance without capital. At the board meeting earlier on the same day the board had allotted only five shares. One of four purchasers was Joseph Bonner, an Ontario Credit Union League director. After the insurance conference, Co-operators' Fidelity directors authorized the investment committee to make a $5,000 mortgage loan. It would cost about $20 to register the still unregistered British Columbia and New Brunswick bonds. On the suggestion of Morrison it was agreed to raise this question at a full board meeting - Savage was ill and two other directors were absent.

Later in June the Ontario Federation of Agriculture held a co-operative automobile insurance conference of OFA directors, county secretaries and insurance committee chairmen. They decided to incorporate an "Ontario Co-operative Insurance Association", which would help to raise capital and nominate directors for Co-operators' Fidelity board. After the meeting Milburn sent a circular letter to county Federations urging them to raise their share of capital, to permit a January start in automobile insurance.

Credit union people were also "talking up" automobile insurance. Most could not get away from their jobs for daytime mid-week meetings, and the League was not strong enough then to pay travel expenses, but on the evening of the next Co-op Fidelity board meeting, July 14, 1948, several board members - president Harman, Milburn, Hallinan and Nicholson - and several staff members met with George Scott, Frank Haffey and Joseph O'Meara (this is the Joseph O'Meara who sang on radio for a number of years with Ernest Bushnell - Mr. Broadcasting).

John M. Hallinan, a bilingual university graduate, had become general manager of Ontario Credit Union League August 10, 1947, in succession to volunteer managing director George W. Scott, a lifelong CPR employee. Hallinan had decided in 1940 against continuing his studies for the Roman Catholic priesthood.

Hallinan explained to the credit unionists the informal plan of representation, and Harman reviewed the visit to Indiana and Ohio, and the desirability of co-ordination of the sale of life and automobile insurance. Hallinan said that half of 250 credit unions in Ontario had committees to promote CUNA Mutual life insurance. O'Meara explained how he acted for CUNA Mutual without remuneration.

Haffey felt that credit union members would be interested in automobile insurance, and Hallinan and Scott felt that it would be more satisfactory to work through credit unions rather than through credit union chapters. Prevailing opinion was that the sale of automobile insurance in credit unions should be voluntary for the first year at least.

Harman hoped to raise the necessary capital to begin business by January 1949. Staples explained the advantages of the six-month premium, but Scott felt that half-yearly premiums would double handling costs, and asked if the company could give a choice between annual and six-month premiums. O'Meara and Haffey preferred an annual premium.

Opinion was against 80/20 collision, explained by Shea. When Harman said it would not be possible to accept all applications, Staples questioned whether credit unions could refuse applications. Scott said credit unions refuse to give loans and could refuse to give insurance. Haffey agreed with Harman that an automobile insurance school would be worthwhile.

This question of underwriting or selection had arisen earlier in the day at the board meeting. Would the company accept a share application from Noisy River Telephone Company, and, if so, would the company's trucks be eligible for automobile insurance? Yes, CF&GA would accept an application for a share, but there was no decision yet about writing truck insurance.

Three future farmer directors, Alden McLean, D. E. Stauffer and Milton J. Brown, were among 24 applicants for one share each. [Brown became a director of Co-op Fidelity and of successor company Co-operators Insurance Association (CIA), the others of CIA.] Dairy farmer leaders Charles Milton and Erle Kitchen bought one share each. One of two applicants for two shares each was Orford Farmers Co-operative, McLean's home co-operative at Muirkirk.

A new member of the staff, Margaret Chambers, attended this meeting on July 14, 1948. She had been engaged at a salary of $45 a week, "on the understanding that she would receive $50 a week in a year's time if her services were satisfactory." A University of Toronto graduate, majoring in mathematics and statistics, she had applied for an advertised job but after an interview at dilapidated 28 Duke Street she felt that she would not be happy in the initial typing and clerical duties, although she thought that "some day the position will amount to a very important and interesting one." However, she had actuarial, data processing and supervisory experience, which would be valuable to Co-operators' Fidelity, and liked "working with people." She was persuaded that the job would liven up quickly.

Her decision proved fortunate for the company. In addition to her experience and skills, she brought to the company a questioning mind, a concern for accuracy and detail, an unselfish interest in the welfare of each member of the growing staff, and a zeal for service to policyholders that contributed in large measure to the character of the successful company that emerged in the fifties and sixties. As office manager and accountant during 1949 and accounting and systems manager in 1950 she brought business experience which may have averted confusion and failure.

Shea said that more office space would be needed for automobile insurance and estimated a deficit of $2,500 for the year - mostly the result of plans for expansion into automobile insurance. In view of plans for joint distribution of life and automobile insurance, Staples said, it would be advisable for Co-operators' Fidelity, Co-operative Life and Ontario Credit Union League to have their offices in the same building.

Shea asked again about registering $9,000 in British Columbia and New Brunswick bonds at a cost of about $20. The decision, on motion of Billy and Milburn, was not to register these bonds, held in a safety-deposit box, but to reconsider in January. Perhaps this annoying expense would "go away" but at least the 1948 operating loss would be $20 less.

Chapter 15

Negotiating "Joint Distribution"

For discussion purposes Harman, as president, at this July 1948 board meeting, presented a memo proposing incorporation of an agency, with two directors appointed by Co-operative Life and two by Co-operators' Fidelity, and a manager who would build an organization to distribute automobile and life insurance. The two companies would contribute equally during the first year, at a maximum rate of $800 a month, and later according to services received and results obtained. The directors of Co-operators' Fidelity would offer to become the Ontario advisory committee of Co-operative Life, but the board and the committee would have different officers.

Morrison questioned so heavy a commitment as $800 a month, and the feasibility of joint distribution. Milburn said he, too, had been doubtful about joint distribution until he had gone to Indiana and Ohio. Harman said that a well-developed distribution system must be built up, whether for each company separately or together, and Co-operators' Fidelity must know its program by October.

"It must be an effective program and well organized to give

71

immediate volume results," Harman said. "The largest volume of rural automobile insurance is sold in January, February and March."

"The basic question is two sets of machinery or one," said Staples. "The same mileage, and the same man, can do both jobs." It was agreed that the executive would prepare a proposal for submission to both the Ontario life advisory committee and Co-operators' Fidelity board.

Harman, Nicholson, Staples and Shea met with "Red" Crofford, Co-operative Life president, later in the month to discuss joint distribution of life and automobile insurance. The term "distribution" instead of "sales" originated in the co-operative ideas of Harman and Staples. The organization would find automobile insurance easier to "distribute" than life insurance - life insurance would have to be "sold."

At an early September meeting Co-operators' Fidelity executive (Harman, Morrison, Milburn and Hallinan) agreed on joint distribution of automobile and life insurance, but preferred to delegate the sale of automobile insurance to Co-operative Life rather than establish a joint agency.

There were also proposals for remuneration of "general" agents - they were not to be "district" agents, it was thought, because they would not have exclusive territories as in Indiana - and remuneration of sub-agents. A general agent would receive 50 percent of automobile policy fees on his own writings, and 20 percent of sub-agent policy fees. A sub-agent would receive 30 percent of policy fees. Co-operative Life would receive 10 percent of automobile policy fees written in rural Ontario. County Federations would receive 20 percent for provision of satisfactory office facilities, and the company would retain 20 percent to cover the cost of issuing the policy.

The executive reported these recommendations to a September board meeting. Harman reported a wire from C. H. Crofford, manager of Co-operative Life (brother of the president): "Our company not licensed to act as agency for CF&GA. Will share services of Ontario manager, representatives and agency system."

Savage, welcomed back in improved health, and Hallinan said credit unions did not favor payments to agents. Harman said that in rural Ontario the problem was how much to pay the agent as a livable wage to get the job well done. Staples said company success depended on establishing well-paid high-calibre agents. Morrison thought the policy fee plan would give an agent too much the first year and not enough on renewal, and questioned the advisability of linking automobile and life insurance together.

Staples and Nicholson moved a resolution authorizing further negotiations with Co-operative Life. Staples wanted to keep Co-operators' Fidelity moving in the direction of joint distribution but, as he was urging an arrangement, likely to be adopted, which would make him in effect an employee of both companies, he tendered his resignation as a director of the casualty company. When it was accepted in October he was invited to continue to attend the board meetings. He was still a director of United Farmers' Co-operative Company. An Ontario Co-operative Union executive member, he was also president of the Co-operative Union of Canada but in this latter capacity under-employed and over-shadowed by secretary A. B. MacDonald.

The executive favored a full-time man and office at the Ontario Stockyards. The insurance company would pay packing plants and commission firms five percent for premium collection. Harman reported that truckers' livestock policies would be ready shortly.

Nicholson reported that United Farmers' board had approved Co-operators' Fidelity board acting as the Co-operative Life advisory board.

One credit union and three co-operatives were among the applicants for shares in September. Three applications were for two shares, 19 for one share. Applicants included W. C. Good, Lawrence Kerr, Clarence Charlton, William Bradshaw, Barrett A. Forbes, Fred A. W. Marsh, Clayton Frey and Russel Knight.

In the absence of the two employees, the board approved their inclusion in United Farmers' group life insurance plan, and increased Shea's salary from $50 to $60 a week. Shea reported CIS, Manchester, had made a deposit in Canada and obtained a Canadian licence. Co-operators' Fidelity would not need to set up a reserve for unlicensed reinsurance. The board approved proposed automobile premiums, presented by Hebb, which included a flat farm rate for passenger cars (which Milburn thought might be too high) of $16 for "ten, twenty and five" ($10,000 for injury to one person, $20,000 for injury to two or more persons and $5,000 for property damage) for six months, although as yet there was no agreement on a six-month premium. The proposed Toronto pleasure rate for 10/20/5 was $29.

Thirty-eight applicants in October for one share each included: Burton R. Baxter, Picton, Robert C. Young, Cayuga; CBC farm broadcasting pioneer Orville Shugg, Alvinston; Ross Parsons, Ilderton; Harry McGowan, Orton; R. S. Heatherington, Milton; and Ethel Chapman, farm magazine editor. Farmers' Insurance Information Association (FIIA), which had been refused the name of Ontario Co-operative Insurance Association, bought two shares from the treasury and eight others by transfer from a shareholder who needed her money, with funds provided by loans by individuals to FIIA of five and 10 dollars each, but there was still a long way to go before it would be possible to secure an automobile insurance licence.

Kenneth M. Betzner, a Waterloo county farmer with bank clerk experience, attended this meeting as a visitor and was elected to fill the vacancy which would result, following the meeting, from Staples' resignation. Nominated by FIIA, Betzner was past president of the OFA and a member of the Co-operative Life advisory committee which was to merge with Co-operators' Fidelity board. Betzner did not think a six-month premium would be acceptable, but Harman and Nicholson had been in Ohio in September and had been strongly advised to use a six-month premium. In addition to a lower unearned premium reserve, and elasticity in adjusting premiums (rate changes would become effective twice as fast), the six-month premium was in tune with the trend to instalment buying. FIIA had approved the six-month premium, Milburn reported. Staples felt more frequent contact with policyholders would be an advantage, and Billy saw six months as very practical. The question was not important to credit unions, Hallinan said, and the board approved the six-month premium subject to discussion with the department of insurance. Betzner promised to canvass farm opinion.

Was Co-operators' Fidelity going to write automobile insurance for persons other companies would not insure? Hebb told the board that it should adopt underwriting acceptability rules that it was prepared to back up. Shea provided copies of the underwriting rules of the Ohio and Indiana Farm Bureau companies and of Canadian General Insurance Company.

The board asked Harman to appoint a committee to report to board members on underwriting rules in advance of the next meeting. There was also discussion of the agent's authority to give immediate coverage - should he be able to "bind" the company? Would the

Association insure employees of farm organizations and co-operatives, and village residents? Who would be eligible to buy co-operative automobile insurance? The committee to study underwriting rules was asked to report on this question too.

Harman reported that Milliken was offering alternative proposals to the Co-operative Life board - that Co-operators' Fidelity pay Co-operative Life 10 percent of automobile policy fees, or 10 percent of policy fees and $1,000 and Co-operative Life would add a third man to its Ontario staff. (Staples had already employed Bill Ritchie, of Simcoe county. William Ritchie was a former wartime rural-film-circuit projectionist for the National Film Board.) Co-operators' Fidelity board now approved and recommended the second alternative.

Savage reported that Ontario Credit Union League board thought that Co-operators' Fidelity should use a comparable share of policy fees for urban and rural promotion.

Staples felt that the agents he would appoint and supervise should send their automobile applications to him - so that he would know what they were doing - rather than direct to Co-operators' Fidelity. Hebb and Shea thought this would mean undesirable delay. Harman, Shea and Staples would discuss and report on this question.

At an earlier meeting Savage had suggested that the company participate in a new company which would purchase or erect or rent a building to house all Toronto-based Ontario co-operative and rural organizations. The solicitor's opinion, now reported, was that the Association could buy shares in a housing corporation only as a current expense (and could not treat them as an investment).

The board asked the USA tour group to report on the division of the policy fee.

At the first of two November all-day meetings the board approved new proposals that the local or special agent would receive 50 percent of the policy fee and the general or district agent (these names were still uncertain) 20 percent over-ride. The district agent (as he turned out to be) was to receive 50 percent in addition to 20 percent on his own writings. This payment of 70 percent to the district agent, when he might be in competition with his own local agents, was contrary to advice from Ohio Farm Bureau, and may have accounted for the early failure of the district-agent/local-agent plan.

The county Federation or credit union chapter would receive up to 10 percent, the provincial sponsor up to 10 percent, and on rural policies the joint agency 10 percent. Agents would receive a three percent payment on renewal premiums, and the county Federation or credit union chapter 12-1/2 cents for each renewal. Payments to sponsors were for their expenses in promotion of Co-op Fidelity insurance.

Staples should go ahead with the other-than-life licensing of agents, the directors agreed. They would have to write examinations. Savage stressed the importance of agent selection, and asked if each application should come before the board. Hebb thought the directors should discuss the type of agent they wanted and then, as they had decided earlier, Staples would appoint agents. Co-operators' Fidelity should recommend appointees automatically. Milburn stressed the need to consult the county Federation committee about appointments in the county. Savage moved a resolution confirming these arrangements, and later another providing for supervision of urban agents by the joint agency. Opinion on this second motion was divided and, on Harman's request, Savage withdrew it.

The board approved an elaborate underwriting report on prohibited and undesirable drivers and policyholders, and prohibited and undesirable vehicles. A rule against accepting as policyholders persons of 70 years or more excluded some shareholders!

The board agreed to offer automobile insurance to employees of the sponsoring organizations, in addition of course to the members. Harman said that the proposal to appoint urban agents increased the desirability of restricting for the present the people whom the Association would insure.

Applicants for shares at this November 5, 1948, meeting included Daniel G. McKinnon, who became an agent, Richard W. Hannam, Guelph, brother of the then president of the Canadian Federation of Agriculture, and Alex Anderson, Wellington county Federation officer. Nine persons applied for one share, and Mitchell Co-operative Association for three shares. Reorganized as the central wholesale owned by 150 local co-operatives, United Co-operatives of Ontario requested transfer of 75 shares to its new name.

[United Co-operatives of Ontario (UCO) assumed the business of United Farmers' Co-operative Company on October 1, 1948, and held its first annual meeting on December 2 and 3, 1948.]

"It is difficult to get a farm committee to move quickly," Milburn had said in October. "They cannot be pushed." Now he invited all board members to attend a meeting on November 19 of directors of Ontario Federation of Agriculture and FIIA voting delegates from each county. Those Co-op Fidelity directors who could do so would attend this OFA gathering. In addition, the board agreed to meet on November 26, to spend half a day with Milliken and the Co-operative Life advisory committee and the rest of the day on company problems and plans. Deadline January was crowding closer!

While the Ontario government, represented by the attorney-general and the superintendent of insurance, was cautious about a brash new co-operative insurance company, the same government, represented by the minister of agriculture, was ready to help farmers' co-operatives. "Tom" Kennedy's office door was wide open to "Viv" Milburn. At that time the minister of agriculture was supervising credit unions, too, even though they were mostly urban. County agricultural representatives felt free to help farmers' co-operatives, and some of them made no distinction between a farm producers' or supply co-operative and the new insurance co-operative. Ralph C. Banbury, agricultural representative in Northumberland county, proposed that co-operatives at Campbellford, Cobourg and Warkworth, and the county Federation of Agriculture, each buy a share, as part of a county quota of 12 shares.

He proposed also that four artificial insemination technicians take up a share each and undertake to sell co-operative car insurance. "I would feel that if they sold 250 car policies each in the year, making a total of 1,000 in the county, we would have made a fair job," he wrote to Milburn. "Since a large number of our agents simply renew the old policy these figures might be a little higher .... All of these men live on farms, have good cars and while the combination is rather odd they would cover this county in a rural way particularly well."

While it would be all right for the co-operatives to buy shares, Milburn cautiously replied that when the joint sales agency was organized in Northumberland the county Federation insurance committee could put forward "suggestions such as you have offered."

At an organization meeting in October, Farmers' Insurance Information Association elected Betzner president, R. A. Stewart and M. J. Brown vice-presidents and Milburn secretary-treasurer. At the November 19 meeting of OFA directors, secretaries of member organizations and representatives of county Federation insurance committees, Harman, Savage, Staples and K. N. M. ("Ken") Morrison presented the Co-op Fidelity story. "Vic" Roy of Huron county, William Newman of Victoria county, a former member of the Ontario legislature, William McCarthy of Dufferin county and OFA vice-president R. W. ("Bob") Morrison of Lambton county discussed how the county Federation members would sell 226 more shares to qualify Co-op Fidelity for an insurance license.

Cheered by the plans made at the OFA-FIIA meeting, and evidence that farm committees had begun to move, Harman, Shea and Hebb visited Cecil Richards, chief examiner, and R. B. Whitehead, K. C., superintendent of insurance, at Queen's Park, to discuss a licence to write automobile insurance. The licence would be forthcoming as soon as the company had the capital, but these officials said that the experience in automobile insurance in the past year had been very bad, and they did not recommend entering the field at the present time.

Told that the company expected to write 4,000 policies in the first year, Richards estimated that premium income would be $120,000, or $30 per policy per annum, and said that the company should have paid-in capital of half that amount, or $60,000, for automobile insurance. In view of the six-month premium, however, the department would require only $25,000 or $30,000 for 4,000 policies, and an additional $10,000 for each additional 1,000 policies. Thirty thousand dollars and the earlier requirements for fidelity and livestock transit insurance totalled $60,000.

The proposed capital requirement was small, only enough to stand an 80 percent loss experience, and many companies had greater losses, Richards said. ("An 80 percent loss experience" meant claims amounting to 80 percent of earned premiums - the "loss ratio." Operating expenses - the "expense ratio" - would be additional.) Both he and the superintendent urged the company to continue to raise capital after securing a licence, or it might be necessary to make a call on the unpaid portion of the shares. The following day Richards said that he had not taken the company's planned reinsurance into account, but that $30,000 was the minimum to secure a licence. The company would have to maintain minimum capital of $60,000 for bonding, livestock transit and automobile insurance. Reinsurance would ease future capital requirements.

When Co-operators' Fidelity board met a few days later - the second meeting in November - there were applications for 117 shares from 110 applicants, most of them active in Farm Forums, farm supply co-operatives or county Federations of Agriculture. Applicants included: five farm co-operatives, applying for a total of six shares, Moore Credit Union, of Corunna, applying for one share; R. S. McKercher, president, Seaforth Farmers Co-operative, a future president of the successor company (CIA); Melville Howden Staples, editor of the UFO's "The Challenge of Agriculture", published in 1921; Charles R. Coultes, Andrew Cumming, Leland L. Pound, Wellington Sutton, Clarence Allin, George C. Feagan, William Brander, Alex Gillies, John M. Goit, and others who became closely associated with the company in one way or another.

Harman dutifully reported the advice and requirements of the insurance officials, and recommended that the company continue to raise capital beyond the $30,000 objective. The board agreed and approved with minimal changes a 20-point emergency first-year program proposed and presented by Harman on "Distribution Program of Co-op Life and Auto Insurance in Ontario."

The "Ontario Co-op Insurance Board," to be both Co-operators' Fidelity board and Co-operative Life advisory committee, would consist of five nominees of FIIA, three nominated by credit unions and one by the Ontario Co-operative Union. The board would nominate one director to the "national Co-op Life board," and would appoint a distribution committee consisting of president Harman (as chairman of the committee), the secretary, Hebb, and the distribution manager, Staples, to meet weekly or more often. Agents would send applications to Co-op Fidelity, not to the distribution manager, and Co-op Fidelity staff would deal directly with the agents concerning applications, underwriting and premiums, but keep the distribution staff informed "by copy or otherwise."

Farm people bought automobile insurance early in the year. The plan was to harvest this business first. The company would pay Co-operative Life $1,000 and 10 percent of rural policy fees toward the cost, and by autumn would aim to spend a corresponding $1,000 and 10 percent of urban policy fees on urban distribution. The "Ontario Co-op Insurance Board" would concentrate on automobile insurance during the first half of 1949, and would bring efforts on life insurance into balance later, "mobilizing the force of the Ontario farm and co-operative movement behind life as well as auto."

Co-operators' Fidelity board authorized an additional staff member, reduction of the proposed property damage retention of $5,000 if it seemed necessary, and zoning of farm rates if it seemed desirable after correspondence with O. C. Griffith, Ohio Farm Bureau. For the next three years Griffith (20 years later general manager of a large company, Shelby Mutual) provided continuous advice by correspondence and made two several-day visits to Toronto without any fee or remuneration.

The same day the board spent the afternoon in discussion of Harman's 20-point distribution (that is, sales) memorandum with R. H. Milliken, K. C., of Co-operative Life, who had been attending a board meeting of the Bank of Canada. With minor clarifications he agreed to seek the approval of the board of Co-operative Life, and to recommend the appointment of a third man to the Ontario staff. Milliken's visits to Ontario were always harmonious and welcomed - "Red" Crofford was inclined to ruffle Ontario feathers.

Chapter 16

December 1948

All over rural Ontario the county Federations of Agriculture or their insurance committees were soliciting share applications or small loans to FIIA. Many people could spare only $5 or $10 - and, of course, they did not know if they would ever see this money again. When Co-operators' Fidelity board met in mid-December there were 197 applications for shares. Except for 54 shares - an application from Victor E. Taylor, Brucefield, for 10 shares, an application from Waterloo county Federation of Agriculture for 12 shares, and 16 applications for two shares each - applications were for one share each. Applicants included two future CIA presidents - Kenneth M. Betzner and Gordon W. Greer - and other farm leaders, UCO director Charles W. McInnis, Leonard Laventure, Sam Hendrich, Eldon D. Weber, Donald Ireland, James Powers, Lloyd M. Kerr, Clayton H. Bender, J. Harvey Taylor, Howard Shuh, Oliver A. Snyder, J. D. McLennan, Harold P. Leslie and W. Erskine Johnston, who became a member of the Ontario legislature. Several of these applicants for shares subsequently became agents. With acceptance of these applications, the directors had allotted 1,235 shares ($50 paid in), to exceed by 35 shares the superintendent's requirement of $60,000.

There was enough capital to obtain an automobile insurance licence but there were questions still to be settled before the company could write automobile insurance - despite two years of investigation and discussion. To expedite discussions, the secretary asked approval to deposit money in a trust company, to register all bonds (bearer municipal and government), to reimburse an agent for his casualty licence fee if he wrote 20 automobile policies within three months of licensing, to authorize signing the automobile reinsurance treaty with CIS, Manchester, to apply for an automobile insurance licence, to authorize writing automobile insurance, to authorize collision, fire and theft premiums comparable with public liability rates already approved, not to write automobile insurance in northern Ontario for the first year, and to use tabulating equipment (in the beginning, UCO's).

Nicholson reported acceptance by Co-operative Life, with one variation, of the 20 points on distribution. Milburn reported on OFA and FIIA promotion of automobile insurance. Staples reported on steps to launch automobile insurance in counties recommended by FIIA.

A motion by Betzner, seconded by Nicholson, that the renewal commission to district agents be changed from three to five percent was lost. Savage proposed, seconded by Morrison, to reimburse an agent for his first casualty licence fee, at the rate of $5 for his first 20 policies issued, and $5 for each additional 10 policies. An amendment by Milburn and Betzner to soften the requirements was lost, and the Savage proposal carried.

Hallinan, general manager of the League, reported a proposal from the League executive, moved by Mitchell and Savage, to appoint "a reasonable number" of agents recommended by the League, that agents and volunteers send automobile insurance applications direct to the company, and that the company provide the League with the names and addresses of credit union members who become policyholders. The company should make payments to the League similar to those made to district agents (20 percent of policy fees if there was an agent, otherwise 70 percent). Savage had to leave the meeting early, and the board approved the proposal only in part, referring the payments proposal to the executive.

Staples asked if an agent already in the field would be allowed to sell co-operative automobile insurance along with other automobile insurance. In reply the board took a first step toward an exclusive agency force, following the practice of Farm Bureau companies and

Canadian life insurance companies. Co-op Fidelity agents would "handle no auto insurance except Co-op with any exceptions to be approved by the head office staff." Exceptions were few - in January Harman and Hebb agreed to Staples' proposal that two State Farm agents could write Co-op automobile insurance for eligible persons and State Farm insurance for others, but State Farm may not have agreed. Both T. A. Cameron of Lucknow, in Bruce county, and H. S. (Harve) Hallman of Blair, in Waterloo county, became valuable exclusive representatives. Hallman was recruited by Betzner.

The board had accepted most of the secretary-treasurer's recommendations but postponed decision on whether to write automobile insurance in northern Ontario. Between issues of the twice-monthly Rural Co-operator, Hebb was developing automobile insurance forms and a rate manual. The application form became part of the standard automobile policy and could not be varied without the permission of the superintendent. Hebb and Shea visited superintendent Whitehead to request permission to show policy fees, rural postal route and county on the application form, and particularly to omit a question about "racial extraction" of the applicant, which they felt would be offensive to some people. Racial origin might be of concern to a life insurance underwriter, but should not matter in automobile insurance. After some probing and questioning, the superintendent agreed to these changes in the Co-op Fidelity application form. (It was not until some years later that the racial origin question was removed from the Ontario standard application used by other insurance companies.) It was perhaps on this occasion that the superintendent advised Co-op Fidelity to obtain a personal credit report on all urban applicants (advice which the staff followed carefully). While the company would incidentally receive some racial information (such as color), the purpose of the report was to check on the applicant's accident record (which people forgot easily) and on living style factors which might indicate the likelihood of accidents or irresponsible driving.

Notably, at the year-end board meeting, the directors had agreed at last to spend $20 to register "all unregistered bonds."

Chapter 17

Zero Hour

The new year was not going to be any easier for board or staff. There were too many questions for decision, too many things to be done.

In preparation for a discussion with the Ontario Credit Union League executive of sharing policy fees, on automobile policies issued to credit union members, Harman prepared a long and methodical memorandum in which he reviewed unfruitful negotiations between Co-operators' Fidelity and the League. There followed 20 points in support of a request that the League executive allow its request for the basic 50 percent of the policy fee to remain pending for a year or more. They included:

"(2) This is a new and unproved project with unproven directors and staff .... Co-op Fidelity may need all the dollars it can possibly retain to show an earning, increase its capital, and strengthen its position. It will take several years of successful operation to put this new insurance company in a relatively safe position.

"(3) Co-op Fidelity is under a moral obligation to pay dividends on its stock at the earliest year possible and to retire its stock in a reasonable period.

"(4) Other organizations as well .... are contributing extensively The Rural Co-operator (financed by United Co-operatives and Federation of Agriculture) contributes extensive staff time .... United Co-operatives contributes office space, a good deal of time by Co-op Fidelity president .... At present these several organizations (including La Caisse Co-opérative de Notre Dame and First Co-operative Packers, each providing the time and expense of its manager as a Co-operators' Fidelity director) are making contributions .... which would total several hundred dollars a month.

"(5) There is doubt as to whether the Ontario insurance branch would permit payments by Co-op Fidelity to the Ontario Credit Union League on such a scale as 50% of policy fees.

"Perhaps, in addition to the above [20] points, it is the caution that comes from feeling this great new responsibility of actually operating in automobile insurance this month ...."

At a mid-January 1949 Co-operators' Fidelity board meeting, Savage volunteered to take Harman's paper to Ontario Credit Union League board. Applications for 64 shares included one from William Dennison, a credit union member and future mayor of Toronto, and an application for 19 shares from Terminal credit union, Toronto. Actually, Terminal bought 20 shares but accepted one of them as a transfer from an estate. The moving spirit behind Terminal credit union was George W. Scott, unpaid secretary and managing director of the League from its beginning in 1941 until Hallinan's appointment as general manager and secretary-treasurer in 1947. Scott, assisted by his wife, gave the League his "spare" time for six years.

From the beginning, friends of Co-op Fidelity provided a market for the company's shares at par. It would be some years before the Association would be strong enough to find easily a purchaser for a block of 20 or more shares, but there was always someone available to buy one or two shares - and the price was always at par ($50), never more than par because of the Rochdale co-operative principle that capital should receive only a fair return. An individual shareholder could get his money back (or an estate could sell one or two shares) at any time (as soon as the board met), but in the early years shareholders received no interest or dividends. Co-operatives and credit unions were patient and did not offer their shares for sale. Prominent farmers among 37 individuals who bought shares in January included Alva

Rintoul of Carleton Place, Frank Marritt of Keswick, Charles Hooper of Gormley and Eldred Aiken of Allenford. Colin Kenneth O. Cameron of Iroquois bought five shares. Some counties had not reached their share quotas and Morrison recommended writing to them. Nicholson proposed new, higher quotas, based on a new sales objective of 2,000 shares. Savage suggested that too much capital might be subscribed and become a liability. If sufficient capital were subscribed, said Shea, the Association might write liability insurance for farmers and personal property floaters for credit union members and others. It was agreed not to set new quotas but to seek additional applications from the counties and the credit unions.

Shea reported acceptance of seven automobile applications, and employment of a third staff member, Vera Burtwell, a graduate in law of the University of Toronto. FIIA had agreed to purchase office equipment for the use of the Association, and CIS, Manchester, had agreed to accept liability for property damage reinsurance in excess of $1,000, instead of $5,000.

After lunch two auditors from Millar, Macdonald and Company reported to the board a loss of only $136 for 1948, and a reduced deficit because a reserve for unlicensed reinsurance was no longer needed. Instead, the chief examiner of the department of insurance required a special (but smaller) fidelity insurance reserve. The chief examiner hoped to have quarterly reports in 1949, the auditors said, but audit fees to date had not met the auditors' costs (a comment which became perennial).

Staples reported that of 35 applications for non-life licences the department had said six were unacceptable; 17 other persons were about to apply.

No insurance was to be solicited in northern Ontario except by approval of the board. A proposal to appoint an agent in Algoma was referred to the distribution committee. Recent shareholder and former UFO club secretary J. D. McLennan at Thessalon was already licensed to sell insurance for Co-operative Life.

People were prepared to believe that a new company without experienced insurance staff could sell and issue policies but there was concern about what would happen to claims. The president and board accepted Hebb's proposal that the company should use a firm of insurance adjusters as the company's claims department.

Policyholders would report their claims to Keddel & Shea, Toronto, who would handle a claim or refer it to another adjusting firm. It became necessary to explain repeatedly that Shea, the adjuster, was not Shea, the assistant secretary.

The January board meeting was not over yet. The directors deleted from the rate manual a statement that implied that Co-op Fidelity would write insurance for members of the Federation not resident on a farm, approved rules for giving binding authority to agents, approved application for a licence extension to permit the company to write supplementary accident insurance (medical payments) with the automobile policy, heard a report from Harman that he and Wilfred Bishop of the Ontario Hog Producers Association had discussed livestock transit insurance with Duff's (a meat packer) at Hamilton. Morrison said that Co-op Fidelity would have to provide service at the "West Toronto" Ontario Stockyards.

In preparation for an annual meeting on Saturday, February 19, 1949, the January board meeting "authorized" work-horse Harman to write a directors' report for scrutiny by the directors on February 9. Harman had been president for almost a year and, although the board was still trying to function as a management committee, Harman was really a managing director. He had held the board together through controversy concerning the first bonding claims, through the first steps into livestock transit insurance, and through innumerable discussions and arguments about automobile insurance. During calendar year 1948 there had been 13 all-day board meetings and 168 board resolutions. Despite the confusion of ideas, the basic opinions developed during the Harman-led visit to Indiana and Ohio had prevailed - integrated selling of life and automobile insurance, six-month automobile premium, policy fee and low renewal commission, district and local agent, exclusive agency force. (A Farm Bureau "district" agent, however, was an experienced agent who selected, trained and supervised "local" agents.)

Although as secretary of United Farmers' Co-operative Company he was heavily engaged in the reorganization begun in 1946 and brought to completion in 1948, Harman had given a great deal of time in 1948 to Co-operators' Fidelity. In addition to insurance board meetings, Harman conducted executive and committee meetings, participated in insurance sponsor conferences, and spent other time in discussion with Hebb, Shea and Staples - in a sense "staff" although only Shea was employed by Co-operators' Fidelity. As secretary since April of Co-operative Life advisory committee, Harman was working (until September) with OFA elected leaders Stewart and Betzner and with four United Farmers' directors: Amos, Good, Nicholson and Staples. Nicholson and Harold Ghent represented the Ontario Co-operative Union on the advisory committee. Merging the committee with Co-operators' Fidelity board was inescapable. Meetings of committee and board with "Red" Crofford and later with Milliken were frequent, leading eventually to the agreement on joint selling plans for 1949.

The February board meeting accepted with minor corrections Harman's draft of the directors' report to the annual meeting. He reported that the League had agreed to promote automobile insurance on the basis set out in his January memorandum. The League executive had agreed generously that it would limit its claims against Co-operators' Fidelity for expenses incurred to 10 percent of policy fees paid by members of credit unions. Chapters, credit unions and credit union members would provide their services without any other reimbursement. This was the beginning of a voluntary help program that later on would make the difference between failure and success and that would grow and grow and grow. The League then had ~~only~~ *fewer* ~~about~~ *than* 50 member credit unions but 15 years later it would have 1,500 *300* member credit unions. For the first few years most automobile insurance applications would come from farm and rural people.

Harman was asked to write an appeal for capital to be sent to credit unions over the signature of Hallinan, League general manager. Milburn would write to county Federations. Billy, who was not present, had resigned as a director. With his employer's permission, Louis Billy had founded a caisse populaire in an Ottawa hardware store where he was a clerk, and, with the encouragement of Hansard stenographer Alphonse Desjardins, built it into a strong institution under its own roof - La Caisse Co-opérative de Notre Dame d'Ottawa.

Savage had persuaded Billy to stand for election to CF&GA board in February 1948. An experienced lender, he helped to develop fidelity bonding of credit unions and caisses populaires. His resignation was a significant loss of contact with French-language Ontarians.

The board allotted 31 more shares. Shea reported issuance of 152 rate manuals, five to 20 automobile applications daily, over a thousand inquiries about automobile insurance in three weeks, and efforts, with employed and voluntary help, to answer all inquiries. The board authorized additional office staff, investment of funds in mortgages or government bonds, renting equipment from FIIA, and preparation of quarterly rather than monthly statements.

Present during the afternoon session, president "Red" Crofford of Co-operative Life explained a national insurance agency which Co-operative Life was now proposing to organize. Co-operative Life had insurance in force of over seventeen million dollars, he said, with a surplus of $27,000 for 1948.

The distribution committee presented an extensive report. A. H. K. Musgrave, of Ontario Co-operative Union staff, was considering joining Co-operative Life field staff. OFA was lending a member of its staff, J. R. Sheane, to Staples for the next few weeks.

The board approved employing board member Nicholson, responsible to Staples, to work in Bruce, Huron and Perth counties, as he was available to the end of March, at $10 a day and expenses, including seven cents a mile for the use of his automobile.

A successful independent agent at Peterborough, proposed by Milburn and the county "ag. rep.", was prepared to write co-operative automobile insurance, and gradually give up writing insurance for other companies. On the recommendation of the distribution committee of Harman, Staples and Hebb, the board approved an elaborate long-term plan to make him an exclusive Co-operators' Fidelity agent. The agent was to agree to submit a monthly report to the Peterborough FIIA committee and Co-operators' Fidelity on automobile insurance sold and renewed, to sell only co-operative automobile insurance to eligible new applicants after two years, and at the end of three years to furnish annually a list of eligible persons insured with other companies.

Apparently this proposed agreement was too restrictive to be acceptable and was taken to the superintendent of insurance, who good-naturedly reprimanded and cautioned Co-operators' Fidelity. The Association was trespassing on "the general agency system" and the right of the agent to represent whatever companies he pleased. There were to be many more inquiries, from general agents, as the years went by, about writing co-operative automobile insurance, but it became the practice to discourage such inquiries tactfully and firmly. Co-op Fidelity accumulated its policyholders in Peterborough and elsewhere without the help of previously experienced agents, except in a few instances. One of these was Harve Hallman, a Waterloo county farmer who stopped selling insurance for State Farm Mutual to sell for Co-operators' Fidelity. He already understood policy fees and six-month premium, and before long he could quote premiums for many prospects and makes of car without looking at his bulky manual. The manual itself was a cause of complaint for many years. Agents wanted a small printed manual, but rate changes were frequent and office staff felt that the company could not afford it, and there never was a compact manual.

The same February board meeting - the last before the annual meeting - decided to send a committee to see superintendent of insurance Whitehead, and the superintendent of agencies, Fred Spencer, about licensing secretaries of county Federations of Agriculture. Another resolution, to carry out instructions from Spencer, said that "prospective agents should be informed clearly that no commission can be paid them .... for business written previous to obtaining a licence."

The Association was learning that the superintendent controlled an Ontario company absolutely. His power to require more capital or to withhold a company licence enabled his staff to make rules in most areas of the company's operations. The superintendent refused to license employees of co-operatives as agents of Co-operators' Fidelity, although they could hold licences (part-time rural licences) for other companies. The theory was that a co-operative or farm organization employee, representing a co-operative and farm-sponsored insurance company, would have "undue influence" over members of organizations by which they were employed. For a while the superintendent licensed secretaries of county Federations (with salaries of not more than $500 a year) but this privilege did not last when general agents began to lose policyholders and complain of unfair competition.

Staples suggested that it would be advantageous to Co-op Fidelity to increase the renewal commission at this time from three percent to five percent. The directors accepted a proposal by Nicholson and Wood that the executive study the possibility of basing an increase in renewal commission on claims experience (loss ratio) and volume.

Chapter 18

Annual Meeting 1949

The annual meeting was uneventful. Shareholders and policyholders each had one vote. As yet there were few individual policyholders.

"Financing was a fundamental requirement in order to get a licence to write auto insurance, so the board set out to raise another $30,000 in cash, which was achieved by the end of the year," the directors said in the report prepared by Harman and presented by Hallinan. "Since farm people had purchased fewer shares of Co-op Fidelity during the first two years, energies to sell more shares were concentrated on farm people through the county Federations of Agriculture. By the end of the year 1,286 shares [inclusive of shares not yet allotted] of Co-op Fidelity were well spread among urban and rural organizations and individuals."

W. C. Good, Brantford farmer-philosopher and co-operative elder statesman, discussed democratic representation of shareholders and policyholders on the board. Good was within a few days of his 73rd birthday and consequently, although a Co-op Fidelity shareholder, not eligible for the company's automobile insurance. Harman explained that free rent and a great deal of free assistance had kept expenses in control. Milburn explained that FIIA was buying and owning furniture and equipment for the company. But J. J. Thurston, of Cameron, questioned the wisdom of not paying directors.

Wilfred L. Bishop, representing Ontario Hog Producers
Association, said that the potential competition of Co-op Fidelity had
already saved farmers an increase in livestock transit premium rates.
Policyholders and shareholders had received with notices of the
meeting a slip which said: "Members .... may wonder how it is going
to be possible for each of several thousand shareholders and
policyholders to attend an annual meeting and participate in the
election of the directors who will conduct the business .... It is
proposed that credit unions and caisses populaires in Ontario should
nominate three of the directors, the Ontario Co-operative Union one,
and a provincial insurance association (representative of the county
Federation insurance committees and of farm policyholders and
shareholders) the other five directors."

The terms were expiring of three directors, Betzner and Milburn,
considered to be representatives of FIIA, and Savage, considered to be
a representative of Ontario Credit Union League. Betzner and Milburn
were nominated. Savage said his health would not permit him to
accept renomination, and nominated as a representative of credit
unions, G. Douglas Hughes, assistant secretary of the Ontario
Co-operative Union. Betzner, Milburn and Hughes were elected.
Hughes was a university graduate and a Canadian air force veteran (of
the second world war) who had been a prisoner in Germany.

Billy had resigned after one year on the board, and had no one to
suggest from the caisses populaires to fill the vacancy. Savage
nominated P. J. Mulrooney, who was editor of Ontario Credit Union
News, a part-time job. An accomplished writer of magazine articles
and stories, he had organized a score of credit unions. Mulrooney was
elected for a two-year term. In a discussion about zone representation,
Savage said that it was not easy to find credit union members who are
able to attend day-time Monday-to-Friday meetings at their own
expense. Farm organizations did not like to meet on Saturdays,
although the historic Good-Fraser-Morrison-Drury get-together in a
Toronto hostelry to found the United Farmers of Ontario had taken
place on a Saturday afternoon in 1913.

The third credit union director was John M. Hallinan. The other
FIIA directors were W. J. Wood, K. N. M. Morrison and Leonard
Harman. Ontario Co-operative Union representative was William G.
Nicholson.

Taking up the problem raised earlier by scholarly Good, a new

United Co-operatives director, Alden McLean, Muirkirk farmer, offered ideas on securing democratic representation on the Co-operators' Fidelity board. While Good had been one of the founders of United Farmers' Co-operative Company in 1914, McLean had just been elected to the UCO board. In 1936 United Farmers' had sent him to a Depression-time world youth congress in Geneva, Switzerland. It was a good investment. McLean was later to become a UCO president and one of the ablest and most constructive directors of CIA, Co-op Fidelity's successor.

Staples, as distribution manager, led a discussion on automobile sales. The farm boy who did not like high school and chose not to go to university was becoming a confident and competent leader. Good had the last word, advising patience in waiting for results in co-operative insurance, but his advice would not be taken.

Chapter 19

Farm Bureau Advice

Contact with the United States Farm Bureau insurance companies was helping board and staff to make good decisions. "Ollie" Griffith, Ohio Farm Bureau reinsurance underwriter, was providing the most extensive and detailed advice. A March 11, 1949, three-page single-spaced letter included: ".... it sounds as though there is a tremendous interest in representing your organization. To have linked up 72 representatives down here in a comparable period of time would be unheard of .... you should be able to operate for a reasonable period .... on your initial plan regarding commissions. When an agent can put business in either of two companies, he usually puts as much as possible in the company paying the most commission .... We strive always for an exclusive agency force, that is, writing for no one but us .... We went for a good many years without any renewal commission .... It is always harder to come down than it is to go up in commissions. You can go up and get a cheer from your agency force at any time, but ...."

Ohio Farm Bureau agency secretary W. T. Allnutt wrote Harman a two-page letter on March 16: "It is true that we do pay an 8% renewal after the first six months or year .... As for your proposal of increasing the 3% to 5% to your district agent, it would appear to me that it would be well to set up a basic amount that is to go to the writing agent rather than increasing the amount that goes to the district agent .... We have a contingent loss ratio bonus which we pay the agent providing .... the district as well as the agent has a loss ratio not to exceed 55% .... A district manager can do a great deal toward developing production in a given area if he spends his time developing agents rather than working on his personal production."

Business pressures, and the growth of staff, were forcing the board to accept committee and staff recommendations and to delegate more authority. Staples was doing a big job in appointing agents. Bernard Shea and Margaret Chambers were under pressure from the inflow of automobile applications. The secretary-treasurer, in a pattern established by Savage, was the manager, and Hebb was trying to keep up with these voluntary obligations as well as those of editor of the twice-monthly eight-page Rural Co-operator. Fortunately, his employers in both jobs were much the same people, but his recommendations to the board did not gain the easy approval which the Savage magnetism had commanded. Operations were more extensive now, and the president, Harman, in his managing director role, and Hebb struggled to gain board acceptance of the steps they thought necessary to success.

They took to a board meeting in March a long agenda with ten recommendations. Happy with progress made, the board (a Co-op Fidelity board but calling itself the Ontario Co-operative Insurance board) re-elected officers and executive, investment (Mulrooney replaced Billy) and distribution committees, set ambitious new share sale quotas, and proceeded to deal with an unending succession of problems.

An informal meeting of members of the board and representatives of other organizations had discussed the proposal of Co-operative Life Insurance Company to establish a national insurance agency, and had produced a six-point proposal for an Ontario agency which would sell life insurance for the Regina company and automobile insurance for the Toronto company. Nicholson reported that Co-operative Life board had referred these proposals to a committee. Staples favored this plan which would make him responsible to an Ontario board rather than to the two Croffords, president and general manager, in Regina. Co-operators' Fidelity board approved the plan as a basis for further negotiation. There would be a meeting with Milliken in Toronto on April 1.

Staples and Hallinan reported on a visit to the department of insurance concerning the licensing of county Federation of Agriculture secretaries.   It was decided to accept the department's offer to license, for a limited period, county Federation employees receiving not more than $500 a year.

Staples then read to the board a surprising and disturbing letter from the department's agency supervisor, Fred Spencer, asking for withdrawal of automobile rate manuals from credit unions. This would be a major set-back.   The executive, the distribution manager and the secretary were to see "appropriate officials of the Ontario government," to seek the help of the solicitor, Mitchell, in preparing a presentation, and to "make every effort to secure a favorable ruling."

Other decisions were expansion of livestock operations, including opening of an office at the Ontario Stockyards, agreement to insure old automobiles (this meant 10 or 12 or more years) and crediting the writing commission of 50 percent of the policy fee on direct business (non-agent) to an approved district agent, to retain himself or to divide with his local agents, as he saw fit.

The latter recommendation of the distribution committee survived an amendment by Morrison and Mulrooney to allow the district agent only 30 percent on direct business and to limit the arrangement to six months.

At this meeting the board approved an arrangement (copying Indiana Farm Bureau Insurance) that with elaborations was still in operation 20 years later.   County Federations could send in itemized bills for expenditures in promotion of insurance up to a limit determined by 10 percent of policy fees paid in the county and 12-1/2 cents on each automobile renewal.   The law did not permit paying a commission to anyone or to any organization other than a licensed agent.

For the present the company would not pay any commissions on livestock transit or fidelity insurance, but would pay, as permitted by the Ontario Insurance Act, a five percent collection fee to packinghouses and livestock commission brokers for deducting livestock transit insurance premiums from payments to farmers. Truckers were the policyholders, but farmers paid the premiums.

Staples reported that A. H. K. Musgrave had joined his staff as an employee of Co-operative Life Insurance Company.   Then 54 years old, Musgrave had been an RCAF training officer during the second world war, and subsequently a member of the staff of the Ontario

Co-operative Union. He was principal of the Union's war veterans' rehabilitation school, training young men for co-operative management jobs. As a student at Ontario Agricultural College he was a champion boxer. After graduation he was a reporter for the Farmers' Sun, sold automobiles and before the second war operated a fruit farm at Clarksburg.

Sixty agents had been licensed to sell automobile insurance, and 74 more were on the way. They were part-time agents, and mostly farmers, but to find so many salespeople in so short a time was an achievement. With co-operative and untiring zeal, Staples and his assistants found these representatives with the help of county Federations of Agriculture, Farm Forums and local co-operatives. Staples was well known among farm people as former national secretary of Farm Radio Forum, and for a brief period as an OFA field organizer.

Appointment of an agent required the approval of the county Federation of Agriculture insurance committee, which was also the local unit of the provincial Farmers' Insurance Information Association.

A guest at the annual meeting of FIIA was Marion E. Foltz, claims manager of Ohio Farm Bureau Insurance Companies. Manager of a farmers' supply co-operative when the Farm Bureau's first automobile claim occurred in his area, he received a telephoned request from Columbus to handle it. The result was an invitation to become the claims manager. Asked at Toronto whether he had lawyers advising him, he said he had a dozen attorneys on his staff, but, "What would we want their advice for? We tell them what to do." His visit was helpful, and added to the knowledge and confidence of directors, staff and FIIA members.

Chapter 20

Wheels Turning Fast

When the board met late in April 1949, automobile insurance was humming. For the previous six weeks the company had been issuing 125 to 150 policies a week. "This is about the volume we hoped would develop, but handling this number of policies means more work than we had anticipated - partly because of our inexperience, partly because of the inexperience of our agents," the secretary-treasurer reported. There were only four full-time staff members, three of them university graduates, and there were three to four temporary typists.

About a dozen automobile claims had been reported so far. "We will need to watch the claims closely to see to what extent our underwriting has been weak, and what risks we should consider dropping," Hebb continued. "We must also be sure that our claims settlements are prompt, fair and friend-making. Some of us came to the conclusion, as a result of the visit of Mr. Foltz, of Columbus, that sooner or later we must get into the claims field ourselves." The dropping of risks, except rarely, did not materialize.

There were now 89 licensed agents, 26 persons who had applied for a licence, and 31 others who had applied for appointment as an agent. Seventeen persons had failed the department examinations. Twenty-seven of the 89 agents held life licences; nine other persons held life-only licences.

There was a new agreement with Co-operative Life, which now undertook to maintain an Ontario field staff of three men. Co-operators' Fidelity reimbursed Co-operative Life to the extent of $1,000 and 10 percent of non-credit-union policy fees. In addition, but not as part of the agreement, Co-operators' Fidelity board accepted a recommendation to engage a fourth man, and to provide an automobile and expenses, who would be responsible to Staples.

Staples had found office space, at 30 Bloor Street West, which Co-operators' Fidelity agreed to rent (1,500 square feet for $275 a month). It seemed expensive, at over two dollars a square foot per annum, but the company needed space badly, and would sublet some space to Co-operative Life for $75 a month. In the autumn Ontario Credit Union League also moved to this new location.

Now the board received a discouraging ruling from superintendent Whitehead. Credit unions could promote Co-operators' Fidelity insurance, and they could canvass their members to find out their insurance needs. They could turn the information over to the company, and they could advise which credit union members were worthy of automobile insurance. But the credit union could not have a rate manual, or quote rates, or receive applications for automobile insurance. The company could provide the individual credit union member with rate information if it was in the form of a pamphlet, but not in the form of a manual, and the pamphlet was not to pass through the hands of the credit union.

In view of the growing volume of business, the prospect of a bigger staff when the first renewals became due in a few weeks, and the plan to move out of the Rural Co-operator office, the secretary-treasurer (and editor of the Rural Co-operator) recommended that the company engage a full-time manager. The board agreed and instructed the executive to do so.

Betzner said the company would have to write cargo insurance for the truckers for whom it was writing livestock transit insurance. As an Ontario Federation of Agriculture executive member and former OFA president, he had addressed a meeting of the livestock section of the Automotive Transport Association. The truckers had said that they were ready to work with Co-op Fidelity.

Betzner's protege in Waterloo county, Hallman, wanted the company to write a medical payments policy, as State Farm and a few other companies did. The department of insurance had approved, and the board at this April meeting authorized selling such a policy. As a courtesy to the medical co-operatives, whose chief business at that time was hospital insurance, the company would pay a hospital bill even if the policyholder was entitled to recover the amount, or had recovered the amount already, as hospital insurance. If the medical co-operative chose to pay the claim, the individual would receive double reimbursement.

During these spring months "the staff" was wrestling with automobile insurance renewal questions. The first policies would expire early in July. In the direct writing tradition of State Farm Mutual, and the Farm Bureau companies, Co-operators' Fidelity would bill policyholders direct. How much time would it allow policyholders to pay? Farm Bureau companies in the United States allowed 10 days, and honored claims for 25 days. To tell a Co-operators' Fidelity policyholder that he could have 10 days after the due date to pay, would renew the policy under Ontario law and, if the policyholder did not pay his premium, it would be necessary to send him a registered letter to terminate the policy.

Although he had put a rural weekly newspaper (with a pay-when-you-please subscription list) on a cash basis, Hebb was in doubt about what to propose. Cut them off at the due date, Shea advised him. Co-op Fidelity president Harman had preached "cash trading" to UCO local co-operatives, and, with other executive members (meeting on June 17 with the livestock transit insurance committee), agreed to a demand for cash on the premium due date.

It fell to Margaret Chambers to turn this confidence in the policyholders into money in the bank. She was ready. When Margaret Chambers joined the staff a year earlier, in 1948, she began with typing, clerical and bookkeeping duties. The company's fidelity and livestock transit insurance provided schooling in insurance accounting. Bernard Shea prepared the financial statements, with the help of the chief examiner, Richards, an occasional and helpful visitor to the shabby Rural Co-operator office. He was exacting about records and had been dubious about the plans for expansion.

Building background for automobile insurance, and taking minutes, Margaret Chambers attended the six long and sometimes contentious board meetings during the rest of the year, but in 1949 she was too busy for board meetings. At the last meeting in 1948 she had explained the advantages in electric tabulating for the volume of business expected in automobile insurance, and the board had approved use of UCO's Remington-Rand equipment. That was how the company became a Univac user (with 90-column punch-cards) although most insurers used IBM (80 columns).

Beginning with the planning of a punch-card code to carry all the information about policyholder, vehicle and insurance - age, sex, district, vehicle type, age and value, insurance coverages, premiums, agent, and so on - which would be needed by the company and required by the superintendent of insurance, Miss. Chambers planned and supervised the 1949 office operations other than underwriting, claims and answering the unending flow of inquiries about automobile insurance. As Shea engaged underwriting help, and Miss. Chambers engaged clerical help, it became necessary to spread out of the Rural Co-operator office - once the UFO and U. F. Co-op board room - into UCO office space. There was a sigh of relief when the company moved in May to 30 Bloor Street West.

Now it became necessary to rent tabulating equipment, and to employ an operator and a key-puncher. Fortunately, Miss. Chambers could operate the equipment herself, and never hesitated to do so - to get the work done or to show others how to do it. During the early months of 1949 she had to improvise records, and find her own way. In May, with automobile applications flowing in, and policies flowing out, claims reported in increasing numbers, and the time for the first renewals approaching, she spent a valuable week with the Farm Bureau insurance companies at Indianapolis and Columbus, and brought back with her the forms, procedures and ideas which were to be the basis of the company's operations for many years to come.

It was with trepidation that the staff sent out the first renewal notices that, after a courteous beginning, said: "Your insurance expires on the date first-mentioned above unless ...."; the other side of the premium notice carried the same stern warning and specified that when the Association received a late payment it would retain the premium for the period when the policy was not in force as a reinstatement fee. There were few, if any, complaints about this blunt request for money. In practice, the company followed the Farm Bureau companies in giving 25 days grace, and honored all claims against lapsed policies when people thought they had renewed their policies or by oversight neglected to do so.

The agents, it was apparent from the response, were doing a

magnificent job of explaining to policyholders that they would have to mail their renewal premiums direct to the company. They were proud of the company they were building and they wanted to spread the news.

State Farm provided its policyholders with a metal emblem to attach to their vehicles. Co-op Fidelity agents were proud of the policies they were writing - they were taking some policyholders from State Farm and other companies but they were also writing insurance for many people who were previously uninsured - and they wanted the company to provide a Co-op emblem. A May 10, 1949, letter from Griffith, Ohio Farm Bureau, included a sample of the Ohio Farm Bureau emblem, which in 100,000 lots could be purchased for about five cents each: "One point to be watched .... The insignia showing up in a photograph of a wrecked car gives away the fact that there is insurance. I don't believe you could count on much help from the insignia in clearing out undesirable risks. The chief value seems to be along advertising lines ...." The Ontario agent demand for these emblems continued for many years, but management was not proud of some of the old vehicles the company was insuring and was not anxious to tell judge and jury that there was insurance, and never succumbed.

In May the board asked for preparation of a by-law which would avoid the necessity of sending each policyholder by mail notice of the annual meeting and a financial statement, approved employment of two directors - Mulrooney in the office for five days at $10 a day, and Nicholson in the field as needed at $10 a day and expenses - and engaged Andrew Hebb as general manager, to begin September 1, 1949 (actually mid-October), at a salary of $6,000 a year. He would continue as secretary and Bernard Shea would become treasurer. There would be an employee pension plan - the first "fringe benefit" - either with the Dominion government or with Co-operative Life.

League general manager Hallinan had been unable to attend the insurance board meeting in April when Hebb, as volunteer secretary-treasurer, recommended appointment of a manager with "effective control over auto agents and auto field work." The board, with only the directors present, instructed the executive "to negotiate to engage a full-time general manager at a satisfactory salary."

Hallinan had been appointed League general manager as first choice among 12 applicants and, had he been present, might have explained the procedure used, and might have suggested posting or advertising the Co-op Fidelity position. In May, when Hebb was appointed, Hallinan was again unable to be present.

At a time when the Ontario Federation of Agriculture seemed to be taking over a credit union enterprise, Hallinan was worried about Co-op Fidelity on several counts. During the latter months of 1948, when the directors had divided uneasily over the handling of a Toronto parish credit union bonding claim, as already related, Hallinan and others thought Hebb and Shea too firm - even dictatorial - in their demand for prosecution of an erring member of the credit union before paying the claim.

When the OCUL executive met on Saturday, July 9, 1949, Hallinan reported 25 new member credit unions. He summarized his concerns as a Co-op Fidelity director:

"1. The appointment of a general manager of CF&GA, salary of $6,000 per annum, without advertising the position.
"2. Discrimination against credit union members when applying for automobile insurance.
"3. A complete investigation is used on applicants for bonds.
"4. Misconception of the original purpose of CF&GA and a complete lack of a co-operative, humanitarian element in the operation of the company.
"5. Directors should set the policy and management carry it out. At present the reverse is true.
"6. Re-emphasize that the sanction and approval must be obtained from the League before any agent can be authorized to solicit credit union business."

On motion of Percy Quinton and "Bert" Savage, Hallinan was instructed to "write a vigorous letter to the president and general manager of CF&GA expressing the concern and dissatisfaction of the League with the present method of conducting the affairs of CF&GA ...."

The other two credit union representatives on the insurance board, Hughes and Mulrooney, were present at the OCUL executive meeting as visitors. Mulrooney had sent in his resignation as an insurance company director, to sell Co-op Fidelity auto insurance in the Toronto credit unions. OCUL executive, at this meeting, nominated J. M. Best to succeed him.

Hallinan, Hughes and Best represented credit unions at an insurance board meeting on July 21. In the course of the day Shea, Staples, Sheane and Hebb were asked to leave the room while the board "discussed a letter from the Ontario Credit Union League regarding the policies and operations of Co-op Fidelity" and a reply written by president Harman. During the discussion the directors agreed that a committee should proceed with a study of underwriting policies. Hebb was invited to rejoin the meeting and Harman reviewed the board discussion of the correspondence.

After Shea, Staples and Sheane returned, Staples reported that there were now 126 agents licensed to sell automobile insurance. Mulrooney, whose home was in Toronto, had accepted appointment as the company's first urban agent, on salary and commission, to develop credit union automobile insurance.

Hallinan explained that new restrictive investment legislation would prevent some credit unions from increasing their ownership of Co-operators' Fidelity shares. Morrison thought agents should not be allowed to buy shares, because agents and employees should not control the company. (Actually, as policyholders they would have one vote, and only one vote, whether or not they bought shares.)

Chapter 21

Cash or Else

To this Co-op Fidelity board meeting on July 21, Shea presented a six-month financial statement and a six-month forecast. It would be possible to avoid a loss for the year 1949 if the company should write 6,000 automobile policies, have a very low loss ratio, and use quite a bit of equipment owned by other organizations. If an insurance company bought a desk and chair for $200, this was an expense of $200. The equipment could not be treated as an asset and be depreciated gradually.

At this meeting the board endorsed the cash renewal plan. Most fire and casualty companies allowed their agents three months to collect and pay renewal premiums. Usually the agent mailed a new policy, at each renewal, to the policyholder, and allowed him to pay for it at his convenience. If he had an accident, or his house was damaged by fire, he was sure to pay his premium, but if there was no accident, or no fire, he might decide not to renew his insurance. He had enjoyed free insurance in the meantime. A company might have 10 or 15 percent of its assets outstanding in unpaid premiums, instead of invested to produce revenue. This was an expensive form of credit, and resulted in higher premiums.

As a result of direct billing and cash on the line Co-op Fidelity's statement of assets and liabilities became an accountant's delight.

[There were no "agent balances" and accounts receivable were negligible. Instead of the usual 10 or 15 percent of assets in accounts due from agents, which in 1971 would have been four to six million dollars, there was cash in the bank or gilt-edge securities (although somewhat tarnished by inflation). The resulting income reduced the cost of insurance.]

From the beginning of 1949 the company insured passenger cars and farm trucks. Usual coverage was $10,000 liability to one person, $20,000 to two or more persons and $5,000 property damage (known as 10/20 and 5).

Chapter 22

Provincial or National?

In this month of July 1949 Milburn, representing Co-op Fidelity, attended a two-day meeting in Winnipeg of the "National Insurance Committee" of the Co-operative Union of Canada. Other committee members in attendance included Lloyd Matheson, Maritime Co-operative Services, Moncton; R. M. Dancer, Canadian Pool Insurance, Winnipeg; J. M. Craig, Federated Insurance Agencies, Regina; F. L. Walters, Alberta Co-operative Wholesale, Edmonton; C. Gordon Smith, CUNA Mutual, Hamilton; H. A. Crofford, Co-operative Life, Regina; A. B. MacDonald, secretary, Co-operative Union of Canada (CUC), Ottawa; A. C. Savage, Ontario Co-operative Union and CUC, Toronto; and A. W. Friesen, president, Co-operative Union of Canada, who was chairman.

Among ten others present were O. H. Edgerton, CUNA, Madison, Wisconsin, and R. G. Wright, Canadian representative, CIS, Manchester.

MacDonald provided background. CUC in 1947 had named a national committee on co-operative insurance, with CUC president Ralph Staples as chairman, which reported in 1948. The 1949 congress of the CUC passed a resolution: Co-operative insurance was developing in Canada "under many authorities and jurisdictions," lacked "national co-ordination and direction," could be "a great

111

financial power in Canada," and the CUC board would convene a national committee to "examine the present co-op insurance operations in Canada and report .... on plans for co-ordination ...."; and the CUC would bear the costs of the committee. The conference reviewed co-operative and mutual insurance development throughout Canada, except Quebec. (Leo Berube, Le Conseil Superieur de la Co-opération, Quebec City, was invited but absent.) Milburn expressed Ontario preference for a provincial fire and casualty company together with an agency which could represent other fire and casualty companies and Co-operative Life. He presented a memorandum entitled "A Pattern for Co-operative Insurance in Canada," prepared by Harman, and a chart to show the Ontario insurance board's concept of an Ontario and national insurance program. Crofford saw a growing demand for fire insurance and automobile insurance, and predicted that unless some co-ordinating agency were set up, a number of small companies would spring into existence. Possible conflict between CUNA Mutual and Co-operative Life, CUC reported, was "frankly discussed .... but with careful guiding and planning the greatest possible co-ordination could be brought about."

Democratic control was a major topic. Mutuals tended to grow away from the people. As Wawanesa Mutual (Manitoba) grew larger, operating nationally, it became more efficient, but it also grew away from the people. A subcommittee consisting of Savage, Crofford and MacDonald was appointed to study two questions: "Is it more advantageous to operate co-operative insurance services on a national, provincial or interprovincial basis? How can democratic control be exercised?"

Milburn reported on Winnipeg at Co-operators' Fidelity's second meeting in July. At the earlier meeting, it was agreed that an attempt should be made to collect from CUC the expenses of the company's delegate to Winnipeg. Failing collection, Co-operators' Fidelity should pay the account.

Harman had reported earlier on a visit to a co-operative insurance company at Minneapolis-St. Paul, and now, at the second board meeting in July, he reported on a visit to Columbus, and discussions with Foltz, claims manager, and Leftwich, secretary, who was then president Murray Lincoln's second-in-command. Ohio Farm Bureau had found fire insurance, which at that time in Ohio had to be written through a separate company, its least satisfactory field of operation. Earning surplus to finance three-year premiums was a problem. The Ohio company retained only $2,000 fire risk on any one local farm co-operative.

Staples reported employment of George Barclay, Ilderton, as an employee of Co-operators' Fidelity, to be a member of the distribution staff. Living on a farm, and formerly a commercial school teacher, Barclay was to make a major contribution in the employment and training of agents. He was a good judge of people, and a few years later employed a young Dutch immigrant who in 1970 became the company's second general manager (Teunis Haalboom).

William Ritchie had become discouraged and had resigned, and Rodney Sexsmith, Napanee, had taken his place on Staples' staff. One day Sexsmith told a road companion that a salesman could sell life insurance to anyone. "See this car coming," he said. "I'll stop him and sell him some insurance." He proceeded to flag down the motorist and, lo and behold, sold him a small life insurance policy. The distribution field staff now consisted of Musgrave, Sexsmith and Barclay, all responsible to Staples.

At this same meeting, on the recommendation of the solicitor and the secretary-treasurer, the board approved a first mortgage loan of $3,000 to one of the directors, but immediately, at the instance of Morrison, passed another resolution to instruct staff to refuse future applications from directors for mortgage loans. However, despite the representations of the solicitor, L. W. Mitchell, the superintendent ruled that the mortgage was not permissible and the loan was never made.

Morrison, Milburn and Betzner were working at livestock transit insurance, and Milburn reported another meeting with the livestock division of the Automotive Transport Association. It was agreed to write livestock transit for truckers to all Ontario meat packing plants by September 1, and cargo insurance for any trucker for whom the company wrote livestock transit.

The board recommended a five-day week to Co-operative Life in Regina for its Ontario office, and authorized the secretary to determine Co-operators' Fidelity office hours. It approved Co-operative Life's formula for membership dues to Ontario Federation of Agriculture and Ontario Co-operative Union, with provision for a minimum payment of $25 to each. The board postponed action on a membership bill of

$100 from the Union to Co-operators' Fidelity. Other topics were automobile policy sales, reimbursement of agents for the cost of their licences, which they had to renew in October, a share of the policy fee for both Co-operative Life and the League on urban agent sales to credit union members, approval of livestock transit insurance for a non-PCV trucker (that is, not licensed as a public commercial vehicle) and authorization of a possible $25,000 mortgage on 409 Huron Street (owned by Ontario Whole Milk Producers League and headquarters for the OFA) which never materialized.

Chapter 23

A Strong Leader

Despite his uncertain health, Savage continued as secretary-treasurer of Ontario Co-operative Union until the end of July, 1949. The four and a half years since organization of the Union, and his original appointment, had been a time of bounding co-operative enthusiasm in rural Ontario. One hundred and fifty farm supply co-operatives were now the owners of reorganized United Co-operatives of Ontario. Farm Radio Forum was at its peak. There were 40 county Federations of Agriculture, and Savage had helped to organize many of the 30 medical (really hospital) co-operatives, following Blue Cross and Toronto's CUMBA, which by this time had 4,200 members.

Liberated from the shackles of the civil service, Savage was free to speak his pent-up criticisms of big business and high finance. There was truth in his words and magic in his voice. People listened, and usually they did as he recommended.

His assistant, Douglas Hughes, became secretary-treasurer, but, in August, representing CUC, Savage spoke in Moncton, New Brunswick, at the annual meeting of Maritime Co-operative Services (MCS). MCS was operating a fire and casualty agency for Wawanesa Mutual, and except for an employee pension plan Co-operative Life had not entered the Maritimes as yet. CUNA Mutual was operating in the credit unions.

Speaking on ownership and control of co-operative insurance, Savage divided Canada into five regions (including Quebec). In each region democratic organizations, owned and controlled by people as individual members or by democratic organizations owned and controlled by individual members, should be the sole owners of the shares in a share capital insurance corporation. These democratic owners would appoint delegates to the annual meeting of the insurance corporation, and the delegates would elect the insurance board of directors. The delegates would also report back from time to time to the representative organizations.

The regional insurance corporations (presumably writing life as well as fire and casualty insurance) would organize a national reinsurance federation, which would co-ordinate regional insurance activities and the exchange of information and meet in conjunction with the annual congress of the Co-operative Union of Canada. This plan would provide "user control" and "permanent ownership by the co-op movement," "maintain local interest," and prevent "control by a few people .... and such co-op insurance corporation from becoming just another insurance company."

For once, however, people were not going to accept advice from Savage - even if an Ontarian inexplicably was advising the "have-not" provinces to keep control of their own affairs and not to throw their insurance into a one-big-company plan which the central provinces probably would dominate. Fellow members of the subcommittee appointed at Winnipeg, Crofford and MacDonald, had made up their minds already that there was to be a centralized national insurance organization, rather than Savage's federation, and Crofford at least did not intend Ontario to dominate it.

At about the same time Co-operators' Fidelity livestock transit committee met in Barrie - Milburn (chairman), Morrison, Betzner, Wood, Staples, Hebb and J. R. Sheane (OFA staff) - and made numerous plans, including engagement of Sheane as livestock department manager. Meeting in Toronto a week later, FIIA approved the proposal to expand the livestock transit program. Milburn was trying to get office space at the Ontario Stockyards. Milburn, Sheane and Cecil Belyea (Federation fieldman) met with the livestock commission firms early in September to ask them to deduct premiums as they were doing already for Hartford Fire Insurance. They were reluctant to have two lots of premium to account for. Sheane engaged a male assistant, Edgar Tebbit, as a typist and accountant. Sheane obtained a list of over 1,300 livestock truckers, and Staples was dividing these names among the company's agents for canvassing. CIS, Manchester, agreed to provide surplus cargo insurance for the excess of $3,000.

Co-operators' Fidelity board confirmed these arrangements and agent commissions on livestock transit and cargo insurance when it met in September, 1949. The directors dealt with major matters like raising capital and minor matters like reimbursement of agents for licence fees. Never before had the Ontario department of insurance had so many applications from one source for part-time licences, and now raised the other-than-life rural licence fee from $5 to $15. The urban full-time fee was $25. In August the board had approved the prospective appointment of Verne Kallio as an agent at Coppercliff in Sudbury district, and now approved another northern Ontario appointment, Ernest Beaudry, at Verner, in Nipissing.

Chapter 24

General Manager Breaks the Rules

Reporting for the first time as general manager at this September meeting, Hebb said that of the first 93 automobile policies due for renewal in July (issued in January) only two had lapsed at September 22, of 197 due in August only two had lapsed, and of 414 due in September, 31 were three days past due and 17 were 10 days past due. The company sent out a lapse notice at three days, and a follow-up at 15 days; if the premium was still unpaid, the file was closed at 25 days.

"Red" Crofford had met individually with Hebb and Harman on a recent visit, and Hebb reported Crofford's concern that, after a contribution of $2,300 from Co-operators' Fidelity, in seven months Co-operative Life had a loss in Ontario of $5,000. Co-operators' Fidelity was now paying for one fieldman and some other joint field expenses direct, and Ontario farm leaders and employees were helping Co-operative Life, and the board declined to make any additional contribution. "Joint distribution" was becoming joint disagreement, with Ralph Staples uncomfortably in the middle.

The general manager reported two departures from the automobile

underwriting rules. Several directors thought he had made a mistake
in "holding covered" two trucks of Ancaster Co-operative as a
temporary accommodation - if there had been an accident the company
and its reinsurer would have been obligated to pay. The trucks had
been insured through the "B. A. Shea Agency" but as a result of an
accident the original insurer withdrew its coverage. In the other
instance the Association had provided automobile insurance for
Savage, although his health did not meet underwriting requirements.

In October 1949, after receiving an audited nine-month statement
showing a loss of several thousand dollars, the superintendent's chief
examiner, Richards, telephoned to express satisfaction with progress
made - if the loss ratio continued to be satisfactory, wiping out the
loss would be just a matter of time - and to suggest that the company
calculate unearned premiums on a 100 percent basis! - instead of the
80 percent used so far. The reason that most companies were allowed
to use 80 percent, he explained, was that they paid agent commissions
of 20 or 25 percent, but Co-op Fidelity was paying practically no
renewal commission. The theory was that if a company got into
difficulties (short of insolvency) another company would be willing to
take over its policyholders and obligations if it received 80 percent of
the true unearned premium. It would regard the other 20 percent as
the cost of acquisition.

The general manager suggested that the department allow the use of
the 80 percent basis for 1949, so that shareholders and policyholders
would not be too discouraged. Richards agreed to withhold his
decision until yearend results were available. On a 100 percent basis,
earned premium in 1949 would have been about $5,000 less. Richards
did not renew this request. (As superintendent in 1965, he asked
Co-operators Insurance Association to adopt a 90 percent basis, and in
1969 CIA voluntarily adopted a 100 percent basis.)

Material prepared for speakers and canvassers, in a campaign to add
$30,000 to current share capital of $65,000, forecast a loss for the year
of at least $5,000, and urged spreading the shares widely "because of
our present inability to pay interest on capital."

Directors took issue, at a board meeting in October, with the
incorrect use of the word "interest," and substituted the word
"dividends." Betzner wondered if dividends could be paid
retroactively. There would be no promises of dividends, it was
agreed, but there should be investigation of the inequity that could

result, when dividends were finally paid, to the persons who had held their shares for a long time.

The company's publicity was conservative. "The Indiana Farm Bureau's highly successful automobile insurance company used up all its capital of $16,000 in its first year of operation and had to sell all its equipment to the parent Farm Bureau so that it could have $50 in the bank at the year's end. But their first couple of years were the hardest .... Our deficit this year may be about $5,000. It may be more. It is not likely to be less. A lot depends on our loss ratio."

When Milburn sent this material out a month later he modified the heading on this section from "What will deficit be this year?" to "There may be a deficit," and changed the text to: "It would be very difficult for a new insurance company to show a surplus in the first year of operation. Co-op Fidelity is no exception. It is too soon yet to make a guess at the figures which will appear on our annual statement."

There could be a call on the shares for the unpaid portion, there was no promise of dividends on capital, and subscribing for a share would not entitle the shareholder to automobile or other insurance, the circular warned share purchase prospects. (At that time insurance companies were exempt from securities law. No prospectus was required and unlicensed individuals could sell Co-op Fidelity's shares.)

Shea presented the nine-month statement, a forecast of results for 1949, and a forecast for 1950 based on possible new automobile policy sales of 5,500, 7,300 or 9,150, consequent variations in the number of renewals, loss ratios of 40, 50 or 60 percent, taking over furniture and equipment purchased by FIIA and the Rural Co-operator, and an automobile purchased by United Co-operatives, and unearned premium at 100 percent. With a 50 percent loss ratio, and 5,500 new policies, the 1950 loss would be $32,700 or with 9,150 new policies $28,900.

These were frightening figures, and with a loss ratio of 60 percent the loss would be $48,300 or $45,600. If the loss ratio were only 40 percent, however, the loss would be $17,000 with 5,500 policies, $11,700 with 7,300 policies and $6,300 with 9,150 policies. (The company did not pay its friends for equipment in 1950, continued on an 80 percent unearned premium basis, wrote 5,700 new automobile policies, and, oh joy! reported a small profit.)

Hallinan showed the board posters prepared by Best, which the League was distributing, in promotion of co-operative automobile insurance. (New Co-op Fidelity director "Joe" Best was an enterprising credit union leader in London. At the April 1949 OCUL annual meeting he was a candidate for president but failed to unseat Cy Watson. Best defeated George Scott for the vice-presidency, vacated by Savage, who was elected a "national" but really international director.) Vera Burtwell, underwriting staff member, had discussed with the executive a file of automobile insurance refusals, many of them because the applicants were not members of the sponsoring organizations. Shea now discussed with the board the borderline risks refused for underwriting reasons. The purpose was to have the board's understanding and approval in meeting the criticisms which were beginning to appear. If the company was refusing to write insurance for its friends, no wonder it was losing money!

Milburn reported that as a result of meeting with a committee from the packinghouses and two meetings with the livestock commission firms, both groups had agreed to deduct premiums for Co-op Fidelity. It was time to inform them that Co-op Fidelity was in business. The board approved issuance of "single trip" livestock transit policies.

Best had familiarized himself with the company's by-laws, and he pointed out that the board should determine the remuneration of the officers it appointed, including the treasurer, Shea. He also pointed out that Shea's actual duties were not the same as those enumerated by the by-laws. The president, Harman, said that it should be clear that only one employee is directly responsible to the board and that other members of the staff are responsible to him. It was agreed to clarify this matter at the next board meeting (when the board passed a resolution that the remuneration of the secretary and the treasurer should be nil, and that the persons occupying these positions, Hebb and Shea, should be remunerated for the services they perform in other capacities, and another resolution delegating the care and custody of the company's funds to the secretary).

October streamlining included a decision "that the management exercise from this date the functions of the investment committee, securing authority and guidance from the board at least quarterly." Other resolutions provided investment guidance for the next three months. The only investments were to be government bonds and Toronto vicinity mortgages; there was to be an effort to build mortgages to 25 percent of assets, and there was to be an independent appraisal for any mortgage in excess of $4,000. By Ontario law the company was restricted as a mutual to trustee investments, and Richards had agreed earlier that because of these investment limitations he would approve 25 percent of assets in mortgages. While there was no statutory limitation on mortgages, prudent fire and casualty companies invested most of their money in more liquid securities.

Chapter 25

Negotiations with Regina

Milliken would be in Toronto on November 24 and 25, 1949, and the Ontario insurance board would meet again at that time. Nicholson had informed Co-operative Life board that Co-op Fidelity would be ready then to negotiate joint selling arrangements for 1950. Co-op Life had entered into a commission arrangement with Maritime Co-operative Services to sell life insurance in the Maritimes.

In reply to a letter from Milliken, Hebb wrote a long letter in preparation for negotiations. "It would seem that there has been some misunderstanding between our two companies arising out of the fact that your contribution to joint distribution in Ontario is known to both of us .... but you do not see what we are doing and we are not rendering you statements to show what we are doing."

Co-operative Life had spent $14,555 in Ontario in 10 months ended September 30, and attributed $7,093 of this amount to expense on automobile insurance. Co-op Fidelity had paid Co-op Life $2,993 in cash, and Hebb estimated Ontario expenditures of various kinds on life insurance at $2,400. In a letter to Co-operative Life he wrote: "That does not seem an unreasonable discrepancy if we bear in mind that (1) you are the established company, and we are just starting; and (2) that the above figures do not include our Ontario expenses prior to December 1, 1948, in helping to introduce Co-op Life in Ontario, nor does it [sic] include a great deal of voluntary help ...."

Barclay had been employed only in August, and had worked full-time on life insurance in October, and in 1950, Hebb estimated, Co-op Fidelity's expenditures on life insurance would be $6,900 and Co-op Life's on automobile insurance $10,800. "If our policy fee payments [to Co-operative Life] should amount to $4,000 we would have equalled your financial contribution to the joint distribution program."

"Ontario people accelerate slowly," the letter continued, ".... it will take us a while to think that Co-op Life is our idea .... the day will surely come when Ontario will be one of Co-op Life's most dependable bastions." The letter concluded with an estimate that, with continuing good luck, Co-op Fidelity would have a loss of $5,000 to $10,000 that year, and perhaps $15,000 to $20,000 the next year, and break even in the third year.

Another long letter, a couple of days later, went to O. C. Griffith, Ohio Farm Bureau Insurance, enclosing the operating forecasts for 1949, 1950 and 1951, and asking numerous questions and for an appraisal of Co-op Fidelity's position and progress.

The first paragraph of a six-point memorandum put before the board on November 24, 1949 - before Milliken joined the meeting - said: "Co-op Fidelity will have its hands full in 1950 with automobile insurance and livestock insurance, with automobile insurance at least likely to lose money in 1950. The Ontario insurance board, therefore, should not assume at the present the financial responsibility for the Co-op Life program in Ontario, that is, should not undertake to distribute life insurance on a commission basis."

Co-op Fidelity's 1950 results would be better than expected - livestock transit would lose money and automobile insurance would make money - but the certainty of loss in 1949, and the expectation of loss in 1950, inhibited generosity toward Co-op Life and western Canada. The directors were not willing to make any additional contribution for 1949, beyond the $1,000 already paid, 10 percent of policy fees, and Barclay's salary and expenses and an automobile provided by United Co-operatives. For 1950 they agreed to offer alternatives: provide a fieldman and his expenses to work under Staples and pay 10 percent of all policy fees other than on credit union non-agent policies, or, if Co-op Life employed Barclay, 10 percent of policy fees plus $6,500. Milliken was fair and charming, as usual, and expressed himself as satisfied with the proposals, and asked that they be sent in writing to Regina.

There were only seven shares allotted at this meeting, although Milburn reported on 40 meetings across the province to promote co-operative insurance and raise additional share capital. Hallinan reported that credit unions were asking individual members to subscribe for shares, rather than subscribing themselves as in the past. However, credit union members did not seem to have $50 for investment, and almost all share applications by individuals in the early years were from farm and rural people.

Staples reported life sales of over a quarter million dollars in a five-week period. There were now 60 life-licensed agents. Staples proposed limited other-than-life licence fee reimbursement for agents who did not qualify for full reimbursement. A letter from district agent W. V. Roy on behalf of Huron county agents proposed renewal commissions of five percent instead of three percent and that 2-1/2 percent go to the writing agent. Roy was also secretary-treasurer of Huron county Federation of Agriculture.

On the motion of Best and Hallinan, the board asked the solicitor to report on paying dividends retroactively at some future time to relieve inequity to early shareholders arising out of non-payment of dividends in the early years. Other matters dealt with were tractor premiums, reduction of the minimum automobile premium from $5 to $2, a proposed employee pension plan held by Co-operative Life, permissible cash to be held by insured credit unions, remuneration of the solicitor, borrowing authorization, and enactment of a by-law to avoid the necessity of mailing to each policyholder a notice of annual meetings (and a financial statement). Annual meetings would be held the last Saturday in February. Shareholders would continue to receive notice and a financial statement by mail.

Chapter 26

Co-operative Politics

One of Staples' fieldmen, Musgrave, had been doing a big job in the company's most productive territory, which included Grey, Bruce and Huron. Enthusiastic and quick to understand the insurance program, he was an effective teacher and an effervescent person with a gift for remembering names and cheering up discouraged agents - the forty-niners were often discouraged. He had a small fruit farm at Clarksburg in the Beaver Valley, in Grey county, and divided western Ontario with George Barclay. In the fall rumors began to reach the office that Musgrave was canvassing for election to the board of United Co-operatives. Harman and Hebb were agreed that it was undesirable for someone who was indirectly an employee of Co-operators' Fidelity to become a director of the province's biggest co-operative organization. Although not nominating Co-op Fidelity directors, UCO was the biggest shareholder and one of the chief sponsors. Staples was not in a position to express an independent opinion because he himself was still a UCO board member and a director of the Ontario Co-operative Union. Five "Ontario Co-operative Insurance" directors - Harman, Milburn, Morrison, Hallinan and Hughes - were employees of provincial organizations, and it would be a complication if their insurance employees were also to become their employers as directors of these provincial organizations.

Hebb made unsuccessful efforts to dissuade Musgrave from running for election to the UCO board. Musgrave had been talking of taking some time from insurance the next summer to work on his fruit farm. Hebb felt that another three or four days a month taken for UCO board attendance and travel would injure the bigger sales program planned for 1950. He wrote to Musgrave that he was also concerned about "the added complication of another member of our Ontario insurance staff becoming a member of the UCO board." (Musgrave was elected for a three-year term at the UCO annual meeting in December, 1949. Co-op Fidelity director Nicholson resigned as a UCO director, and C. Foster Rice, manager of Temiskaming District Co-operative, New Liskeard, was elected in his place for a two-year term. Among the unsuccessful candidates was Co-op Fidelity director W. J. Wood, who had lost his U. F. Co-op board seat in 1947. At this UCO annual meeting A. C. Savage led a discussion on "cash policies," that is, cash trading in the local co-operatives.)

In western Canada, an employee of one co-operative was often a director of another co-operative, or the farmer president of a major co-operative like the Saskatchewan Wheat Pool might become a full-time "employee." In Ontario a different viewpoint was developing - employees should not become directors, or make policy pronouncements, and directors should not become full-time paid officers. An elected, paid full-time officer would be an employee without a boss. Co-op Fidelity faced no such danger as yet because it was not able to pay directors for attendance at board meetings. But Co-op Fidelity directors did not want the company's "employees" to be directors of the organizations by which Co-op Fidelity directors were employed.

As a result the board adopted a series of nine recommendations, prepared by the general manager with approval of the executive members and amended by the board after discussion with Staples. All key employees in co-operative insurance would be employed on a full-time basis; no employees would serve as directors of any provincial or national farm or co-operative organization; and Co-op Fidelity would be regarded as, in effect, a joint subsidiary of other Ontario co-operative and farm organizations. The remaining recommendations asked Staples and Musgrave to become full-time employees by May 1, 1950 (that is, to resign from the UCO board), asked Co-operative Life to increase their salaries for full-time employment to $5,000 a year for Staples and $3,600 for Musgrave, and authorized the general manager to agree to any additional contribution by Co-op Fidelity to the costs of joint distribution that might be necessary to secure the recommended salary increases.

The general manager reported to this December meeting that Co-operative Life had accepted the 1949 arrangements for sharing joint distribution costs, and for 1950 had elected the arrangement under which Co-op Fidelity would employ one fieldman who would be responsible to Staples, and pay Co-op Life the equivalent of 10 percent of automobile policy fees on other than credit union non-agent policies. The solicitor, Mitchell, had advised that in the payment of dividends on shares there would be no way to discriminate between recent purchasers and those who had held their shares for a long time.

With an operating loss in prospect, and a probable demand by the department of insurance for more capital, there were only 25 shares allotted at this last meeting in 1949. Among the purchasers were Blair Gray, Komoka, and William James Stinson, Chesley, successful agents, Barbara Ellen Liscumb, a new staff member, and Ernest Moores, a UCO employee who had agreed to become Co-op Fidelity office manager beginning in January 1950. Co-op Fidelity director and Ontario Co-operative Union secretary Hughes had written personal letters to local co-operative officers, and Milburn had written to county Federation presidents and county insurance chairmen asking for share subscriptions.

Chapter 27

Yearend 49

Chosen from the top ranks of the sponsors, Co-op Fidelity directors were not afraid to disagree, as they did on the delicate matter of "eligibility" at this all-day board meeting four days before Christmas 1949.

The board agreed not to cancel a policyholder's automobile insurance because he had attained 70 years of age, but could not agree on continuance of insurance for "retired farmer" policyholders who were no longer eligible as members of the Federation of Agriculture. The general manager proposed that a retired farmer should continue to be eligible if he did not undertake other full-time employment. Best and Hughes moved that a policyholder should continue to be eligible as long as he kept his automobile insurance continuously in force, but by a Milburn and Nicholson amendment the decision was postponed until the next meeting.

Harman introduced, and Staples explained, proposed incentive sales payments by Co-op Fidelity to the three field managers, and to writing agents. (The district agent plan was not working well. The district agent was not taking responsibility for the appointment and supervision of local agents.) There was also an effort to have casualty-only agents improve their incomes by taking out life licences. If the writing agent had five or more automobile policies issued in a month he would receive an extra five percent of the policy fee, but if he were an active life agent an extra 10 percent; for 10 or more automobile policies, he would receive 10 percent or 20 percent. The proposals, approved by the board without change, included payment of the three percent renewal service fee (the Indiana Farm Bureau name for renewal commission) to the writing agent in any month in which he had three or more automobile policies issued.

Two members of the staff had particularly difficult jobs in 1949, Margaret Chambers and Bernard Shea. With responsibility for policy issuance and records, policy renewals, and accounting records, Miss Chambers had built up a staff of about 15 persons by the yearend. In an effort to lighten her load the general manager had engaged an office manager, Carl Yelland. A capable person with co-operative sympathies, but critical of internal operations, he resigned after only a few months. Shea had the difficult job of refusing many automobile applications sent in through volunteers or by agents. He did so courageously, tactfully and patiently.

Sometimes it was necessary to make explanations to prominent friends who were helping to raise capital or were sending applicants to agents. A director of the company and vice-president of Ontario Credit Union League, Joseph M. Best had sent in an application for a vehicle nine or more years old, and he "was more than surprised" that the applicant had been asked for a garage mechanic's report on the condition of the vehicle. "It seems to me," he wrote to the general manager, "that it's hard enough to get people to switch from their present coverage to CF&GA without throwing more obstacles in their way." The general manager explained that the company was insuring many old vehicles not acceptable to other insurers.

A resourceful and cheerful staff, sharing problems and answers, included Olive Bandy, Margaret Howard, Helen Morrison, Zita Whitehead, Trinka (Kit) Tuinema, and other capable people like Artur Ekbaum, who had been a co-operative leader in his native Estonia. He and his novelist wife Salme had fled from Soviet domination. Fan Galway, on Co-operative Life staff, was secretary-lieutenant to Ralph Staples.

Chapter 28

Public Supervision

Department of insurance officials tried to be helpful. Although he was a prominent member himself of the Queen's Park Civil Servants credit union, Richards, the chief examiner, could not understand why non-professionals would want to get into the insurance business with all its hazards and difficulties. He saw failure as a possibility, or even a probability. He did not encourage entry into bonding insurance in 1946, or automobile insurance in 1949, and 10 years later, when asked how much capital would be necessary for life insurance, he would say, "Why would you want to go into life insurance? You don't want to do that?" But once Co-op Fidelity was into a new line of insurance, he was a helpful public servant. Superintendent Whitehead was less fearful of disaster - he was apparently content to allow Richards to worry over a new company's solvency - but he advised the general manager to require a personal credit report concerning every urban applicant for automobile insurance, and this advice the company followed scrupulously for 20 years.

Spencer, the agency superintendent, was under direct pressure from Ontario Insurance Agents' Association. Arguing ably the right of people to get together to provide themselves with insurance co-operatively, Staples found Spencer sympathetic, but unyielding in his defence of the private enterprise position of the general agent. Life

Top,
  Kenneth M. Betzner

Bottom,
  Ralph S. Staples

Top,
  Herbert H. Hannam

Bottom,
  Andrew O. Hebb

Top,
  Hassil E. Schenck

Bottom,
  Leonard Harman

Top,
 Vivian S. Milburn

Bottom,
 Margaret Chambers

Top,
  John M. Hallinan

Bottom,
  A.C. Savage

Top,
  Leonard W. Mitchell

Bottom,
  Bernard Shea

insurance agents and life companies were not concerned about competition from a new life insurance company, because an additional life insurance policy did not replace an existing policy. But, although many Co-op Fidelity automobile policies were for persons previously uninsured, general agents were losing some policies to "the Co-op" - they were particularly incensed about part-time agents. Spencer made new rules about not licensing farm and co-operative employees, and secured the superintendent's support for the withdrawal of rate manuals from credit unions. (But it was his proposal, in 1952, to license "voluntary representatives" who successfully wrote the automobile section of the agent's examination.)

John Edwards, the department actuary, was a good friend. In November 1949 he informed the general manager confidentially that Canadian Underwriters Association ("the tariff companies") was proposing to the superintendent certain automobile insurance premium changes, but that the Independent Conference companies did not agree. The two groups sold their insurance through the same general agency system, and sometimes through the same agents, and uniformity was almost essential. The superintendent suggested that they return when they had reached agreement. Edwards explained that the superintendent had no authority to set rates, and that the two rate organizations met annually with the superintendent to inform him of their plans. Each company was theoretically free to set its own rates. Edwards provided the general manager with the CUA premium proposals. (Occasionally, in later years, the rating organizations would want some information about CIA, and Edwards would telephone and ask for it.)

Murray Maxwell, an ex-serviceman and a law graduate of the University of Toronto, joined the underwriting staff under Bernard Shea in November 1949, and soon became interested in the closed claims files which adjusters Keddel & Shea were forwarding. "I haven't the least doubt but that you were wise in handling your claims in this manner in the earlier stages," Ohio Farm Bureau claims manager Marion Foltz wrote in December. "We had around 5,000 policies in force when I came in January 1927 to set up our claims department." The proper time to take over claims service, he said, would depend on the quality of service given by the independent adjusters, and the cost per claim.

Co-op Fidelity had 4,431 automobile policies in force at the end of

1949 out of over 4,458 issued during this year. Most agents were farmers and only part-time salesmen. Many prospects did not buy collision insurance; renewal commissions in the second half of the year were minimal; and total remuneration covered little more than automobile expense. In addition, most agents were classified as "local" and a portion of the commissions on their sales went to "district" agents. Perhaps a quarter of the agents did not renew their licences at September 30. Of those who did not, some had sold only a few policies, but a few were good producers, including Theodore Grimble with 43 policies, Robert French 23 and Lawrence Read 19.

Of those who renewed their licences many were enthusiastic Farm Forum, co-operative or Federation of Agriculture members who were determined to make a success of co-operative insurance, even at a considerable personal sacrifice. Others liked the friendly reception they received as Co-op agents, and saw co-operative insurance as a possible part or full-time career.

The leading producers of automobile insurance for 1949 (in order of the number of policies) were: George White, T. A. Cameron, Barrett Forbes, R. M. Peck, Wilfred Glazier, Ed Logel, Edward Lang (who became a staff member), J. D. McLennan, Blair Gray, Elmer Beckett, James Stinson, Russel Knight, Ross Francis, Edward Engel, H. S. Hallman, P. J. Mulrooney (only urban member of this group), Orville Taylor, W. V. Roy, Elgin MacNab, Charles Johnston, James Coultes, Lyle Branscombe, Stanley Coverdale.

In a Christmas bulletin to agents, Staples wrote: "North America is smothering in surplus food ($3 billion worth held by the government of U.S.A. alone), while most humans are underfed .... The co-operative movement stands in solid opposition to the principle of competition and scarcity which is so incompatible with the welfare of modern man. As never before, co-operative workers can be justly proud of the fact that they are definitely and actively building, in a most practical and effective way, that world of peace and goodwill."

Staples' co-operative ideas as distribution manager, and the Farm Bureau sponsorship plan, were more effective in automobile insurance than in life insurance, but life insurance played its part. Staples had done a splendid organization job but not from a standing start in 1949. Staples and the Co-operative Life advisory committee had established an agent base in 1947 and 1948, and without this earlier beginning and

Co-op Life's partnership in 1949 it is questionable whether Co-op Fidelity would have done well enough to pull through the controversy ahead - although fewer policies in force would have meant lesser capital demands from the department of insurance.

One of the most successful agents, T. A. Cameron, Lucknow, in Bruce county, in January 1950 wrote to the general manager that he had been talking to a policyholder who had not seen or heard from an independent adjuster at Walkerton supposed to be settling a claim for him. "So I got a little hot under the collar and wrote a letter to Mr. Ralph Staples last night, which no doubt you may have the opportunity of reading," Cameron wrote.

Keddel & Shea had received a report of the accident on December 28, obtained a report from the policyholder by mail, and then assigned the claim to the adjuster at Walkerton - a slow process - and it was now January 18. Bernard Shea and Murray Maxwell began to think that they could do a better job than Keddel & Shea on the out-of-Toronto claims.

Shea and Hebb had lunch with Richards, chief examiner of the department of insurance, on January 3. They told him that on an 80 percent unearned premium basis the company was likely to have a loss of $5,000 for 1949 - although the adjusters had not as yet provided an estimate of outstanding claims - and to lose $15,000 in 1950. On a 100 percent unearned basis, as urged earlier by Richards, the 1949 loss might be $10,000, and the 1950 loss $20,000. They suggested that he allow the company to calculate unearned premiums at 80 percent for a period of five years, and then change gradually to a 100 percent basis. He withheld his decision.

Turning to capital requirements, Richards said there was a question whether $65,000 was sufficient to support automobile premium income of, say, $200,000 - expected in 1950. He provided three capital rules-of-thumb:

(a) capital and surplus should equal unearned premium reserve;
(b) capital and surplus should be at least as large as incurred losses;
(c) premium writings should not be more than double capital and surplus.

Informed later in the month that the audited statement for 1949, on an 80 percent unearned premium basis, showed a loss of $9,339, Richards permitted use of 80 percent, but was concerned about the future. Bringing with him a letter signed by the superintendent,

R. B. Whitehead, K. C., Richards attended a Co-op Fidelity board meeting on January 24, 1950.

The letter required the company "to furnish without delay additional paid-in capital of $50,000." Richards, who undoubtedly wrote the letter, said that to raise the money in three to six months would be satisfactory. The superintendent would be prepared to consider, the letter said, in answer to an earlier inquiry from the company, in lieu of share capital, "loans which would rank as liabilities of the company only after the claims of policyholders have been satisfied."

Applicants for 40 shares allotted at this meeting included Graham G. Griffith, Sarnia, Barrett A. Forbes, Wyoming, and Bertram W. Klopp, Zurich, early agents, Leonard Laventure, Glasgow Station, an agent later on, and the manager of Belgrave Co-operative Association, Charles R. Coultes.

Co-operative Life no longer needed the special expense fund which Ontario people had lent without receiving any written promise to repay, and the amounts were now to be returned with interest. Ontario Co-operative Union was requested to suggest to these lenders that they invest the money in Co-op Fidelity shares. Co-op Fidelity would seek a loan of $100,000 from CIS, Manchester, to be repaid prior to "retirement or reduction of the guaranteed capital stock." The Association would also invite policyholders, when renewing their policies, to subscribe for shares. Still another resolution approved payment of a commission to licensed agents or credit union members approved by the League, of $5 per share for sale of up to five Co-op Fidelity shares to an individual or for enough shares to bring his or her holdings up to five shares.

The board approved a proposal to write insurance on trucks used for certain commercial purposes within a 25-mile radius of the owner's home (described as "semi-farm trucks"). Shea reported that county Federations of Agriculture would be able to submit accounts for expenses in promotion of insurance up to a total of $2,883 - 10 percent of non-city policy fees in 1949.

Hebb and Staples had disagreed about whether a person should become eligible to buy automobile insurance if, not belonging to one of the sponsoring organizations, he purchased Co-operative Life insurance. Staples said that he thus became a member of Co-operative Life Insurance Company and therefore eligible for automobile insurance. Hebb thought it to be the policy of Co-op Fidelity to follow the Indiana Farm Bureau Insurance companies in writing life insurance for anyone, but automobile insurance for only certain eligible persons, and asked for confirmation of his viewpoint. The board agreed with Staples and passed a resolution accordingly.

Chapter 29

National Insurance Shadow

Fluttering over the heads of the harassed directors, and casting an additional shadow on an as yet unprofitable enterprise, was the possibility of a "national" other-than-life co-operative insurance company. Towering and persuasive A. B. MacDonald, secretary of the Co-operative Union of Canada, and Lloyd Matheson, insurance manager, Maritime Co-operative Services, Moncton, probably on his way to Regina for a board meeting of Co-operative Life Insurance Company, visited Toronto on February 13, 1950. They met at 30 Bloor Street West with Harman, Staples, Milburn, Hughes, Betzner, Hallinan, Shea and Hebb.

The CUC's committee on co-operative insurance, when it met at Winnipeg in January, MacDonald reported, had agreed that a fire and casualty company should be organized nationally, although a subcommittee had reported disagreement (MacDonald and H. A. Crofford in favor of national organization, Savage of Ontario in favor of regional organization). MacDonald also said that the national committee had agreed with the subcommittee that Co-operative Life should operate nationally and that CUNA Mutual should be recognized as a national co-operative insurance company operating in the credit unions and among credit union members. The national fire and casualty company would provide for delegate representation, but there was no decision yet between a mutual and a joint stock basis. It was to be explored whether Co-operative Life could be reorganized as a joint stock company, MacDonald continued. The committee recommended establishment of an advisory council in each region.

The visitors wanted Ontario to participate in the proposed national fire and casualty company. "Co-op Life should be the national company in life insurance, with CUNA Mutual operating in the credit unions," Harman stated as the Ontario position. "But we will vote against a national fire and casualty insurance company, and we are not prepared to participate, at the present time at any rate, in such a company. If other provinces wish to operate in fire and casualty insurance, good luck to them." Ontario's many local farm fire mutuals had proved themselves more efficient than a company like Wawanesa, operating nationally, and these fire mutuals entered into the Ontario preference for local and regional operation.

French-language credit unions in Quebec had organized recently a co-operative bonding company, said Hallinan. The Maritimes haven't enough automobiles to launch a regional automobile company, Matheson commented.

Would Ontario consider participation in a national company if means could be found to make regional control effective? asked MacDonald. Ontario favored regional organization both for control and efficiency, Harman replied.

"It would not be possible to get the same 'people-participation' in a national company," said Milburn.

"What about developing Co-op Fidelity into a national organization?" queried MacDonald, not as a proposal but as a test of Ontario's convictions.

"We would lose the sense of participation," said Harman, adding that Co-op Fidelity already had a big job on its hands, and inadequate capital.

"CUNA Mutual has tried two forms of control - mail ballot and area control - but neither plan has worked except in Ontario, where there is a higher number of individual policyholders," said Hallinan. He felt that national or international organization offered "less control but more service."

Staples did not share the Ontario position stated by Harman. "Canada is none too large for a single insurance operation," he said. "Being small doesn't assure being democratic, and a national organization might be more efficient. I would not want Ontario to stand in the way of a national development."

"While the Ontario viewpoint is clear now, it may be different at some future time," commented Betzner. "We might prefer to operate on a national basis rather than to have another national casualty company that might come into Ontario."

Despite disagreement, the exchange of views was friendly. The visitors departed to continue their large plans on behalf of "have not" provinces. The Ontarians were unaware that their preference for provincial or regional insurance organization, with its greater policyholder participation, was about to undergo a severe test. They had not reckoned with the possibility that there could be more participation than a struggling semi-mutual company could absorb.

With less business experience than their farmer allies, urban credit unionists were more critical of the underwriting rigidities and money-losing operations of Co-op Fidelity. At an Ontario Credit Union League (OCUL) executive meeting a month earlier - on Saturday, January 14, a resolution moved by George Scott and Percy Quinton instructed the League's representatives on Co-op Fidelity board to oppose a suggested limitation on the company's credit union blanket bonds. Co-op Fidelity staff was proposing not to provide bonds for credit unions which retained as cash on hand more than $1,000 for more than 48 hours.

This OCUL executive meeting also discussed the proposed amendment of Co-op Fidelity by-laws to avoid mailing notice of the annual meeting and a financial statement to policyholders. The day of the annual meeting - the last Saturday in February - would be printed on policies and renewal notices. Notice and a financial statement would still go by mail to shareholders. Co-op Fidelity co-founder Savage moved a resolution, seconded by George Scott and carried, to oppose confirmation of the by-law at the approaching annual meeting and to "make every effort in our power to get the policyholders to attend the meeting for the purpose of voting against this by-law amendment."

An OCUL directors' meeting the next day approved a Co-operative Life pension plan for League employees, contributed $100 "to the library being built in Nova Scotia to honour a great co-operative leader, Father Tompkins," and appointed League vice-president Best as the OCUL voting delegate at Co-op Fidelity annual meeting on

February 25. Popular C. J. Watson of Windsor advised the directors that he would not be a candidate for re-election as president of OCUL.

If Co-op Fidelity had been national, with its head office in Regina or Moncton or Ottawa it is likely that there would not have been so many troublesome complaints. They were annoying. They had to be answered carefully. If it was not possible to satisfy the policyholder, it might be possible to keep him. If it was not possible to keep him, it might be possible to disarm him - so that he would not broadcast his criticism. There were the automobile underwriting criticisms which had begun early in 1949; there were the premium criticisms which had begun with the first renewals at mid-year; later on, there would be claim criticisms. Criticisms, of course, might disturb manager and staff, but kept them alert.

In January 1950, for example, a rural clergyman forwarded $39.65 to renew his policy for six months, but he was "getting a little bit disillusioned .... And unless I am given better terms on my car insurance policy you may be sure I shall not apply for more insurance from your company." He provided some food for thought. Co-op Fidelity was the first insurance company in 26 years to surcharge him because he was wearing a hearing aid. "If you imposed a surcharge for an alcoholic, one could understand it. But I am an abstainer .... and people of my degree of deafness are usually more alert, and have better sight, than those with perfect hearing. How many people do you penalize because of imperfect eyesight? .... Hearing aids are worn by people who are very slightly deaf, and by those who are almost stone-deaf. I think you have been very unfair to me, and I would ask you to do something about it."

He got a soft and painstaking answer, but no concession: "....for the present at least, because of the need of economy we must rely to a great extent on rough rules which are hard on some people." About alcohol he was told: "We just do not take drinking drivers insofar as we are able to weed them out. Our agents have turned down hundreds of persons on this ground, and we have turned down others when we were aware of the facts. Undoubtedly, some have slipped through, and we have had to cancel two policies for driving while drinking."

Chapter 30

Operating Problems

On February 15 the board studied a detailed report to the directors by the auditors, Millar, Macdonald & Company. Fidelity insurance, they said, had been profitable, livestock transit and automobile unprofitable. "The livestock underwriting loss is the result of overhead expenses," said comments written by the accountant in charge of the audit, J. B. Barker. "At present, two employees are engaged full-time in the livestock department. In the face of premium reductions offered by other companies it is evident that your Association will have to reduce the direct expenses of this department if further loss is to be avoided."

Concerning automobile insurance he wrote: "The use of tabulating equipment is not essential in an operation as small as that of your Association. The cost of this equipment, including salaries and supplies, would average at least $600 per month. While this equipment can produce a considerable variety of statistical information, the usefulness of this information should be compared with the cost of its production. We do not suggest that the use of tabulating machines be arbitrarily discontinued but we do recommend that the entire system of office routine be reviewed to ensure that the most effective use is being made of all facilities and that expenses are controlled so as to produce the best possible results with the lowest reasonable cost."

These comments were disturbing to the directors. Hebb and Margaret Chambers defended the use of tabulating. (Subsequent opinion obtained from Millar, Macdonald & Company's only other insurance client, Canadian General Insurance, supported Barker's viewpoint - Canadian General's chief accountant thought a million dollars in premium was needed to justify tabulating. However, Canadian General dealt with agents only; Co-op Fidelity required cash with each application - had no agent accounts - and collected renewals directly from policyholders.)

Co-op Life's president, H. A. Crofford, had visited the joint offices at 30 Bloor Street West and had advised some of the Co-op Fidelity directors (and Co-op Life advisers) that the Ontario insurance company's purchase of steel desks was extravagant. In July the board had authorized the secretary to buy equipment as needed.

The other directors agreed with Hughes at this February meeting that there should be continuing study of the relative merits of six-month and annual automobile policies. Despite the auditors' comments on livestock transit insurance, the board approved a recommendation by Milburn, as chairman of the livestock transit committee, to rent an office at the Ontario Stockyards for $30 a month, and adoption of the same livestock rates used by Hartford Fire Insurance Company.

Back in 1948 O. C. Griffith, Ohio Farm Bureau Insurance, had recommended that the company retain $5,000 of automobile property damage risk, but the chief insurance examiner, Richards, had permitted a retention of only $1,000. Now the department had agreed to an increase from $1,000 to $5,000 per policy per accident, and the board approved a request to this effect to reinsurer CIS, Manchester.

Shea reported that Brompton Pulp and Paper Employees' credit union was dissolving, but he believed that a purchaser had been found for the credit union's five shares.

The general manager recommended no change in automobile premium rates, except for vehicle age and value ratings. Premiums were a difficult question - presenting perhaps a choice between 10 percent fewer policies with more premium per policy or more policies with less premium per policy. Only one policy in four included collision insurance. Any increase in premium should be in PL/PD (public liability/property damage). The true loss ratio for 1949 was not yet known - many claims were still unsettled. A rate increase at mid-year would not produce much earned premium in 1950. The company would update rate manual automobile age and value ratings for collision and fire and theft insurance. These changes would be necessary once a year to let premiums fall as vehicles became older. To apply these new ratings to business in force would have been a lot of work, with a loss of premium of two or three hundred dollars. Richards, the chief examiner, had agreed that the company need not apply the changes to policies in force, unless the policyholder changed his coverage or his vehicle, until the company made a general change in rates or until the beginning of 1951, whichever was sooner. This was "discriminating for a short period between old and new policyholders," Hebb reported, but since other companies were increasing their collision rates it was "not particularly unfair to policyholders."

The board was giving the general manager more leeway, and left automobile premium revision with him. The general manager wrote to Griffith, Ohio Farm Bureau, that, following advice of a year earlier from Griffith, he was asking the reinsurer, CIS, Manchester, for an increase in the commission on premiums ceded, and, beginning in 1950, a 35 percent profits commission. He also asked for a reduction in the reinsurance premium itself. Hebb informed Co-op Fidelity president Harman, but apparently did not tell the board about this request. (With his usual generosity, Robert Dinnage, the English general manager, granted these requests. The additional revenue would make the difference between loss and profit in 1950.)

The board received at this February 1950 meeting the first of many recommendations which would come from county Federations of Agriculture. Huron county Federation insurance committee proposed a change in agent commissions but the board felt it unwise to disturb so soon the new plan of paying the renewal service fee to the local writing agent in any month when he wrote three new policies. The county insurance committees were close to the agents and their recommendations kept the staff alert to problems.

The board authorized the distribution committee to appoint agents, but not to promote automobile insurance actively, in northern Ontario, approved reimbursement of some agents for their licence fees, and approved a monthly $10 prize to encourage writing of complete coverages (policy fees amounting to $9).

The board reviewed a 15-page double-spaced directors' report, to be presented to the annual meeting on Saturday, February 25, prepared by Harman and Hebb, but made no changes.

"The directors of your Association stand before you in pride that this is a real annual meeting," the report said. "They take pride in the fact that they must account to you as shareholders and policyholders ...." The directors approved the lengthy report, on the motion of Milburn and Best, asked Hallinan to present it to the annual meeting, and asked newly appointed office manager Ernest Moores, a graduate of the Ontario Co-operative Union's war veterans rehabilitation training school, to conduct the election of directors.

At this February board meeting Harman reported interviews with Staples and Musgrave. Staples would like until December 1950 to decide whether to undertake full-time insurance service or terminate his insurance employment. Musgrave intended to complete at least a year on UCO board, and probably the three years for which he was elected. He would like to continue in insurance work and he would give up working on his farm in the summer if necessary.

"This matter has proven an extremely awkward one for your president both because of the interlocking complications of directors and staff in UCO and insurance, with your president finding himself in the middle of the muddle, and also because of long and close association in various aspects of the farm and co-operative movement with the persons concerned," Harman wrote. He suggested either that the "Co-operative Insurance board" press Staples and Musgrave for decisions, or that the board "re-state the principles of (a) having insurance staff on a full-time basis and (b) having no co-op insurance employees on the boards of organizations sponsoring co-op insurance in Ontario," urge Staples and Musgrave to undertake full-time insurance at the earliest possible date, and select June 1, 1951, as the latest date for putting into effect the stated principles. The board agreed to deal with the president's report in March.

Meanwhile O. C. Griffith of Ohio Farm Bureau was carrying on what amounted to an insurance "correspondence school" for Co-op Fidelity staff. The day after the board meeting a 10-page closely typed letter arrived, reviewing 1949 operations, analyzing forecast expenses and revenues for 1950 and 1951, and answering a list of questions sent to him concerning underwriting, claims and reinsurance. Study of this letter was good preparation for the impending annual meeting. Staff members were getting to know more than directors about insurance, and certainly more than the shareholders and policyholders who attended annual meetings, although it might be difficult for them to think so as long as there were operating deficits.

"I should think you could expect to break even or possibly make something in 1951," Griffith wrote. "We lost about $19,000 in our first year of operation .... It does appear that your present expense ratios are too high .... You are probably wise not to tinker with the rating just at this point .... Even if you do change your rates for new writings, there are some situations in which it is not unfairly discriminatory to postpone mass reclassification .... You should perhaps consider handling your own claims .... I am wondering if your independent connections may not possibly be a little lax and perhaps paying more for such claimant goodwill than it is worth just at this important period .... Your sales department must assume responsibility for rapidly adding agents who will increase the volume immediately out of the loss point .... Everyone has to make sacrifices in order to get a company started soundly. It is hard for me to see how you can increase your acquisition expenses at a time when you have not reached the break-even point. If the pressure is so great that you are beginning to lose your agency force or failing to gain volume rapidly enough, something may have to give ...."

The rate manual prohibited writing policies for "aliens or unnaturalized persons or any others not acquainted with usual motor vehicle laws and who would be difficult to defend because of language difficulties." This prohibition followed the Ohio Farm Bureau manual. There were many Dutch immigrant farmers in southwestern Ontario, and agents and others were critical because the company was not accepting them as policyholders. Griffith said: "If attributes along character lines were entirely satisfactory, one of our underwriters might occasionally be persuaded to take an alien or unnaturalized person for merely the physical damage coverages, that is, fire, theft and collision .... Facts might be brought forward in an occasional case to overcome our objections ...."

Discussing automobile loss ratios, Griffith said: "High rates repel good risks .... and tend to make for high loss ratios and expenses. My own idea is a middle course .... not charging the highest rates nor gambling by charging the lowest rates, but pitching somewhere in between and doing the kind of an underwriting job which will remove the few risks from the portfolio that cause the disastrous or high frequency losses. Since your loss ratios are as high as they are out of the first year, it looks to me as though you should aim for somewhere between 42% and 47% in 1950. It looks as though this will almost be a requirement ...."

Chapter 31

Gentlemen's Disagreement

The fourth annual meeting took place at the King Edward Hotel, Toronto, in a room known as "Vanity Fair," on Saturday, February 25, 1950. Policyholders and shareholders had received financial statements, and at least some were critical of the operating loss. Although the directors had anticipated, since automobile planning began, a loss in 1949, and perhaps in 1950, their annual report in 1948 included nothing to prepare shareholders and policyholders for a 1949 loss. Perhaps such realism would have made the selling of shares too difficult.

There were 64 individuals present who were entitled to vote either as policyholder or shareholder or as both, but with only one personal vote in any event, and there were 33 persons, some of them entitled to vote as individuals, who were entitled to one vote as delegates for corporate shareholders or policyholders.

Hallinan presented the directors' report. It had been necessary to send a financial statement and a notice of the annual meeting to 5,000 policyholders, and the board asked for approval of a by-law that would make it unnecessary to send a personal notice of the annual meeting and a financial statement to policyholders. "It may seem at first, inconsistent with democratic principles and practices," the report acknowledged, but "it would be an important economy." There might be 10 to 12 thousand policyholders another year. Announcement of annual meetings would appear in the Credit Union News and the Rural Co-operator. The meetings would be held on the last Saturday in February. Shareholders would receive individual notices and financial statements. Everyone would know about the meetings, through premium notices and publicity, and the directors hoped that a representative number of policyholders and shareholders would attend annual meetings and would elect to the board of directors the persons nominated by the sponsoring organizations.

The automobile six-month premium made possible a strictly cash direct-from-policyholder-to-Association renewal plan, with results "beyond our expectations." The six-month policy, however, made a lot of work which "fell heavily on a new organization .... We had about 20 persons employed by the end of November."

Hallinan explained that the board functioned as "the advisory committee of Co-op Life in Ontario," and that "when we speak of your board in its double capacity we call it the Ontario Co-operative Insurance board." As the advisory committee in Ontario, "we have the responsibility of getting Co-op Life established on a self-sustaining basis in Ontario .... Co-operative life insurance made satisfactory progress in Ontario in 1949 .... Insurance purchased by individuals reached a total of $707,000 - almost double the figure for 1948 .... 79 life agents were on the job at the beginning of this year."

During the year there had been discussion of Co-op Life organizing a companion national other-than-life company, the report continued. "It has been suggested that Ontario join in such a plan, but your board has taken the position that, while a national co-operative company functions efficiently in life insurance, provincial or regional companies will be more appropriate, democratic and successful in other-than-life insurance."

Over 4,400 new automobile policies were a "highly satisfactory result .... Legal requirements that urban agents must be full-time, and legal restrictions on credit union insurance committees making voluntary sales of auto insurance are obstacles in the way of the rapid development of credit union auto insurance .... Credit union insurance committees have directed many applicants to us .... Our rural agents have done a great deal of work for which they have not received adequate remuneration."

Expenses claimed too big a proportion of the premium dollar for profitable operation, Hallinan continued, but the expense percentage would go down with increased dollar volume and a higher proportion of renewal premium. In the first year automobile premium was two-thirds new and one-third renewal. "In our second year it will be more like one-third new and two-thirds renewal. In the third year (1951) the more cheaply handled renewal business may make up more than three-quarters of our volume."

Explaining the superintendent's request for $50,000 additional capital, the directors said: "If two years ago we could have foreseen the difficulties and obstacles in 1949 and 1950 which we can now see clearly, we might never have gone into automobile insurance. Fortunately, however, your directors believe, we were able to see more clearly the results which we shall be achieving in five and 10 years than we could see the difficulties of the launching years .... Our expense in auto insurance in 1950 will be at least double our expenses in 1949 .... Your board is aware of the possibility that, in spite of making all reasonable progress in 1950, we can have a substantially larger loss in auto insurance this year than last year .... We are confident, however, that we will have your support in raising the additional capital required .... The building of user-owned and controlled business institutions is something we can all do - patiently, carefully and with all our faith and energy."

After some discussion of the report, former Co-op Fidelity director A. C. Savage, of Bolton, who had sold his city home to live in a rural area, and Paul E. Meehan, Toronto, secretary and manager of CUMBA Co-operative Health Services, moved that election of directors and consideration of the proposed by-law take place at 3 p.m. but withdrew this motion when J. J. Thurston, of Cameron in Peterborough county, protested that he hoped to be on his way home by 3 p.m..

A resolution by E. C. Cardy, Toronto, seconded by Savage, to hear the guest speaker during the morning, rather than after lunch, as scheduled by the agenda, was carried. Lynn Matteson, secretary, Mutual Service Insurance Companies, St. Paul, Minnesota, explained a new plan of representation and control being put into use by these companies. In answer to a question by Co-op Fidelity solicitor L. W. Mitchell, Matteson explained the advantages of the six-month automobile policy used by Mutual Service: first, a larger percentage of the premium is earned; second, "we can adjust the rates and get results more quickly; and third, in direct billing we find that the policyholder will pay the premium more readily."

After lunch Bernard Shea presented the financial statement and auditors' report. The directors' report had explained that United Co-operatives, the Rural Co-operator and Farmers' Insurance Information Association had purchased and lent the company $6,000 worth of equipment. The company itself had purchased $7,000 worth of equipment. Did this $7,000 appear on the balance sheet, questioned H. M. Shannon, of Holy Rosary credit union, Toronto. An insurance company was not permitted to show furniture and equipment as an asset, Shea replied. The amount appeared only as an expense.

Following adoption of the financial reports on motion of Savage and Sam McFarlane, of Keen credit union, Hamilton, discussion returned to the directors' report. Clayton Bender, Gowanstown farmer, as a member of Perth county Federation of Agriculture insurance committee, criticized the way a claim had been settled in the summer of 1949. Harve S. Hallman, Waterloo county agent, stressed the importance of good claims service.

The company's high expenses were a matter of concern to the directors of CUMBA Co-operative, and they had asked him as secretary to discuss these expenses at Co-op Fidelity's annual meeting, Paul Meehan said, which he did quite strongly and at some length, supported by David Leah, a CUMBA director. (CUMBA president L. W. Mitchell, Co-op Fidelity solicitor, did not participate in the acrimonious afternoon session. Leah was a member of St. Edward's parish credit union and of Queen's Park Civil Servants credit union.) Wagging a finger at the directors, Meehan asked if they could give an assurance that earned premiums would be sufficient to take care of claims and expenses in 1950. Harman as president replied that the company expected to incur a loss in 1950.

After further discussion the meeting by motion proceeded to the election of directors, to be conducted by office manager Ernest Moores. As secretary, Hebb explained that, in accordance with the representation understanding, Ontario Credit Union League was nominating Joseph M. Best, London, for a three-year term, and that FIIA, at a meeting the previous day, had agreed to nominate Leonard Harman, Toronto, and M. J. Brown, Norval, for three-year terms, and K. N. M. Morrison, general manager, First Co-operative Packers,

Barrie, for a one-year term. Morrison was out of the province and unable to attend the meeting.

Moores, as election chairman, asked the meeting to elect three directors for three-year terms first, and then elect one director for a one-year term. Leah moved, seconded by J. P. Manning, member of a parish credit union in London, that the meeting elect the four directors at once, the fourth highest person to serve for one year.

At Harman's request the secretary explained the "gentlemen's agreement" concerning representation. Legally the meeting could elect anyone it pleased but it was hoped that the meeting would honor the agreement and elect the persons nominated by the sponsors. Harman said that if the motion carried the representation agreement would be upset. The motion was put and defeated.

First three nominations were Best, Harman and Brown, in accordance with the representation plan. Then Leah nominated J. E. O'Dell, Corunna; Meehan nominated C. M. Yelland, Toronto, former Co-op Fidelity office manager; Harold Ghent, Newmarket District Farmers' Co-operative manager and Ontario Co-operative Union president, nominated Savage; and Harry Cook, manager of a Kitchener consumer co-operative, nominated Meehan. All nominees, except Meehan, agreed to stand for election.

In accepting nomination Savage said that he entered into the "gentlemen's agreement" on the understanding that the business would be conducted in a certain way. A lot of policyholders were present protesting against the way the business was being conducted, and therefore he no longer felt bound by this "gentlemen's agreement."

After discussion it was agreed, by motion of Betzner and Savage, to put the names of the sponsoring organizations on the blackboard after the names of those persons nominated by organizations. Waiting for the result of the ballot, the meeting appointed auditors for the current year and, by motion of Savage and A. E. Dodson, Tilbury, accepted the directors' report.

Harman explained the by-law to dispense with mailing each policyholder a notice of the annual meeting. Shareholders would still receive a notice by mail. Lorne Cragg, of Garden City Press Co-operative credit union, Toronto, and William J. Buchanan, Downsview farmer, moved approval of the by-law, but Savage, who was co-founder of the company, did not agree, and he moved an amendment, seconded by Clayton Bender, who was licensed as a

Co-op Life agent, that struck out most of the by-law, and left only the proposal to hold the annual meeting on the last Saturday in February. Shannon and Ghent spoke in favor of the amendment, and it was carried. The by-law was then carried as amended - and gutted!

Moores then announced election of Best, Harman and Savage for three-year terms. One of the FIIA nominees, Brown, had been defeated. Hardly containing his anger, president Harman said that what had happened was highly undesirable and that he was going to make an issue of the matter. He was going to insist that this insurance company be controlled through democratic organizations. Milburn told the meeting that he was disappointed and confused.

Harold Ghent, who had just completed a year as president of Ontario Co-operative Union, commented that he never thought the arrangement would work. He had nominated Savage and had spoken against the money-saving by-law!

Milburn, Hebb and others got together to discuss whether to nominate Brown or Morrison for the one-year term. Morrison had been a valuable member of the board for two years. On the other hand, FIIA had nominated Brown for a three-year term and Morrison for a one-year term. It was decided to follow the FIIA preference and nominate Brown. Brown's presence at the meeting, and Morrison's absence, may have influenced the choice.

Moores called for nominations. R. S. Heatherington, Campbellville, nominated Brown. David Leah nominated J. E. O'Dell, Corunna. An RCAF veteran of overseas service, O'Dell was secretary and fieldman of Lambton county Federation of Agriculture and manager of Lambton Co-operative Medical Services. An Ontario Credit Union League director, he had been the runner-up for appointment as OCUL general manager. O'Dell declined to stand, however, and Brown was declared elected for a one-year term.

The representation agreement had not been thrown out the window, Savage commented after Harman resumed the chair. There was not going to be ill-will between town people and farmers. There was displeasure and dissatisfaction with the directors' report, and he did not believe there was any other reason for the change that had taken place.

Board members now were Milburn, Harman, Betzner and Brown, representing FIIA; Hallinan, Hughes, Best and Savage, representing credit unions; and Nicholson, representing the Ontario Co-operative

Union.

Elected reeve of Simcoe county's Essa township, in his 75th year, CF&GA's first president, William John Wood, had declined nomination for another three-year term.

In a conciliatory gesture, Meehan seconded a vote of thanks to the board of directors, moved by Lorne Cragg. The meeting concluded with a recommendation, moved by O'Dell and district agent B. A. Forbes, Wyoming, Lambton county, to review the automobile insurance eligibility rules, and to insure Federation of Agriculture members who resided on the farm whether or not their income was derived from the farm.

With the defeat of the by-law which was expected to avoid the expense of mailing meeting notices to over 10,000 policyholders the next year, and the breakdown of the not necessarily democratic representation plan, the directors and managers felt that the sky had fallen. As it turned out, however, this annual meeting was to be a turning point in the history of the company (if Co-operators Insurance Association succeeding Co-op Fidelity may be considered the same company). Policyholders and shareholders would turn their backs on a mutual company, which might be controlled by agents, employees, urban or rural factions, or by a self-perpetuating board of directors, or by whatever group happened to turn up at an annual meeting.

A subsequent analysis showed that while there were fewer than a hundred votes at the meeting, over five thousand people and organizations were entitled to vote if they could have afforded the time and expense to attend. While there were over three hundred persons and organizations in Toronto entitled to vote, there were over seven hundred in Grey county alone, and an annual meeting in Owen Sound might have turned out quite differently.

Chapter 32

Aftermath

The disturbed directors of FIIA held a special meeting in Toronto on March 13, 1950. They and the county Federations had put two years of effort into raising money to write automobile insurance, and by agreement they were to nominate five of nine directors. Now, unexpectedly and incredibly, the annual meeting of policyholders and shareholders had rejected one of their nominees.

After discussion, with Betzner as chairman, they addressed two resolutions to the president and directors of Co-op Fidelity, probably drafted by FIIA secretary Cecil Belyea with Milburn's help. One resolution requested that Co-op Fidelity board

(1) reaffirm support of the "gentlemen's agreement" for nomination of directors,

(2) ask Savage "to resign at once" to permit the board to appoint the FIIA nominee (K. N. M. Morrison), and

(3) "commence study at once to devise a more satisfactory plan for administration of Ontario's co-operative insurance now handled by CF&GA."

The other resolution asked Co-op Fidelity to convene a meeting of the boards of the four sponsors along with the board of Co-op Fidelity.

Savage was seriously ill in Sunnybrook Hospital in Toronto when the insurance board met a few days later. Harman presented two long memoranda which he had prepared, "A Review of Co-operative Insurance in Ontario," and "Possibilities in Control of Co-operative Insurance in Ontario."

In the first paper he outlined the history of the company, development of the representative control plan (and "gentlemen's agreement"), endorsation of the plan by four sponsors (UCO was an indirect sponsor, nominating one FIIA director who would become a Co-op Fidelity director), acceptance of the plan at the annual meeting in 1949, raising capital for automobile insurance, guidance from United States insurance co-operatives, joint distribution (with Co-op Life), livestock transit insurance (saving farmers thousands of dollars a year), and the annual meeting in 1950.

"Yet board and management have been subjected to incessant barrages of severe conflicting criticism," Harman's memorandum continued. "But this insurance venture should be regarded as co-operative business deserving of patience and support by all co-operators. It cannot be primarily a debating club or a shooting gallery. It is unfortunate that much energy will be required for attempts to re-establish some suitable representation to continue throughout 1950. And the larger job must proceed, of reorganizing the basic structure so as to ensure long-term stable control in the user's interest."

The paper on "Control" set out the need for an Ontario other-than-life insurance company and also an agency (replacing the Bernard Shea agency) to write classes of fire and casualty insurance not written by the Ontario company and to represent Co-operative Life on a commission basis. Company and agency should have "identical management and board and ownership and control."

"We must have a stable operating situation with management accountable to a united responsible body which possesses broad understanding and a reasonably clear sense of direction," the Harman paper said. "Let us compare Ontario insurance management at present to a person who finds himself surrounded not only by one or two mothers-in-law, but by half a dozen mothers-in-law. Somehow we must put Ontario insurance management in a position to operate a modern insurance business. On the other hand, we must ensure that Ontario co-operative insurance will not go the way of most mutuals and be lost to the general farm and co-operative movement .... We are forced to the conclusion that direct control by policyholders is not practical in Ontario. Control must be established on some indirect basis through one or more democratic 'people's organizations'."

Harman then reviewed various types of control by other organizations: a joint stock subsidiary, like Co-operative Insurance Society of Great Britain, owned by the English and Scottish Co-operative Wholesale Societies, or Pool Insurance in western Canada owned by three Wheat Pools; a mutual controlled by an interlocking directorate, like Indiana Farm Bureau Insurance controlled or dominated by Indiana Farm Bureau and Indiana Farm Bureau Co-operative, or like CUNA Mutual with directors from various credit union leagues, and insurance services confined to credit unions and credit union members; and a mutual controlled through policyholder proxies in the hands of a companion organization, like Mutual Service Insurance Companies, St. Paul, Minnesota.

With the eventual plan perhaps forming (or possibly already formed) in his mind, Harman thought there was "little likelihood of developing a stable and harmonious insurance program under sponsorship as varied and as unaccustomed to joint action as the Credit Union League and the Federation of Agriculture. Then we must look to one of the four sponsoring groups for major responsibility."

Possibilities were merger into the national casualty company proposed by Co-operative Union of Canada to "parallel Co-op Life," control of the board by Ontario Credit Union League either now or over a period of three years - "which could be expected to swing the program rapidly in an urban direction .... even with the rapid growth of urban credit unions the advantage of volume and of spreading of risks and of having rural auto risks would eventually lead it into operations beyond its own membership" - control by Ontario Federation of Agriculture, "which could claim to represent some nine-tenths of the present policyholders," or control by Ontario Co-operative Union, "through proxies of individuals to their local co-ops or credit unions .... even here a division might readily arise between rural co-ops and urban credit unions."

Harman's final alternative was: "United Co-operatives of Ontario might be asked to form a joint stock insurance company of which it would control all of the voting stock. A board might be composed of persons appointed by UCO board and might include persons nominated by Ontario Co-operative Union, Ontario Credit Union League and Ontario Federation of Agriculture."

The Co-op Fidelity board decided, as requested by FIIA, to set up a committee to devise a more satisfactory plan for administration of Ontario's co-operative insurance, and to convene a meeting of the sponsoring organizations. The board also asked the sponsoring organizations to reaffirm their support of the present system of nominating directors until a new basis was agreed upon. Betzner and Brown moved that the board request Savage to resign so it could appoint a director as nominated by FIIA. Placed on the agenda with the prior approval of Harman as president, this FIIA proposal was perhaps an effort to make the informal representation plan into the "more satisfactory plan for administration of Ontario's co-operative insurance." If Savage resigned, to permit the appointment of Morrison, nominated by FIIA, the representation plan would be stronger than before, although probably not satisfactory in the long run.

The eight board members present divided evenly on a motion to table by Best and Hughes. Harman voted against to tie the vote, and voted again to declare the motion to table lost. The original motion was changed to include the words "and the resolution should not be forwarded to Mr. Savage until he returns home in improved health." Nicholson shifted his position to vote for the resolution, which was carried by a five-three vote.

Harman was re-elected president and Milburn vice-president in voting by ballot without prior nominations. A resolution added Hallinan to the executive. The board appointed the executive together with Nicholson as a committee to study reorganization.

Authorization of any two of six named staff members to sign cheques included three women university graduates, Margaret Chambers, Anita Soni and Norah Carruthers. With Vera Burtwell in underwriting, and Barbara Liscumb in policyholders' service, there were at least five women university graduates in a total office staff of perhaps twenty persons. Previous insurance experience might have been more harmful than helpful for a company following in the unorthodox trail of the Farm Bureau insurance companies, but the busy new company needed, and had, a resourceful staff.

The board was participating less in day-to-day operations. Harman's recommendation not to reappoint livestock transit and distribution committees was accepted. (A livestock transit insurance committee would have lacked Morrison's expert leadership.) Staples was in the middle of Co-op Fidelity disagreement with Co-operative Life, and the distribution committee of Harman, Hebb and Staples was not as harmonious as formerly.

Chapter 33

Board Pressure for Full-time Sales Manager

At this long and distressing meeting in March 1950 the board adopted an 18-point resolution, accepting a report from Harman, which asked Co-operative Life for full control over its Ontario sales program, pressed the distribution manager, Staples, to become a full-time career employee and asked Co-operative Life not to make his new basic salary of $4,200 (increased from $3,600) effective until he resigned from all provincial and/or national farm and co-operative boards. There was no objection to commissions he was to receive on Ontario life sales. Staples was to spend at least two days a week in the field, with at least one day in actual selling, and he was to have until the end of the year to become full-time. Musgrave would not have to make a decision until Staples did so, provided he confined his UCO board activities to the minimum necessary.

Staples was ready to agree "that Ontario co-op insurance employees should not be members of provincial or national farm or co-operative boards of directors, and that key employees should be full-time employees," but he was prepared to spend only "from one to two days a week perhaps" in the field, he wished to retain the use of a company automobile (which he considered to be part of his income), and he wanted until December 15 to make any decision or commitment, with no interference with his remuneration in the meantime. Although disturbed by "the chain of events which has led to this impasse," Staples "conducted all negotiations with dignity and restraint," as he said in a letter to the insurance board. The advisory committee had not discussed or questioned his membership of several boards when recommending him to Co-operative Life for appointment as its Ontario manager.

Musgrave's election to the UCO board had triggered a "chain of events" which included, despite success in the sale of automobile insurance, growing doubts, on the part of some "Ontario Co-operative Insurance board" members, whether Ralph Staples, without previous sales or insurance experience, could manage a life insurance sales program .... especially if he were not giving it his full time and thought. Musgrave had had extensive experience in selling automobiles; Staples' sales strength was his Farm Radio Forum renown and his fervent belief in co-operatives.

When the board met in April six applicants for one share each included Harman, Hebb and Staples - each purchasing his second share. Another was Earl Grose, UCO fertilizer manager. It was agreed to mail to the Federation of Agriculture mailing-list, offered by Milburn, an appeal for the purchase of shares. Best suggested use of the Credit Union News; Betzner did not think general publicity would sell shares.

Distribution arrangements took up most of the day, with the board meeting separately with Hebb and Staples. After Hebb and Staples reported on sales progress, Staples and Shea left the meeting and Hebb reviewed discussions between himself and Staples concerning the board's 18-point March resolution. Then Hebb left the meeting and Staples gave his interpretation of the situation. Hebb was invited to the meeting in the afternoon when, in effect, the board asked only that Staples pay his 1950 "per diems" from UCO to Co-operative Life, and that he decide "not later than June 1, to be clear of United Co-operatives by December 15, 1950, and of other provincial boards by early 1951." If he did not so decide by June 1, the board would secure someone else as distribution manager by September 1. Hebb left the meeting again and Staples returned for additional discussion between himself and the board.

To answer annual meeting criticism of office operations, it was decided to invite the president of CUMBA, Leonard Mitchell, to have the CUMBA manager, Meehan, spend a day or two in study of Co-op Fidelity office operations, in view of the criticisms of extravagance and inefficiency Meehan had made at the annual meeting. Meehan accepted this invitation but never found time to go to the Co-op Fidelity office to make the proposed study. In later years David Leah made the claim that the criticisms had been effective and had turned the tide for the company - at least to the extent that they contributed to Harman's determination to reorganize Co-op Fidelity as a joint stock company, this was true.

As a result of reinsurance arrangements with CIS, Manchester, and occasional visits to Canada by directors of the CIS owners - Co-operative Wholesale Society (CWS) and Scottish Co-operative Wholesale Society (SCWS) - Ontario co-operative insurance directors and leaders were becoming more aware that CIS had become one of the biggest and most successful insurance companies in Britain as a joint stock subsidiary of the two wholesale societies. A few perhaps were aware that CUNA Mutual Insurance Society had considered in the early forties reorganization as a joint stock company. "From the beginning many leaders of the movement had wondered if the credit union insurance company should not be a stock company, with CUNA national board holding control of the stock," said a CUNA Mutual folder (probably published in the early fifties). In the mutual an individual policyholder and a big credit union had one vote each, and "in 1939 concern about control became widely felt and action was demanded." After a three-year study, during which individual policies were not sold, it was decided to abandon voting by mail in favor of area meetings or, if the state of Wisconsin would not authorize area meetings, to reorganize as a joint stock company. "If the movement had it to do over it would probably have made its insurance company a stock company, to provide maximum control by the movement itself."

After Co-op Fidelity's April board meeting, UCO general manager Hugh Bailey became concerned about the pressure on Staples, his second vice-president, perhaps because of discussion with him, or perhaps because of discussion with Stauffer, his president, and rumors that Staples might challenge Stauffer for the presidency. At any rate, Bailey asked Hebb to arrange some easing of the Co-op Fidelity deadlines. With the agreement of Harman and other board members,

Hebb informed Staples that he would have until August 1 to make a
decision about full-time insurance employment, and until November 1
as distribution manager if he should decide against resigning from
UCO board.

At about this time Margaret Chambers provided the general manager
with cheerful news. Of almost $24,000 in automobile claims
supposedly incurred in 1949 (excluding reinsurance) about $15,000
had been unpaid and estimated at the year-end. This was the probable
cost of 120 unsettled claims, as estimated by the adjusters, Keddel &
Shea. They had settled 47 of these claims during January and
February. Estimated at $3,859, they had cost only $3,093. This was a
gain of $766. Assuming that the remaining claims cost no more than
estimated, the company had over-stated its operating loss in 1949 by
this amount. This was helpful information to pass along to Richards,
chief examiner. The remaining claims might be overestimated too.

At its annual meeting in London on Friday and Saturday, April 28
and 29, 1950, the Ontario Credit Union League turned down, by a vote
of 108 to 82, a proposal to hold future annual meetings in "June or
July, preferably June," as an accommodation to "farm people," who
found meetings in "late April or early May" difficult to attend.

Best was elected president by acclamation at the directors' meeting
which followed, and Savage was elected to the executive. Newly
elected vice-president Aubrey S. Dalgleish of Hamilton took the chair
for discussion of "a letter from CF&GA asking whether the OCUL
intends to live up to their Gentlemen's Agreement." After reports
from Best, Hallinan and Savage, and discussion, the directors adopted
a resolution moved by Cy Watson of Windsor and Arthur Briggs of
Toronto: "we instruct the manager to reply that this board of directors
has never agreed to the so-called Gentlemen's Agreement and does not
now agree to it; and feels that it has no authority to enter into any
agreement that will disenfranchise any shareholder or policyholder
except on a basis that can be legally enforced and is fair to all users of
the company's services."

The League directors adopted a resolution moved by L. W. Mitchell
and newly elected director John Homer of Hamilton "that if
Mr. Savage sees fit to continue as a director of CF&GA that we pay
him his expenses and per diem allowances," and also a Savage and
Watson motion "that the OCUL will be prepared to consider any
equitable system of voting that they wish to submit to us" but that a

proposal to hold a joint meeting of the boards of directors was not practical.

CUNA representative Gordon Smith asked the OCUL board "to give instruction" to its "national" directors on an upcoming request of Employers Mutual Insurance Company for approval to "sell automobile insurance to credit union people." By motion of Homer and Mitchell, the directors told the "national" directors "to use their own common sense in this matter."

Chapter 34

Capital Requirements

At the next Co-op Fidelity board meeting, early in May, 1950, Milburn reported arrangements for a visit to Ontario by Marion E. Foltz, Ohio Farm Bureau Insurance claims manager. Both Milburn and Foltz were former farmers. Applicants for 64 shares included Wm. J. Buchanan, Downsview farmer, buying two additional shares, Austin McQuarrie, Shelburne, Daniel E. Stauffer, president of UCO and a future president of the insurance company, who bought two shares, Charles W. McInnis, Iroquois, UCO director and president of Ontario Hog Producers Association, Hugh M. Bailey, UCO general manager, Victor B. McCalpin, Gananoque farmer, Harold D. Ghent, Newmarket co-operative manager and Ontario Co-operative Union president, and Colin G. Groff, Ottawa, secretary, Canadian Federation of Agriculture. Most purchases were one share ($50 paid), but William N. Alves, Brooklin, in Ontario county, purchased 20 shares.

Practically all applications were from farmers and farm organization employees, but one of the applicants on this occasion was Mrs. Violet Davis, New Toronto, an ardent credit unionist, who later became a successful CIA agent. The city was extending away north to Downsview, eating up the farms, and Toronto District Rural Co-operative (of which UCO staff member Fred Newton was manager) was winding up for lack of farmer members. Through the leadership of William J. Buchanan, who probably was the president, and possibly on the suggestion of Harman, who was UCO organization manager, this co-operative generously gave part of its surplus, in the form of $1,800 in UCO preference shares, to Co-op Fidelity. This gift was a major lift to the struggling insurance company.

The superintendent of insurance had secured for Co-op Fidelity an amendment to insurance investment law which permitted it as a mutual to invest in UCO, and the company had purchased $5,000 in UCO four percent debentures. With the $1,800 gift of UCO preference shares, the mutual would have in UCO the maximum permitted investment of five percent of its assets in one company (insurance assets had been $112,000 at 1949 year-end).

Shea presented a first quarter financial statement and a revised budget for 1950. The automobile loss ratio for the first quarter was 61 (claims cost as a percentage of earned premium), but with a 50 percent loss ratio (not predicted) for the rest of the year the company could have a small profit.

The board nominated Nicholson again to be the Ontario director of Co-operative Life Insurance Company. The department of insurance had not softened its demand for $50,000 additional capital as a condition for renewal of the company's licence at June 30, and CIS, Manchester, had agreed to lend $100,000 on a basis that would satisfy the department, but the loan was dependent on British Treasury approval. Co-op Fidelity had raised only about $8,000 in share capital in three months of effort.

On behalf of the reorganization committee, but "without endorsation," Milburn presented a 12-point proposal for a joint stock insurance company, and an incorporated insurance agency, with UCO the majority owner of both. UCO would be invited to invest $75,000 to $100,000, and to continue to buy additional shares as others purchased shares, to maintain a majority position. The UCO would nominate five of nine directors, the Ontario Credit Union League and the OFA two each. The three organizations and the Ontario Co-operative Union would be sponsors, and it would be an objective of the company to reimburse the four sponsors for services provided and expenses incurred in promotion of insurance.

It also would be an "objective to pay dividends on capital over a period of years equal to not more than five percent per annum from the time of organization of the company." The company would "co-operate in every practical way with CUNA Mutual Insurance Society and Co-operative Life Insurance Company." The Ontario co-operative insurance program would recognize the provision of life savings and loan insurance in Ontario credit unions as the exclusive field of CUNA Mutual. The new agency would "integrate the distribution of Co-op Life insurance" with automobile and other insurance. With all nine directors present at this May 3 meeting, the board agreed unanimously but reluctantly to ask the OFA, the OCUL and the Ontario Co-operative Union to support these proposals, and the UCO board to study them.

Savage was in better health and had written to Co-op Fidelity that he hoped to answer at this board meeting the request that he resign. He now said that he would have to defer his decision until he had consulted other persons responsible for his election.

Now that there was a measure of agreement on the reorganization proposal, however, discussion shifted, from control on behalf of policyholders as the reason for reorganization, to the need for capital. There were no "whereases" in the 12-point reorganization proposal or anything to indicate that control was the principal objective. Without the background of the annual meeting someone reading the resolution would assume that the purpose of reorganization was to secure additional capital, and that UCO was to have control to enable it to watch over its money. After all, the resolution needed the support of the directors and all the sponsors, and emphasis on control going to UCO was not going to advance it with either the OFA or the League.

(No one suggested that UCO, with share control, should content itself with three directors, and allow OFA and OCUL, who had provided shareholders and policyholders, three nominees each. This would have been fairer and, to OFA and OCUL, more acceptable. No one questioned the need to match UCO share control with UCO board control.)

When Hugh Bailey, UCO general manager who was also company secretary, mailed the 12-point reorganization proposal to UCO board members early in May, he also sent a memo prepared by Harman which reviewed Co-op Fidelity's share capital history and the requirements of the department of insurance. Again there was no mention of a control problem.

Co-operators' Fidelity board instructed the general manager, in view of Lambton county representations at the annual meeting, to interpret liberally membership in the Federation of Agriculture to qualify an applicant for automobile insurance.

Meeting a few days later, the Ontario Federation of Agriculture executive studied Co-op Fidelity operations, and the reorganization proposal, and said: "Go slow!" The OFA president at this time was J. C. Brodrick, St. Catharines; vice-president, R. A. Stewart, Almonte; second vice-president, Wesley C. Down, Hilton. "Before any changes are made in the present organization every possible method of financing should be investigated," the executive said. The matter should be referred to FIIA.

"No move should be made at present to close the office of the livestock transit insurance branch at the Stockyards, and the present set-up should be continued if at all possible," the OFA executive also requested.

Chapter 35

An Accommodation
Between Managers

It was springtime in Ontario but only Harman was clear about the future of Co-op Fidelity. He had done a tremendous amount of work to advance the joint stock company. But Savage, the founder, had been asked to resign from the board, and Best, president of the League, had no enthusiasm for proposed UCO control. Nor did Milburn, Betzner and Brown like the idea - the Federation of Agriculture had raised the money for automobile insurance, and it was going well, with profitable operations in sight. Hebb was close to Harman and Bailey, and went along with the Harman proposals, but he was close to Milburn and Betzner too, and he shared their misgivings about control by one sponsor. In addition, he had some personal concern about how difficult it might be to work for the new bosses.

In addition to capital and control problems, there was the sales problem. There was little future for a co-operative automobile, fire and casualty company, without integrated life insurance sales to reduce agent costs, but there was little agreement with Co-operative Life. Co-op Fidelity was trying to be generous about costs, but Co-op Life also felt it was being generous. Co-op Life did not agree about the desirability of regional fire and casualty companies, and was going to organize a national companion company - not a regional company but a national company. In addition, Co-op Life was not supporting Co-op Fidelity in its request to Staples and Musgrave to resign from the UCO board.

Staples had done a big job for Co-op Fidelity in automobile insurance but perhaps was not as successful in selling life insurance for Co-op Life. Second vice-president of UCO, he was openly critical of Stauffer as president, and was suggesting that he himself should become a full-time UCO president. Staples was a highly intelligent and extremely able person, with a firm belief in co-operatives and a co-operative social order, and confidence in himself as a leader. Nevertheless, he was modest and open-minded, and he admired his close friend, Leonard Harman, for his greater sureness and his certainties. Staples was the son-in-law of self-sacrificing CCF leader J. S. Woodsworth, and not unlike him, but he stood on his own feet and went his own way.

[Staples was one of a half dozen "kindred spirits" Herbert Hannam and reform allies had elected to U. F. Co-op board to transform the company into a central co-operative owned by local co-operatives, as long advocated by W. C. Good, the company's first president in 1914. For many years, until 1935, the annual meeting of U. F. Co-op, with the terms of all nine directors expiring annually, had been a cut-throat lottery, with frequent changes in board personnel and company policies. Even a president could lose his seat on the board. Clergyman-farmer W. A. Amos was an exception. Elected and re-elected to the board from 1927 on, he was president for six years from 1930 to 1935. Absent from the board since 1920, Good was elected in 1932 and became vice-president. Re-elected in 1933, he was defeated in 1934.

[Breaking new ground as secretary of companion UFO, Hannam intervened in 1935 and succeeded in electing to the company board himself, W. C. Good and pioneering female member of parliament Agnes Macphail, with whom he had become acquainted 15 years earlier when they both taught in rural schools in East Gwillimbury township near Newmarket. Hannam retired from the board in 1936 to become U. F. Co-op secretary, but he and fellow reformers were able to elect in his place UFO president William G. Nicholson. In 1937 they elected Agnes Macphail's brother-in-law, Hugh Bailey of

Dundalk, and in 1938 Vivian S. Milburn of Peterborough, to establish clear control of the board, and to work with "good guys" Amos and R. J. Scott, who needed no election help, to develop the "affiliation" of local co-operatives and UFO buying clubs. The "affiliates" were accepting some of their patronage dividends in the form of U. F. Co-op voting shares, and United Co-operatives of Ontario (UCO) was in the making. At the 1940 annual meeting Hannam and his allies mustered enough votes to dismiss former U. F. Co-op president Harold Currie of Strathroy and to elect Staples in his place. Milburn retired from the board in November 1941.

At an annual meeting on December 5, 1944, the directors asked for and received "the power" to pay the president by "annual salary" instead of "per diem." Later the same day they re-elected Scott president, for an unprecedented eighth term, but on January 30, 1945, they told him that they had lost confidence in his leadership and on March 6 they asked for his resignation as president.

[Hugh Bailey became co-operative company president in March, 1945, in succession to R. J. Scott, and, as proposed by Hannam from Ottawa and persuaded by his fellow directors, general manager on December 7, following the annual meeting, when Miss. Macphail and of course Bailey had retired from the board.]

When the Co-op Fidelity capital and control problem arose in 1950, the farmer and meat-packer from Dundalk had managed U. F. Co-op (now UCO) successfully for four and a half years.

Unassuming and thoughtful, Bailey believed whole-heartedly in co-operatives and a co-operative social order, although not as inflexibly as Staples, and as general manager of UCO he did not want a full-time president - least of all Staples, much as Bailey admired him, for he would have been no seat-warmer. Bailey was much more comfortable with Stauffer, a part-time president. Not one to interfere in operations, but colorful, Stauffer was a full-time farmer and part-time drover - rushing from farm to market to farm meeting, where he interjected sometimes witty, sometimes sweepingly radical and often obscure but always brief remarks. (Supporting a 1945 proposal to limit directors of the proposed United Co-operatives of Ontario to two consecutive three-year terms, Stauffer said, "The son may have more brains than his dad," and added, "If a man is indispensable he can be used in some other capacity.")

Bailey had a difficult job managing a complex business and a nine-man board of directors, and Stauffer would do whatever Bailey suggested ("Bailey's a money-maker," Stauffer said), and yet here were Harman and Hebb and the Co-op Fidelity board, in April 1950, putting pressure on Staples to resign from UCO board or to resign as insurance distribution manager - perhaps pushing him into the UCO presidency, and maybe full-time. If they wanted greater UCO participation in the insurance program, they would have to be easier on Staples.

Bailey and Hebb had a long and amicable discussion, probably in May. Bailey was worried about Stauffer and Staples. Hebb was worried that the UCO would play too strong a hand in the insurance company, perhaps to the personal discomfort of himself as general manager, and not leave enough room for OFA and the League.

Hebb summarized their discussion in a 16-point memo to Bailey written the same day. The first seven points were:

1. Staples to agree not to contest UCO presidency in December 1950 or December 1951.
2. Staples to be allowed to continue as both an insurance employee and on UCO board until December 1951.
3. Musgrave would resign from insurance employment before May 1952 if he intended to be a candidate for re-election to the UCO board in December 1952.
4. Neither Staples nor Musgrave to accept UCO board executive positions or to devote more than the minimum necessary time to UCO board work.
5. Neither Staples nor Musgrave to be eligible to serve on the insurance board.
6. Neither Staples nor Musgrave to accept any new national or provincial farm or co-operative board positions while continuing as insurance employees. Staples to resign from boards of Ontario Co-operative Credit Society and Ontario Co-operative Union by early 1951.
7. It would be agreed that no insurance employee should serve as a member of any provincial or national farm or co-operative board.

Point 8 provided for the possibility that Staples might agree only not to contest the presidency in December 1950, and points 9 and 10 dealt with remuneration. Some other points arose out of Hebb's concern that the insurance company, under UCO control, should continue to be independent. The final points sought to retain the support and participation of the Federation and the credit unions despite reduced board representation. The Federation was "particularly" important to the automobile insurance program. It would continue to be an objective to strengthen the Federation financially, and "to bring all the sponsoring organizations into closer and more effective working relationships."

Bailey would discuss these proposals with Stauffer and perhaps other UCO board members, and negotiate with Staples, and, if agreed upon, Hebb would try to secure approval of Co-op Fidelity board.

A week later, with Harman's approval, Hebb and Ernest Moores, from Co-op Fidelity, and, with Bailey's approval, Harvey Giles and T. E. Brady, both of United Co-operatives staff, attended a personnel school at Granville, Ohio. Harman had persuaded Bailey that employing staff was a specialized function, and had employed Giles, a personnel specialist, whose expertise and ideas gradually revolutionized employment practices in UCO and became a major influence on the insurance company. The Granville personnel school was sponsored by Ohio Farm Bureau Insurance, and arranged by a new personnel executive, Herbert Evans, who was helping president Murray Lincoln reorganize Ohio Farm Bureau Insurance.

Griffith's boss, C. W. Leftwich, had been Lincoln's right-hand man until Evans' appointment, but, now that the Ohio Farm Bureau insurance companies were firmly established, Evans and others would help Lincoln reorganize them as Nationwide Insurance and take them in new directions. During this visit Hebb and Moores went in to Columbus to see Griffith, review with him Co-operators' Fidelity's first quarter financial statement, and discuss capital requirements. Ontario's chief insurance examiner Richards had added another rule-of-thumb - "capital and surplus should be half of earned premiums" - not quite as tough as "premium writings should not be more than double capital and surplus" but for Co-op Fidelity and its successor, Co-operators Insurance Association (CIA), an impossible standard which (except for 1949 when year-end capital of $59,000 equalled earned premium of $59,000) the company would not attain - even at year-end 1951 with its capital almost doubled by UCO (capital and surplus $168,000, earned premium $352,000).

Moores and Hebb returned to Ontario much wiser. In addition to new ideas about staff selection and training, they had learned not to give rides in the United States. In Columbus they asked a pedestrian where they would find Farm Bureau Insurance, and the pedestrian offered to get in the car and guide them. When the pedestrian had reached his destination, he said that they would find Farm Bureau Insurance just around the next corner - but it was several miles away. "We don't pick up strangers in the United States," said Griffith.

Chapter 36

Agreement on Reorganization

Although nominally a credit union representative on Co-op Fidelity board, Hughes did not share either League or OFA doubts about the reorganization proposal. He wrote that the executive committee of the Co-operative Union of Ontario conveys "our appreciation and approval of the action taken and our hope that this matter can be brought to completion in the near future."

Moving away from the "go-slow" attitude of a week earlier, Cecil Belyea, OFA employee and FIIA secretary, forwarded a cordial resolution: "To allow CF&GA to fail would reflect seriously on all present and future co-operative enterprises in Ontario .... The proposal for reorganization .... would provide assured control of the insurance company .... would provide assurance of sufficient capital to meet insurance department requirements .... would tend to unite more firmly the Ontario Federation of Agriculture and the United Co-operatives of Ontario, thereby strengthening the growing farm movement, in view of which fact the Ontario Federation of Agriculture would promise to continue to support the insurance program and to sell more shares, encourage increased support and loyalty to the co-operative movement, and encourage closer integration of all of our mutual projects."

(A month later, on June 16, 1950, the Ontario Federation of Agriculture executive approved the FIIA's action in supporting reorganization and withdrew its earlier recommendation to retain Co-op Fidelity's livestock transit office at the Ontario Stockyards. The OFA and the UCO had been alienated, and the insurance project was bringing them together.)

On May 22 a letter arrived from Robert Dinnage saying that he had been "unable to persuade the British treasury to allow C.I.S. to deposit sterling securities for the purpose of increasing your society's reserves, nor will they allow us to purchase any of your society's stock with the small amount of dollars which we have accumulated in Canada in connection with our reinsurance arrangements. I am extremely disappointed .... I had a personal interview with the official at the Bank of England who is responsible .... It is simply one of those problems with which this country is faced at the present time."

On May 23 Harman and Hebb attended a special meeting of UCO board to discuss the proposed reorganization. Hebb explained the insurance company's capital needs, and read the letter from Dinnage that said the British treasury would not permit the proposed loan of $100,000.

(A month later Dinnage wrote that "although I do not hold out any hope that we shall for a moment be able to get the decision reversed, we are seeking a personal interview with the Chancellor of the Exchequer in regard to this and another matter.")

Discussion with the UCO directors included the Harman memo on controlling co-operative insurance in Ontario, the Co-op Fidelity financial statement for the first quarter and forecast for the year, the January letter of the superintendent requiring $50,000 additional capital, contributions of Co-op Life and Co-op Fidelity to joint distribution costs and the proposed incorporated agency, the significance of partly paid shares, a report by Harman on reorganization discussions with Hollingshead, a companies branch official, Richards, chief insurance examiner, and Mitchell, company solicitor, views of the other sponsoring organizations, and relationship of Farm Bureau insurance companies to Farm Bureau membership organizations and Farm Bureau wholesales.

Financial charts showed a Co-op Fidelity loss of $7,000 in the first quarter of 1950, and $3,000 in the second quarter, but forecast a profit of $2,500 in the third quarter and $5,000 in the fourth quarter (in contrast with an $8,000 loss in the fourth quarter of 1949). There would be a loss of $2,500 for the year, according to this forecast, but expenses (excluding claims) were declining from 76 percent of earned premium in the second quarter of 1949 to 63, 59, 45 and 42 percent in the four quarters of 1950 - if the loss ratio (claims) continued to be moderate the company would be turning the corner from loss to profit during the latter part of 1950.

There had been most satisfactory agreement on policy between Co-op Life and Co-op Fidelity, but difficulty had arisen concerning the proper contribution of each toward the cost of joint distribution, UCO board member Staples commented. Replacing the Co-op Fidelity informal representation plan, the proposed formal arrangement with UCO would permit good representation of policyholders, he said.

After Harman and Hebb left the meeting, Bailey said that the board should put a definite money recommendation before a special meeting of UCO member organizations to enable them to make a decision. It was agreed that it would not be wise for Co-op Fidelity to try to call the unpaid portion of its shares. The board, by resolution, asked Bailey to prepare for the next meeting a recommendation which, if endorsed by the board, would be presented to a members' special meeting "at the earliest possible date."

By this time Bailey had talked with Staples and UCO president Stauffer about Co-op Fidelity pressure on Staples to resign from UCO board to give full time to insurance. Staples was to have until September 1, 1951 (instead of February 1) to decide.

"The request for postponement does not, in this instance, as you know, originate with me," Staples was able to write to Hebb, probably with an inward smile. "There are those who think they see an advantage to the co-operative movement in having that decision postponed. If the decision is postponed until a mutually satisfactory date, I have undertaken to place no obstacle in the way of a second term for the president of UCO and that is the only undertaking I wish to give. My understanding was that I would be permitted to finish my three-year term as a director of UCO (ending at the annual meeting in 1951) and that there would be no interference with present levels of remuneration ...."

Harman was keeping out of these negotiations because of his difficult relationship to Staples - a personal friend who was a director of the company which employed him (Harman) and, in effect if not in fact, an employee of the Ontario Co-operative Insurance board of which Harman was president. On behalf of OFA, the League and Ontario Co-op Union, Harman was negotiating with Bailey and the co-operative company board a "reincarnation" of Co-op Fidelity, and at the same time doing his own demanding UCO job as organization manager.

Marion Foltz, Ohio Farm Bureau claims manager, who had been a much liked guest at the FIIA annual meeting in the spring of 1949, returned in May 1950, to spend three days with fellow farmer Milburn, FIIA and Co-op Fidelity staff. Automobile underwriter Murray Maxwell had been studying the closed claim files sent to the company office by Keddel & Shea, the independent adjusters who were acting as the company's claims department. Foltz suggested that the company staff handle some claims.

This suggestion became the subject of controversy when Co-op Fidelity board met at the end of May. An applicant for one of 24 shares allotted was UCO past president N. M. Marshall, the more than qualified manager of Norwich Farmers' Co-operative whom the central co-operative company had tried to entice to Toronto as assistant or general manager. Ralph B. Allen, Mount Forest, bought five shares.

Hebb and Shea explained to the board a recommendation that policyholders be asked (on identification cards) to report property, collision, fire and theft claims (but not bodily injury) direct to the Association. Staff would then decide whether to handle the claim or to refer it to Keddel & Shea or other independent adjusters (as Keddel & Shea were sometimes doing). Savage and other board members said that the company was not ready for this step, and the board took no action on the recommendation.

"We have moved too fast before," said Savage. "Let's not make the same mistake again." However, the board approved Hebb's recommendation to use $200 as prizes to encourage the sale of automobile insurance.

Savage and Nicholson moved that the Association express to Dinnage appreciation of the efforts of CIS, Manchester, to help and his promise of future help when permitted by the British treasury. Study of the financial history of Indiana and Ohio Farm Bureau insurance companies indicated that in their early years they did not have as much capital as was being required of Co-op Fidelity. Harman and Hebb reported presentation of the joint stock company proposal to UCO board, and distributed copies of the charts and other material used on that occasion. Harman's painstaking memorandum on his meeting with Hollingshead, Richards and Mitchell said that authorized capital in a joint stock company probably would be for $500,000. It could be increased later by supplementary letters patent. Partly paid shares meant additional security for policyholders, and enabled the board to control transfers.

Richards was asking for $25,000, to support the present mutual company, before the end of June, a second $25,000 as soon as a new charter was granted, and a third $25,000 at the beginning of 1951. With this additional $75,000, the company could continue to grow through 1951 and 1952 without more capital. Richards would not object to use of the first earnings to pay dividends on capital.

Notice of a meeting of Co-op Fidelity shareholders and policyholders to agree to the sale of its assets to the new company would have to go to over 7,000 persons. Savage felt it important to know whether decisions made at such a meeting would be binding on policyholders and shareholders. There should be a clause in the letters patent of the new company to prevent transfer of shares without the board's consent, he also suggested.

Hebb read the letters from FIIA and the Co-operative Union of Ontario approving reorganization. Newly elected president Best of the Ontario Credit Union League said that the League did not favor the plan but had no alternative to offer.

Nicholson reported that five of 11 directors of Co-operative Life were from outside Saskatchewan. C. H. Crofford, general manager, wrote that it was not practical for a life insurance company to provide a profit-and-loss breakdown by provinces. Hughes reported talks with labor unions at Windsor on bonding their employees - these unions, he said, paid their own claims to avoid publicity. There was unresolved discussion of the underwriting rule against writing automobile insurance for unnaturalized citizens - Ontario's numerous recently arrived Dutch farmers.

At the afternoon session of this May board meeting of Co-op Fidelity, Best announced that the League would join the other organizations to make a unanimous recommendation to UCO. A resolution moved by Savage and Nicholson unanimously requested UCO "to participate in the financing and control of the co-operative insurance program on the basis of the 12 points .... of May 3, 1950." (At an FIIA meeting at 409 Huron Street on May 18 Co-op Fidelity president Harman reported that "the question of Mr. Savage's resignation from the board of CF&GA had been deferred owing to the more pressing problem of capitalization.")

At September 30, 1949, business year-end, UCO's total assets had been $3,166,000, and 1949 savings (before patronage dividends and income tax) were $322,000; and so $75,000 was a lot of money for UCO to invest in one non-farm-supply venture. No one took for granted UCO participation on the enlarged scale requested, and Harman and Hebb were authorized to investigate possible additional CIS reinsurance, or Ohio Farm Bureau reinsurance, loan or investment to meet the capital requirements of the Ontario department of insurance.

Meeting for the next two days, in the same board room at 28 Duke Street, UCO directors did not have much difficulty in deciding to hold a special meeting of its member co-operatives at the King Edward Hotel, Toronto, on Thursday, June 29. (They would also discuss at the special meeting payment of dividends on common shares allotted to member co-operatives as patronage dividends.) But they were not as ready to recommend investment of $75,000 or $100,000 to acquire control of an insurance company which had lost money in each of the four years of its existence, was likely to lose money again that year, and maybe would continue to lose money. Co-op Fidelity board did not include one business manager, now that COPACO's Morrison was gone. The insurance general manager was an editor, not an insurance man, and he had lots of queer ideas. He had been publisher of a weekly newspaper in Newmarket for 10 years. The president, Harman, was good at preparing memoranda and charts, but he was a writer and organizer, with limited business experience, and he had made no secret of his belief that managers of local farm supply co-operatives should not be UCO directors. As a result of some of general secretary Harman's uncomfortable ideas, sometimes conflicting with the general manager's, Bailey had taken Harman's place as secretary (which necessitated attendance at board meetings) in 1949. Harman became "organization manager" at that time. "We were both trying to run the business," Harman reminisced with a smile many years later.

UCO board included four managers of local farm supply co-operatives (J. Errol Nephew, Irvin Anderson, C. W. McInnis and C. Foster Rice), two farmers (Stauffer, the president, and Alden McLean), a clergyman and former farmer (W. A. Amos, who was also a past president of both the UFO and U. F. Co-op and leader of a farmer march on Ottawa in 1918 to protest cancellation of conscription exemption for farm boys, and who had served in 1948 on the Co-operative Life advisory committee) and two members of the co-operative insurance distribution staff (Staples and Musgrave) who were under pressure from the insurance board to resign from UCO board. The latter two would not be eligible for appointment to the proposed new insurance board, but no doubt some of the other seven were intrigued by the prospect that five of them might be insurance directors. The general manager, Bailey, was sympathetic but cautious - he had held off construction of a much-needed office building and a modern warehouse in deference to board expectation of a post-war economic collapse like the one that almost crushed United Farmers' Co-operative in 1921.

Although cautious and practical, and anxious for UCO to make money under his management, Bailey was personally unselfish and a sincere believer in co-operatives. Starting in the depression, with nothing but $25 promissory notes from the first members, which he pledged at the bank for cash, he had built Dundalk Farmers' Co-operative into a successful business. Older now, he was as radical in discussion as he was conservative in business. Although he found Harman difficult at times, he liked and admired him, and probably thought that UCO board should recommend the reorganization proposal to the members' special meeting, but he was not one to impose his ideas unnecessarily. "Let's have Leonard in tomorrow," he probably said.

With Harman's participation, and a "thorough discussion," as recorded by the minutes, UCO board recommended "purchasing a majority of the common stock" and "assisting in the election of a board made up of nine persons: five nominated by UCO board, two nominated by OFA (perhaps through FIIA) and two persons nominated by the Ontario Credit Union League."

Silver-tongued Charles W. McInnis would present the board's views to the special meeting. A self-educated reader of English literature and oratory, McInnis was, except for his disregard for grammar, the most gifted speaker Ontario farmers had produced in a generation. On Harman's suggestion, Griffith, of Ohio Farm Bureau Insurance, would be asked to speak to the delegates.

No time was lost in sending word to the member co-operatives. The UCO board met May 30 and 31. The materials were dated May 30 (a formal notice including the resolution approved on May 31), May 31 (three pages of "Information on Reorganizing Co-operative Insurance in Ontario") and June 1 (delegate information and notice of discussion of dividends or no dividends on UCO common stock allotted as patronage dividends).

Harman's carefully prepared three pages of information explained that the insurance company had raised only $8,000 of an additional $50,000 required by the superintendent, that unless it obtained $50,000 the insurance department had said the superintendent would not renew the company's licence after June 30, and outlined "the need for a stable and suitable system of control or government for co-operative insurance in Ontario."

"Nowhere in America or Britain can we find an insurance company serving an area as large as Ontario operating under direct control of the policyholders on a satisfactory representative basis," Harman wrote.

The first two of five expected benefits were:

(1)   Efficient insurance service at low cost, and
(2)   Considerable sums of money available eventually to invest in other co-operative developments.

Co-op Fidelity and UCO boards had agreed on the 12 points but there were three changes from the original proposals. Point 3's "sufficient shares in the new company to have a majority of shares" no longer included the explanation "(that is, $75,000 to $100,000 paid in)" but there was a statement elsewhere in the "Information" mailed to local co-operatives that UCO "would need to invest $75,000 by December 1950 to provide the capital required by the insurance branch to cover operations for 1950 and 1951. On the basis of present operations and prospects this amount of capital, together with other amounts from sale of other shares in the province, should see Ontario's co-operative insurance through 1951 and 1952."

Reference to $100,000 might frighten the local co-operatives and its deletion would strengthen the proposal, but Harman did not mention this omission in a memorandum to Co-op Fidelity directors concerning two other changes in the 12 points. The co-operative company, the Co-operative Union of Ontario (formerly Ontario Co-operative Union), the OFA and the League were to "be regarded as continuing sponsors of the Ontario co-operative insurance program" but the UCO directors struck out the second clause, "and that it be an objective of the insurance company to reimburse these organizations for services provided and expenditures made in promotion of insurance." This powerful idea of Indiana origin - farm and co-operative organizations taking in each other's washing - needed to be seen to be appreciated.

In a memorandum to Co-op Fidelity directors Harman explained that, he had been told, UCO directors "did not want to commit the new insurance organization to probable repayment of money which already has been spent by the sponsoring organizations or is being spent. For instance, the United Co-operatives should not expect to go to the new insurance company and expect to collect the couple of thousand dollars which it will cost United Co-operatives of Ontario to hold this members' meeting on June 29th."

Harman had "felt it necessary to take hasty action" in agreeing to this change and undertaking to secure the approval of Co-op Fidelity directors. Another change, which did not seem important, was deletion of the statement that the proposed agency would use "the same staff" as the new insurance company.

"A message on developments is being mailed to all Co-operators' Fidelity shareholders," Harman reported. Hebb prepared a letter for mailing by Milburn to county Federations of Agriculture and a similar letter for Hallinan to send to credit unions. Hallinan reported to Hebb that League president Best "is very much against sending out any circular from the League on proposed reorganization."

The UCO special general meeting would take place on June 29 at considerable expense to the UCO. It was Harman's idea to bring to the meeting someone who would be regarded as an authority on insurance. In addition, he should come in time to familiarize himself with the operations and be in a position to answer questions that might be asked.

C. W. Leftwich, vice-president and secretary of Ohio Farm Bureau Insurance, agreed that O. C. Griffith would come for a full week, but he was careful to explain that Griffith's personal experience was in underwriting, and that he had no personal experience in capital or financing questions. He also knew Farm Bureau's co-operative relationships story quite well, but he had not been intimately associated with it.

Leftwich provided copies of Farm Bureau's twenty-fourth annual report for use at the UCO meeting. Concerning Co-op Fidelity's capital problem he wrote "we are still suffering from a similar situation in our fire company, although it has been in operation more than 15 years."

"Our operating position is very satisfactory," Harman advised Co-op Fidelity shareholders. "Our claims are not out of the way and, as we build up an increasing volume of business, our expense ratio continues to decrease, so that we may be operating at a profit in automobile insurance in the last half of this year." But the department of insurance "insists that we raise $50,000 capital to secure renewal of our licence on June 30."

The insurance company executive of Harman, Milburn and Hallinan met with Bailey, Hughes and Hebb to consider a name for the new company. The name was necessary to begin five weeks of advertising in the Ontario Gazette required before applying for letters patent. Participants in this meeting agreed that the deputy provincial secretary would not approve the use of the word "Co-operative," in view of the Companies Act restriction on the use of "co-operative" or a derivative, but to attempt to retain the use of the word "Co-operators," although the new company would be neither a mutual nor in law a co-operative. They also agreed on six names beginning with "Co-operators" (with "Co-operators Insurance Association" at the head of the list), and Rochdale Casualty Association as seventh choice. Directors of the various sponsors were asked to indicate preferences by mail. The memo included advice from solicitor Leonard W. Mitchell, that the approval of "Co-operators" for a joint stock company was unlikely.

The League's preference, forwarded by Best, was "Co-operators Casualty Association." As a UCO director, Staples' first choice was Co-operators Insurance Association, and, if it was not possible to use "Co-operators," he preferred Rochdale Insurance Association.

Savage noted "with concern the attitude of the companies branch towards use of the word 'Co-operators'. They claim such word to be a derivative of 'co-operative' and therefore an offence under section

140(3) of the Companies Act."
Savage offered an etymological argument to the contrary. "Co-operators Insurance Association" was his preference and the popular choice, and Mitchell argued successfully for its use, and proceeded with the advertising.

Chapter 37

Six Months' Reprieve

Now came anticlimax. There was no certainty that the UCO members' meeting would agree to put up $75,000, and Harman, Milburn, Hebb and Bailey went to see the superintendent of insurance, R. B. Whitehead, a week before the big UCO meeting, scheduled for Thursday, June 29. Whitehead was a big, strong, friendly and helpful person, who did not get excited about delegations from the Ontario Insurance Agents' Association, and he was not nearly as concerned as Richards about the possibility of the new insurance company not being able to meet its obligations to claimants and policyholders.

But perhaps he was responsive to political pressures. Earlier that month Milburn and the Ontario Federation of Agriculture appealed to agriculture minister Tom (T. L.) Kennedy against the superintendent's mid-year requirement of an additional $50,000. Starting with $15,000 in 1926, Ohio Farm Bureau Automobile Insurance Company had a deficit of $4,783 at the end of its first year, Milburn related, but a surplus of $36,910 at the end of its second year. There was "every reasonable indication that in another year or two we will be in an earning position and be able to supplement our capital both by earnings and by easier sale of shares to our members and friends." Kennedy was not one to make promises concerning something under another minister's control but he would see what he could do.

Possibly influenced by Kennedy, or prompted by his minister, or perhaps impressed by the company's progress and extensive support, and by Bailey's quiet and cautious competence as UCO general manager, Whitehead agreed to renew the company's licence for six months without additional capital if the UCO meeting did not agree to the reorganization plan. If the loss ratio rose dangerously the UCO would make a trust deposit of $25,000 or Co-op Fidelity would increase its reinsurance with CIS, Manchester, and thereby reduce its own risk retention.

For Harman it was still imperative that the UCO special general meeting approve the proposal to form a joint stock insurance company. He had made the proposal in the first place to stabilize control, with provision of capital important but incidental. Obtaining money from UCO had been emphasized increasingly as it became evident that the company was not going to raise more than $10,000 from other sources in the first half of 1950.

Although the credit union representatives on Co-op Fidelity board had joined in the request to UCO to acquire a majority of shares in the insurance company, they did so without the formal approval of the Ontario Credit Union League. Now president Best wanted to be in a stronger position for participation in the UCO special general meeting. At an OCUL executive meeting on Saturday, June 24, Savage asked for approval of the reorganization plan as "an opportunity of getting efficient operation of CF&GA, such as changing personnel and changing management (the present management being without insurance experience)." He said that he was expressing "some of the thinking of the members of the UCO board."

On motion of Savage and Watson, the OCUL executive approved the proposed reorganization on the understanding that the invitation to UCO "to maintain such majority position as additional shares are sold" be deleted.

As the June 29 UCO special meeting drew nearer, with the prospect of a friendlier board of directors taking control of the insurance company, Savage said no more about resigning as a Co-op Fidelity director. He had a good relationship with the UCO directors. When he came to U. F. Co-op from Canada Customs (postal section) in 1944, he brought with him, as the co-operative company directors soon found, valuable knowledge of organization, taxation, employee pensions, government and business. In addition, he had a farm background.

Born in Puckeridge, Hertfordshire, England, he came to Canada by himself at age 15 with the equivalent of a grade 8 education, and worked on a Peel county farm. Twenty years old when war came, he enlisted and served in France as a sergeant until he lost his right arm at Vimy Ridge. One of his many activities after his return to Canada, employment by Canada Customs, and his marriage in 1919, was organization of the Toronto Civil Service Association. He was one of the organizers of the Ontario Credit Union League in 1941. In the election of directors at the annual meeting in Windsor, in April 1947, both he and Cy Watson received 101 votes, one from each and every delegate - a perfect score!

Savage was almost the same age as UCO president Stauffer, who had supplemented grade 9 schooling with reading and experience. Needed on the farm, Dan Stauffer was excused from war service after one of his older brothers was killed in action. Married in 1920, he bought the family farm in 1932 from three brothers and a sister. Stauffer would preside over the UCO special meeting.

Griffith arrived in Toronto on Sunday, June 25, 1950, to play his part in a big week for Co-op Fidelity. Monday and Tuesday he spent at 30 Bloor Street West studying the company's operations. Co-op Fidelity and Co-op Life shared the same offices. There was an interview room and a meeting room but no one had a private office. (Ontario Credit Union League was on an upper floor. Ontario Co-operative Credit Society had been in existence over a year and shared office space with the League. Parented by the League and Ontario Co-operative Union, the Credit Society was full sister to Co-op Fidelity, with, as one might expect, a troubled life ahead. Savage was president, and Hallinan secretary-treasurer and manager. Mitchell was vice-president. Staples was a director and would become the second president. Other directors were A. B. MacDonald, OCUL past president C. J. Watson, UCO president D. E. Stauffer, W. G. Nicholson and David Leah. A bus driver at Windsor, Cy Watson had been a driving president of the League for four years, until Best was elected in April.)

In Margaret Chambers, a University of Toronto graduate, and Bernard Shea and Ernest Moores, both graduates of the Co-operative Union's Co-operative Rehabilitation School for ex-servicemen, managed and taught by Musgrave, Griffith found intelligent and capable young leaders. Shea and Moores were beginners in insurance and in office supervision, and were anxious to learn. For Shea, who was eager to develop a claims program, Griffith brought information from Foltz which Shea had requested by letter. "I am not sure I can manage this business successfully," Hebb said, inviting Griffith to be frank in his assessment of people and operations.

Griffith's discussions with Staples concerning "joint distribution" - Ontario co-operative language but "sales" to Griffith - developed into open disagreement as the week went on. Griffith did not see much merit in Ontario's version of multiple-line operation. Co-op Fidelity should be controlling its own sales, and so should Co-op Life. "Who will own this joint agency force?" he demanded.

This question had not occurred to the Ontario co-operative insurance directors or to staff members - in fact, at first, they did not understand the question. How could a company own an agent or agency force? What did Griffith mean? But this was the issue which would settle joint selling arrangements between Co-op Fidelity and Co-op Life - after another year of discussion.

On Wednesday, Griffith, Harman and Hebb attended a long insurance discussion with the UCO board at 28 Duke Street. Griffith discussed the joint sales program, underwriting, office operations and claims - he felt it was time for the company to handle some of its own claims. Board members had lots of questions. They liked Griffith and his answers. While making it clear that he had no personal experience in life insurance or in sales, he stressed Co-op Fidelity's need for a rapidly growing volume of sales, to push the company beyond the break-even point into the safety of the law of large numbers.

After Griffith, Harman and Hebb left the meeting, the board elected by ballot the five directors who would serve as directors of the new insurance company. Apparently they were confident of the outcome of the morrow's special general meeting, and anxious to assume their new responsibilities. Elected were Stauffer, the president, J. E. Nephew, UCO first vice-president and manager of Oxford Farmers' Co-operative Company, Woodstock, W. A. Amos, a U. F. Co-op past president, C. F. Rice, manager of Temiskaming Co-operative, New Liskeard, and Irvin Anderson, manager of Oxford-on-Rideau Egg Producers Co-operative Association and a director of Ontario Co-operative Union.

"Mr. Amos," as he was addressed by everyone except former

director W. C. Good, was the respected dean of the UCO board. Now 74 years old, he was in his 23rd year as a director. In December 1949 he had been re-elected for a three-year term under a new electoral plan introduced in 1946. He had served again as president during Bailey's difficult first year as general manager. No longer a farmer, he was an occasional Sunday preacher in rural churches. To the new insurance company board he would bring, in addition to obvious qualifications, a long acquaintance with automobiles. He had purchased his first automobile on May 24, 1922, a nifty two-tone Chevrolet sedan, and, after a short lesson from the dealer, drove it home and soon mastered spark lever, crank and clutch.

Chapter 38

A Life-Giving Amendment

Later in the day, Wednesday, June 28, 1950, Joseph Best, Co-op
Fidelity board member and president of Ontario Credit Union League,
met with the UCO board to propose deletion of the second half of
point 3 of Co-op Fidelity's 12-point reorganization plan. As adopted
by Co-op Fidelity on May 3, 1950, point 3 was: "That the United
Co-operatives of Ontario be asked to subscribe for sufficient shares in
the new company to have a majority of shares (that is, $75,000 to
$100,000 paid in), and that the United Co-operatives of Ontario be
invited to maintain such majority position as additional shares are
sold." Someone, probably Harman on Bailey's suggestion, had
deleted the section in parenthesis when mailed to UCO member
co-operatives. Now Best wanted to omit "and that the United
Co-operatives of Ontario be invited to maintain such majority position
as additional shares are sold."

The implication was that UCO would not necessarily continue
indefinitely as the controlling shareholder. The board invited Harman
to join the meeting and after further discussion deleted the clause by
motion. Harman agreed to clear this action with Co-op Fidelity board,
if possible, before the special general meeting the next day.

The stroking out of this clause was the subject of discussion at the
UCO meeting the following day with Stauffer presiding. Did it not

mean that UCO might not have control later on? asked Emerson
Swain, manager of Simcoe District Co-operative, Barrie. While the
League had approved the reorganization proposal, Best replied, the
League felt that there should be only one co-operative insurance
program in the province, but that it was not wise to ask one group to
maintain absolute control. However, he said, it was within the power
of UCO to maintain control for as long as it wished to do so.

(Deletion of the continuing UCO control clause gave greater
flexibility, strength and potential to the future joint stock insurance
company, for within 10 years there would be more non-farm than farm
policyholders, and the company would try to maintain its democratic
character through increasing participation in voting share ownership
and board representation by credit unions and the Ontario Credit
Union League. Other deletions by the UCO board, concerning the
same staff for the company and the proposed agency and concerning
reimbursement of sponsors for expenses in promotion of insurance,
didn't make much difference. The new board of directors did use the
same staff for the company and the agency which was incorporated
later, and the new company was fair in the reimbursement of sponsors.
In fact, when the secretary of FIIA, Cecil Belyea, incorporated the
original unamended 12 points into his annual meeting report in March
1951, no one detected the error. This publication of the invitation to
the UCO to maintain control may have contributed to subsequent
growth of the idea among farm people that the company was a farm
company, that farmers had started it, and that it should remain a farm
company.)

Point 7 was still intact: "That county Federations of Agriculture,
local co-operatives and credit unions be regarded as local sponsors of
the co-operative insurance program." Milburn presented the Co-op
Fidelity rescue plan enthusiastically, without reference to the six
months postponement of the superintendent's capital demand. The
co-operative insurance program could co-ordinate, and help to
stimulate interest in, the local co-ops, the Ontario Federation of
Agriculture and the credit unions.

In an eloquent presentation of the UCO board recommendation,
"Charlie" McInnis said that the UCO directors had moved slowly,
because of prejudice against a joint stock company, because insurance
was something entirely new, and because of the additional burden on
UCO directors and management. They were accepting the proposals,

not to save CF&GA or UCO's investment in it, but because there was an opportunity and a challenge. The insurance program would perhaps render more service than any other co-operative program yet introduced. Discussion and questions followed lunch. In answer to a question about the size of the staff, Hebb explained the various jobs to be done, and adoption of the six-month premium plan on the recommendation of the Farm Bureau insurance companies. In answer to another question, Griffith said that restriction of automobile insurance to Federation, co-operative and credit union members was hampering the growth of the company, although the company had come through a reasonably successful year.

Chapter 39

School Days

Asked for recommendations, Griffith emphasized sales, office staff economies, and that the company should soon start to handle its own claims. UCO general manager Bailey, COPACO general manager K. N. M. Morrison, whose defeat at the Co-op Fidelity annual meeting had led to the joint stock company proposal, and OFA vice-president R. A. Stewart, from Almonte, probably representing Perth farmers' co-operative, urged support of UCO's increased participation.

"Many of our co-ops may be needing temporary financial aid," said Morrison. "They are being given an opportunity to build for themselves a financial institution that will help many of them over a hard period."

Was it the proper thing to operate this company along with another company such as Co-op Life? asked N. M. Marshall, UCO past president but no longer a board member. It might work but Griffith was doubtful. It was necessary to know who the agency force belonged to and who was responsible for making sure that sales quotas were reached.

How would the new arrangements affect the income county Federations now receive from Co-op Fidelity? asked Robert S. McKercher, Seaforth, a future president of UCO and of the insurance company.

UCO board had struck out of the 12 points, it was true, the statement that it would be "an objective of the insurance company to reimburse these organizations for services provided and expenditures made in promotion of insurance," but Harman replied that no doubt the new organization would continue to develop relationships with the Ontario Federation of Agriculture and the credit unions. A motion by Morrison and Stewart to organize a new company, as proposed, was carried unanimously.

Griffith spoke again. The board of the new company would have to face the question of broadening eligibility for automobile insurance. Leading a discussion on how local co-operatives could help the insurance program, Staples said agents had to handle both automobile and life insurance to make a success of it. There were also economies in a combined distribution staff. Perhaps insurance headquarters could be established in the local co-operatives. The fact that a co-op employee could not sell insurance did not mean that he could not talk about it or discuss rates. Savage saw a bright future in the fact that the meeting had endorsed the new proposal unanimously.

Meeting away from 28 Duke Street for the second time (the first time was at COPACO, Barrie, in 1948), the Co-op Fidelity board gathered at 409 Huron Street, OFA headquarters, the following day. Among 19 applicants for 23 shares were Clarence R. Charlton, able manager of a big farm supply co-operative at Ilderton, and W. G. Nicholson, Co-op Fidelity board member, buying a second share. Allotment of these shares meant another $1,150 which the UCO would have to match if it was to hold at least half the issued shares.

Griffith attended the meeting. The board approved the 12-point proposal on reorganization in the amended form in which it was presented to the UCO special general meeting, authorized Harman and Hebb, in consultation with UCO, to organize the new company under the name "Co-operators Insurance Association", proposed that Hugh Bailey, UCO general manager, and nominees to the board of the new company be invited to attend the next Co-op Fidelity board meeting, and heard a report from Hebb that Co-operative Life was not inclined to act on Ontario requests concerning the retirement of Staples and Musgrave from the UCO board.

Hebb and Shea left the meeting while Griffith discussed with the board the insurance operations. By resolution, moved by Hughes and

Best, it was decided, in view of reorganization, to defer action or requests for action concerning distribution staff members Staples and Musgrave acting as UCO directors.

After lunch two of the UCO nominees to the new board, Irvin Anderson and Foster Rice, Hugh Bailey, and staff members Staples, Shea, Moores and Hebb joined the Co-op Fidelity board to participate in a discussion led by Griffith on "the functions, and interrelation of, distribution, underwriting, claims, management and board."

Chapter 40

Office Operations

In July 1950 Margaret Chambers spent three days in the offices of Mutual Service Insurance Companies (automobile, fire and casualty, and life), at St. Paul, Minnesota, and brought back much useful information. At that time Felix Rondeau (of French-Canadian descent) was Mutual Service president, and Lynn Matteson, who had spoken at the Co-op Fidelity annual meeting, was secretary. This company, like the Farm Bureau companies, had no secrets, and took an interested visitor like Margaret Chambers through all its office operations in detail. This was the first of a number of staff member visits to Mutual Service.

Rondeau, Matteson and W. L. Sanford, office manager (who would succeed Rondeau 20 years later as president and general manager), in a luncheon discussion with Margaret Chambers, were agreed that Co-op Fidelity should have made a beginning in handling its own claims. Rondeau outlined a plan for moving into claims (which Miss. Chambers brought back with her) and enumerated the faster settlement and cost advantages.

A Mutual Service claims supervisor, Roman Eller (who succeeded Sanford as president in 1970 following Sanford's death shortly after his appointment), told Miss. Chambers that $150,000 in premiums annually would justify Co-op Fidelity handling some of its claims -

automobile premiums that year amounted to $239,000. It was characteristic of Margaret Chambers that she brought back with her (and typed) detailed notes on the Mutual Service claims department organization and procedures - as she did concerning underwriting and policyholder service (collection of premiums, changes in coverage) departments. It was helpful that Mutual Service, like Co-op Fidelity, but unlike the Farm Bureau companies, was using Remington-Rand 90-column punch-card tabulating.

Mutual Service, like the Farm Bureau companies, was following the policy fee and six-month premium plan developed by State Farm. State Farm was the leading writer of automobile insurance in the United States, with $86,000,000 in premiums in 1949, followed by annual-premium companies, and then by another policy-fee-and-six-month company, Ohio Farm Bureau, 10th with $39,000,000. By 1970 CIA, operating only in Ontario, was writing $29,000,000. But in 1950 apparently a Toronto semi-monthly fire and casualty insurance magazine - Canadian Underwriter - had not heard about State Farm's success and wrote:

> It is a pleasure for this page to get away from Saskatchewan's screwy auto scheme for once and pass comment upon another one that is calculated to tax editorial credulity .... Writing policies for a 6-months term, the 'Co-op' collects the money, looks after renewals .... even it, let alone the agent who placed the insurance, is not interested in losses (apart, presumably, from paying): these must be reported to a firm of Toronto adjusters direct - and does its business on a 'policy fee' system that is far-fetched, feckless, even by Saskatchewan standards. Here is the gen given on this 'fee' flummery: 'The applicant for insurance will pay a policy fee on each major coverage the first time it is written ....'

Canadian Underwriter also said:

> The Ontario Insurance Agents' Association has viewed the rumblings of co-op automobile insurance with a jaundiced eye for the past 18 months or so, and has rightly engaged in top-level discussion and inquiry regarding what appears to be an automobile insurance development directed against its own and the public interest. Force is given to propriety of the Agents'

Association attitude by considering the spate of advertisements that have been appearing in Ontario's country newspapers, representing as a rule that such-and-such a county Federation of Agriculture 'requires four or five part-time township agents to sell co-operative life and automobile insurance.'

Chapter 41

Prospective New Owners

With an office at the Ontario Stockyards, and two men employed, livestock transit insurance was losing money, and, urged by Harman, Hebb reluctantly closed the office in June or July. UCO directors were critical of the office and its two steel desks, Harman said. Livestock transit manager J. R. (Jack) Sheane returned to his former employment with OFA; his assistant, Ed Tebbit, a capable photographer, lost his job through no fault of his own. There was also the over zealous deletion by UCO board, from Harman's reorganization 12 points, of provision for payment of the sponsors for services. There were other indications, Hebb felt, that the UCO directors were too eager to take over and implement their own ideas.

Harman and Hebb attended a UCO board meeting on August 2. Harman reviewed steps taken by Co-op Fidelity since the UCO special general meeting. It was possible to organize a new company without the approval of Co-op Fidelity policyholders and shareholders, but it was necessary to secure their approval for transferring the business from one company to another. There were various opinions, Harman said, about when and how a meeting of Co-op Fidelity policyholders and shareholders should be held. Hebb urged the need for additional study before applying for letters patent.

The UCO board recommended that the prospective members of the new company board be provided with copies of insurance company financial statements, and that "CF&GA secure official sanction from its membership toward the formation of the proposed plan of reorganization."

Returning by invitation the next day, Hebb presented a seven-page double-spaced memo, with the opening thought: "In my opinion, it is unwise to seem to be in haste about the reorganization .... eagerness now would seem to be likely to bring about an unfavorable reaction. There also seems to me to be a lack of appreciation of what the present insurance board has done. The thought that it is necessary to move in fast and change policies to improve the company's position is not necessarily well-based."

Hebb did not agree with Griffith about the desirability of selling insurance to everyone. "He may be right - Mr. Staples has been of the same opinion from the beginning, Mr. Harman for a considerable time." But restriction "may have saved the company from the disaster which the insurance department expected, and which our reinsurers, CIS, feared as a possibility because of our inexperience in underwriting."

Co-op Fidelity had been following Indiana Farm Bureau, and UCO should invite Hassil Schenck, president of the Indiana companies, to come to Toronto for a couple of days of discussion of insurance. The present directors and such former directors as Morrison and Wood were "turning over to their successors a going concern in a healthy condition." A number of directors had given their time, for 12 meetings a year for two, three and four years, without remuneration or expense allowance. A new director, Brown, selling shares and promoting insurance without any monetary return or expectation of it was "just one of hundreds of Federation and co-operative members throughout the province who have given their time to put this new co-op project on its feet."

Milburn had been "one of the hardest workers." Harman, "as president for the last two and a half years of a struggling, inadequately financed and sometimes torn and disagreeing organization .... has had an extremely difficult role, which he has handled with ability and distinction .... During the past winter and spring he has been under extraordinary pressure and strain."

Hebb had hoped that UCO would nominate Harman and Bailey as directors "to provide the utmost continuity in control and development of the insurance company." "Have you thought of the danger of becoming too dependent on the judgment and knowledge of an insurance manager and insurance employees? It may take two or three years for a new director at the insurance board to be reasonably sure that he understands the matters with which he is dealing."

In preliminary discussions Bailey, Harman, Staples and Hebb had agreed that to make minority representation and participation mean anything, the five UCO directors should take their places on the new board not as a group or caucus but as individuals. "If the five UCO directors should go to the new board in the spirit of 'This is a UCO subsidiary, we are running it,' then we will not develop the farm organization solidarity, we will not advance urban-rural co-operation, we will not strengthen the Federation and the credit unions and the co-operatives, and we will not build the UCO and the insurance company nearly as rapidly as we might. The UCO directors should assume their places at the new board, in my humble opinion, with the intention of sharing with the other representatives the decisions and the responsibilities and whatever honors there may be."

The UCO decision to participate was wonderful, Hebb concluded, "and, if the insurance project goes reasonably well, a future historian of Ontario's co-operative movement will have to give a special place to the UCO board of 1950 (as also to Mr. Savage as the person whose initial enthusiasm got us all started in insurance). But, at the moment, or when reorganization takes place, it will be appropriate for the new insurance organization to pay tribute to the old organization and to the retiring directors who have served so selflessly."

(Confusing as it may have been to the UCO nominees to the prospective new insurance board, Hebb did not want them to share "responsibilities and honors" with co-founder Savage. His honors were to be bestowed by "a future historian"! Surely everyone knew that Savage had upset the apple-cart!)

In suggesting that Harman and Bailey might have been directors, Hebb was being practical rather than theoretically sound. His proposal was good sense, but not good political science. If the directors of Co-operators Insurance Association were going to represent the policyholders, although indirectly, elected leaders rather than employees of UCO should undertake this responsibility. From a practical point of view, however, it was discouraging to the prospective manager that UCO was nominating five green directors.

There was no knowing what they might do: yield to the clamor for an annual policy, allow credit, increase agent commissions, ease underwriting rules, abandon policy fees, or write insurance for everyone. They lacked the Farm Bureau background and the painfully gained knowledge and experience of the previous two years.

The Federation (OFA) and the League (OCUL) were able to fill their board seats without nominating green directors. OFA secretary-manager Milburn would drop out - Betzner and Brown would be "CIA" directors. General manager Hallinan would bow out - Best and Savage would be "CIA" directors. [In the Ontario Credit Union News in July Ontario Co-operative Credit Society (OCCS) president Savage announced the appointment of OCUL president Best as part-time OCCS assistant manager. Best lived in London.]

A month after his return to Columbus, Griffith wrote: "I do not have the slightest doubt that in our own early years we were not anyway near as streamlined as you folks are. However, we had the advantage of a little more leeway in rates and regulatory supervision." His summarized suggestions included:

"1. Possible need for grouping operations of the same relative difficulty into individual jobs.

"2. Potential need over the long run for then fitting people in such jobs rather than current practice of creating an interesting job for a certain person. [Reference was to the company's attempts at 'job enlargement.']

"3. Setting up more of a continuous flow of work without backtracking.

"4. Possibilities for greater use of machines and equipment.

"5. Continuous elimination of unnecessary operations and forms. There is a reason for everything being done now but the real problem is whether there is also a basic need and how much expense can be tolerated.

"8. Taking over claim functions with own employees as soon as reasonably possible ....

"9. Volume in order to get a proper spread on the loss side and proper expense ratios on the administrative side.

"10. Teamwork and responsibilities between sales, underwriting and claims."

An Ohio Farm Bureau Insurance agents' convention in Toronto in

August 1950 was another opportunity to discuss Ontario insurance problems and plans with experienced insurance executives. Discussion included the question Griffith raised: Who will own the sales force?

Chapter 42

Planning the New Company

To co-ordinate plans and developments Harman prepared a 22-item "Calendar of Reorganization of Ontario Co-operative Insurance." May 1 to August 8 was "action taken"; August 21 (when Co-op Fidelity directors would meet) to January 2 was "action proposed". The calendar began with a May 1 demand by the insurance branch for additional capital by June 30 (or else), not with the breakdown of representation at the annual meeting, and ended with the proposed transfer of business to the new company January 2, 1951. Mitchell had reported that the superintendent would not permit the old company to be wound up until all its insurance obligations were discharged - several years - but it would not need to be licensed. Mitchell was preparing a petition for incorporation of Co-operators Insurance Association but he needed information and decisions on a number of points.

At a meeting of the Ontario Credit Union League directors in Fort William on Sunday, August 13, 1950, with president Best in the chair, Savage asked for the approval of the proposed Co-operators Insurance Association. Citing the department of insurance demand for $50,000 in additional capital, he said that "the United Co-operatives of Ontario, a democratically controlled organization, offered the only possible alternative for CF&GA, and that in this new company it is hoped that a more sound system of mechanics will be set up." In reply to a question, president Best said that Ontario credit unions had invested about $40,000 in CF&GA.

On motion of Cy Watson of Windsor and John Homer of Hamilton, the directors approved "the setting up of the proposed Co-operators Insurance Association," and on motion of Arthur Briggs and Robert Macdonald, both from Toronto, approved Best and Savage as "directors-to-be" of Co-operators Insurance Association.

The directors divided on an automobile insurance proposal from CUNA representative Gordon Smith, in a letter to the League. Watson and Kenneth Tench of Ottawa moved "that we do not invite Employers Mutual Casualty Company into Ontario at this time." Jim Davidson, Kenora high school teacher, and Arthur Briggs moved "to table to permit further discussion at the January board meeting." The motion to table was defeated, and the original motion was put and carried.

Davidson asked that his dissenting vote be recorded. He was a Rhodes Scholar who had attended St. Michael's College and received an arts degree from the University of Toronto. At Kenora high school he taught French. (In retirement years he would become the mayor of Kenora.)

OCUL vice-president Aubrey Dalgleish took the chair to enable Savage to report that J. M. Best had been appointed manager of the Ontario Co-operative Credit Society.

"The insurance which some of our agents are writing for other companies is becoming more and more of a problem," the general manager informed a Co-op Fidelity board meeting on Monday, August 21. The company did not permit its agents to write life insurance for companies other than Co-operative Life, or automobile insurance of a kind written by Co-op Fidelity, for other companies, but they could write other lines. Some did so through the Bernard Shea Agency, but the level of commissions paid to them might be an embarrassment if Co-op Fidelity, with its lower commissions, began to write these other lines. There was a danger of losing agents who built up other insurance business.

"The U.S. co-ops stress the importance of an exclusive agency force," Hebb reported. Shea presented a revised and more cheering financial forecast for the year - over $2,000 profit if the July-to-December loss ratio was 60 percent, $13,000 if the loss ratio was only

50 percent. Co-op insurance agent Robert Young, of Caledonia, buying two shares, was among the purchasers of 12 shares.

Nicholson and Best moved a management recommendation modifying the rules for writing automobile insurance for aliens. Savage moved an amendment to reduce two years' Canadian residence to one year, but there was no seconder, and the recommendation was adopted without change.

In the afternoon, Amos, Rice, Anderson, Stauffer, Bailey and Staples joined the meeting. Staples was invited to state his viewpoint on the incorporation and control of an agency to sell the life insurance of Co-operative Life in Ontario.

The meeting agreed, as a basis for discussion with Co-operative Life, to organize an agency with the same directors as Co-op Fidelity's successor, Co-operators Insurance Association, which was soon known as CIA, to take over Co-op Life's Ontario staff and equipment and to sell life insurance on a commission.

There followed on that same day the first of two conferences on reorganization. Present were Harman, chairman, Hughes, Betzner, Brown, Rice, Nicholson, Milburn, Stauffer, Amos, Bailey, Savage, Anderson, Shea, Best and Hebb. Harman's "Calendar of Reorganization" got everyone on the same chord. A document entitled "Preliminary Proposals on Incorporation of Co-operators Insurance Association," prepared by Harman and Hebb as a reorganization committee, set out questions which the solicitor wanted answered and suggestions for the new charter. The meeting reached agreement on 13 points or questions. There should be provision for preference shares - Richards said later that he had never heard of an insurance company with preference stock but he agreed to it. Could and should the dividend rate on common stock be limited? Objects set out in the letters patent should not exclude life insurance. Provision should be made for the payment of commission on the sale of shares. Provision should be made for the removal of directors.

The meeting then considered a document entitled "Points for Consideration in Drafting By-laws of Co-operators Insurance Association." Directors should be elected for a one-year term. There was much concern that a joint stock company could become a profit-making organization rather than a co-operative - or that individuals could demand a pay-out of accumulated surplus. Sections 8 and 9 of the 12-point proposal for reorganization should be included in the by-laws if possible. Section 8 gave the primary objective of the insurance company as the provision of a high level of insurance service at the lowest cost consistent with sound business practice, and section 9 said that it should be the objective to pay dividends on capital over a period of years equal to not more than five percent per annum from the time of organization of the company. (That was 1946.)

The question of how directors should be remunerated should be left open for the present, it was agreed. There should be provision in the by-laws, if possible, for participating policies or the payment of patronage dividends. The reorganization committee was instructed to inquire into the incorporation of an insurance agency.

Following this reorganization conference Savage attended Co-operative Union of Canada meetings in Quebec city and the 50th anniversary at Levis, across the river, of the founding of the first Canadian caisse populaire or credit union. On his return Savage wrote from his home in Bolton that R. H. Milliken, K. C., and CUC secretary A. B. MacDonald would like to meet with Co-op Fidelity board on Saturday, October 14, when Milliken would be east to attend a Bank of Canada board meeting. Maritime Co-operative Services had written several thousand automobile policies through Wawanesa Mutual and would like to turn this business over to a co-operative company. There were difficulties in the way of licensing a Saskatchewan fire and casualty company in the Maritimes, and, Savage understood, Milliken thought Co-op Fidelity should offer its services in the Maritimes.

The second reorganization conference took place in early September. All five UCO nominees for the insurance board were present. The solicitor, Mitchell, also attended and brought with him a long memorandum on the details of incorporation.

Mitchell had already advertised the intention to organize a company that would write all types of insurance other than life insurance, and he was doubtful that the superintendent would approve a charter to write both non-life and life insurance. The meeting dropped the proposal to ask for a charter that would include life insurance. It was agreed not to ask for a limitation in the letters patent on common share dividends - it could go into the by-laws.

There should be no proxy voting except by a director, officer, employee, member or shareholder as a delegate for a corporation. It was agreed to press for the right to pay patronage dividends. Mitchell said it was unnecessary to provide for making deposits in the Ontario Co-operative Credit Society - the insurance department could prohibit deposits in any depository which it thought unsafe.

In the afternoon there was discussion of the proposed meeting with Milliken and MacDonald, to discuss the possibility of writing automobile insurance in the Maritimes. This raised the whole question of relations with Co-operative Life, Harman said, and he asked if the meeting would hear a memorandum on "Co-operative Insurance Structure for Canada" which had been prepared (probably by Harman and Hebb) after consultation with Milburn and Bailey.

This was a 12-page discussion of democratic control, policyholder participation, and efficiency of operation. It recognized that the new joint stock company would not be "truly co-operative." It would not provide for direct policyholder representation and control and would not provide for any legally enforceable representation by minority participating groups or organizations. The plan to give one organization legal control and to make it an informal trustee for minority groups "could not very well serve a national insurance company." Seven or eight regional co-operative wholesales, either by themselves or together with other co-operative organizations, might own a national joint stock insurance company, but there would be difficult questions about regional representation.

To "combine as many as possible of the advantages of national unity with as many as possible of the advantages of regional autonomy .... we should accept the fact of a national life insurance company now operating in most of the provinces, but base the national life insurance company on autonomous provincial or regional distribution organizations such as the proposed incorporated agency in Ontario." A regional agency would have the same board of directors as a regional other-than-life insurance company. This board would "elect the [region's] directors of the national life insurance company and eventually perhaps of a national other-than-life reinsurance company" (with the same persons as directors of both national companies).

The memo concluded that "prudence would seem to advise against" Co-op Fidelity (or CIA) accepting "several thousand automobile policies" from the Maritimes, and that Maritime co-operative effort should continue to be partly an effort to keep in the Maritimes control of Maritime business.

Two pages of accompanying charts proposed that Ontario would

228 Management by Majority

have two directors on a national board of eleven. Three other regions, British Columbia, Quebec and the Maritimes would also have two each, and the prairie region would have three directors.

While he favored regional development of co-operative insurance, Savage felt that MacDonald and Milliken should have an opportunity to present the Co-operative Union of Canada viewpoint in favor of a national other-than-life insurance company. After hearing the Harman memorandum, and studying supporting charts, the meeting recommended that the board-to-be of the new company meet with Milliken and MacDonald.

The conference approved a motion by Savage and Best to incorporate "a regional insurance agency for Ontario called Co-operative Insurance Service, to make arrangements with Co-op Life to sell life insurance in this province under a general agent's agreement, with a vested interest in renewal commissions, which would assure Ontario control of the Ontario agency force and regional autonomy within a national co-operative insurance development."

The conference referred the memorandum on "Co-operative Insurance Structure for Canada" to the new board and instructed the secretary to send copies to Milliken and MacDonald.

Returning to plans for the new Ontario insurance company, the conference approved a motion by Savage and Nephew to include in the application for letters patent a provision for removal of a director or directors by a vote of three-fifths of the shareholders present (although the intention was shares represented) at a meeting called for that purpose.

Chapter 43

In the Meantime

At the time of the annual meeting Matteson had told the staff how
Mutual Service built up its medical payments coverage by adding it to
automobile insurance premium notices, and inviting those who did not
wish this protection not to pay for it. Most policyholders paid for it
and the result was a worthwhile increase in premium, against which
there were claims but little other expense. Matteson urged that Co-op
Fidelity do likewise. This procedure seemed a little unethical to
Co-op Fidelity's managers but in the spring of 1950 they had been
able to justify it to themselves as in the interests of the company and
policyholders as a group, and decided to go ahead, without asking for
board approval, in view of board turmoil at that time. As office
manager, Ernest Moores was in charge of premium billing.

   Despite some criticisms from policyholders and agents, the response
was excellent - about 75 percent of policyholders accepted and paid
for the new coverage. As there was no policy fee, and it was a new
coverage, agents did not receive any credit until the first renewal.
Medical payments was a separate accident policy but was treated as
part of the automobile policy - Margaret Chambers had to find a place
for it on the tabulating punch cards.

   This increase in premium, with little expense, and a low automobile
loss ratio in the second quarter (claims were only 34.6 percent of

earned premium), compared with 60 percent in the first quarter, contributed to a substantial underwriting profit of over $8,000, which more than wiped out an underwriting loss of nearly $7,000 in the first quarter. Investment income was about $1,000 a quarter but for the year 1950 would average $1,250 a quarter.

Earned premium was growing rapidly, from $29,375 in the first quarter to $42,122 in the second, with $51,000 and $61,000 forecast for the remaining two quarters. Expenses were going down as a percentage of earned premium. If the automobile (and company) loss ratio were not more than 60 percent for the next two quarters there would be a profit for the year, unless Richards renewed his request to calculate unearned premium at 100 percent.

Both automobile and life sales were better than in 1949. Life insurance sales were over $900,000 at the end of June, compared with $800,000 for all of 1949, and half as much in 1948. But there were 90 life-licensed agents, and many of the sales were of $1,000 policies, and often term insurance at that. As Staples explained, during Co-op Life's "Million in May" campaign, a $2 bonus per $1,000 of life insurance, applicable to the agent's expense in attending a sales meeting, was not payable on term insurance or family income benefit, "not at all because these are undesirable types of insurance, but because premiums charged for these types do not permit any further expense." There were 3,111 new automobile policies issued in the first six months of 1950, compared with 2,443 in the first half of 1949. In June, Staples launched an automobile insurance prospecting contest called "Push the Summer", despite the efforts of his less imaginative colleagues to talk him out of this intriguing contest name. Ed Lang, Grey county, wrote the most applications (19) and Thomas Wharf, Essex county, wrote the most full coverages (11).

Credit unions contributed about 500 policies in the first half of 1949, but only about 250 policies in the first half of 1950 (most of this business without commission cost) - perhaps because of the forced withdrawal of rate manuals from credit unions. The company had only two urban agents, Mrs. Violet Davis, in New Toronto, and Jeff Bradford, in Toronto. Mulrooney, the forerunner of CIA's salaried representatives, had resigned to become manager of CUMBA Co-operative Health Services.

Harold A. Dodge, an Ohio Farm Bureau regional sales supervisor from New York state, was the big contributor to Staples' two-day

September sales meeting at 409 Huron Street. It was for "district" agents and Co-op Fidelity contributed modestly toward their expenses. Shea and Staples reported on the progress of the casualty and life companies. Milburn welcomed the agents, and Harman spoke on "Co-op Insurance as a Career". The three field supervisors, Musgrave and Sexsmith, employed by Co-op Life, and Barclay, employed by Co-op Fidelity, participated. Dodge made four presentations, at afternoon and evening sessions the first day, and at morning and afternoon sessions the second day, and did it all without remuneration (other than his expenses). Dodge estimated the cost of selecting and training a successful agent at $3,000 to $6,500.

Chapter 44

Keeping
"Ontario Folk in Line"

"If in the next two years in Ontario we successfully establish 20 full-time agents, we might estimate the cost of doing so, or the value of those agents, at 20 times $3,000, or $60,000," Hebb wrote to Savage at the end of September 1950. "Whose $60,000? Co-op Life's or Co-op Fidelity's?"

Responding to Co-op Fidelity's memo on a "Co-operative Structure for Canada," Milliken (by mail) and MacDonald (in person) had indicated that they had no proposal for Co-op Fidelity to write insurance in the Maritimes, and Hebb was writing to Savage that the October 14 meeting would deal with other matters.

"My impression is that it was more or less of a good-will mission we were going on, in order to keep the thinking of the Ontario folk in line with what is being attempted nationally by our co-operative insurance leaders," Milliken wrote. "I must confess that it is a new idea to me that we were to come to Toronto to discuss Ontario taking over fire and automobile insurance in the Maritimes."

After quoting Milliken, Hebb's letter to Savage continued: "Mr. Milliken told me in August that Co-op Life would not agree to our having a vested interest in life renewal commissions. Obviously we are going to have a difficult session if we hope to get Mr. Milliken to agree to Ontario control over Ontario life business."

Harman would be chairman, "because of his experience in this matter .... whether or not the new board has been organized by that time," Hebb wrote. "That may mean that the burden of the Ontario argument will rest with Mr. Milburn, Mr. Bailey and yourself." As an insurance company employee, Hebb assumed that he should not play a major role but he was ready to discuss with Savage beforehand "the problems that may arise," either at the office or out at Bolton where Savage lived.

Most of the directors of the old and new companies, and employees Staples, Shea and Hebb were present on October 14. Harman invited the visitors to present their ideas.

MacDonald reviewed the activities of the CUC's "national committee on insurance co-ordination" organized three years earlier. "We want just one co-operative life insurance company in Canada," he said. "We also recognized CUNA Mutual Insurance Society in the credit union field."

There also should be a national other-than-life company "linked up with Co-op Life," MacDonald continued. "We were to seek delegate control and to make it as democratic as possible. If we are going forward in a big way, a scientific way, a strong way, in the co-operative movement and in co-op insurance, then we must be unified in our thinking." A group of Co-op Life agents had undertaken to raise $80,000 capital for the new company, MacDonald added.

MacDonald had helped Coady and Tompkins of St. Francis Xavier organize the co-operatives of eastern Nova Scotia, and he had his own ideas about economic democracy and delegate control. Milliken's ideas were a little different. He had been discussing with M. C. Holden, managing director of Wawanesa Mutual Insurance Company, the possibility of Wawanesa becoming a national co-operative company. From its home office in the Manitoba village of Wawanesa, where it was once controlled by its local policyholders, Wawanesa had extended its operations across Canada under the guidance of a self-perpetuating board of directors.

Milliken said that Wawanesa had applied recently for membership in the Manitoba Federation of Agriculture and Co-operation. (Manitoba co-operatives had avoided the formation of a provincial co-operative union separate from the provincial Federation of Agriculture.) "I would be perfectly satisfied, if Wawanesa became a member of the Co-operative Union and got a few outside directors," he said, "to have it become the national fire and casualty company that we recognize as such, but apparently the Maritimes and some of the people in Manitoba are not satisfied with Wawanesa."

Milburn said that Ontario would not be happy to have Co-op Life and the Co-operative Union endorse a competitor in Ontario of the Ontario casualty company. Milburn had worked for a local farm fire mutual during the great economic depression of the thirties. Barn fires had increased out of hand, as fires do during bad times, and the local farm fire mutuals had been forced to make calls on their premium notes. Milburn and others resented Wawanesa's choice of that time of difficulty to try to establish itself in rural Ontario. Both Milburn and Betzner were critical of Wawanesa's competition with Ontario's mutuals. Suggesting that the CUC was pushing for a national other-than-life company at the instance of Co-op Life, Savage did not think that MacDonald and Milliken could persuade Ontario people to abandon a provincial plan in other-than-life insurance.

After lunch Shea read a Co-op Fidelity proposal for a general agent's contract between the proposed Ontario agency and Co-op Life. Milliken suggested revision but agreed to take it up with Co-operative Life board.

When the visitors had gone it was agreed by motion to ask Co-op Life board for permission for an Ontario committee of three persons to present a case for a general agent's agreement. Milburn and Brown moved that the committee consist of Harman, Bailey and Hebb, but Savage disagreed. The agreement with Co-operative Life was "a matter of policy and should be worked out by board members, not employees." Harman did not think he should go to Regina unless it was the unanimous wish of the conference that he should go, and did not put the motion to a vote. Nominees to the new board should deal with the matter at the next joint meeting, he suggested.

It was also agreed to consider at that time an Ontario viewpoint resolution, introduced by Betzner, which included "hearty disapproval of any arrangements to recognize Wawanesa as the other-than-life co-operative company in any part of Canada." The resolution urged regional development of other-than-life insurance, but Ontario would not object to other regions (Maritimes, prairies, B.C.) combining to organize one company.

In a subsequent note to Harman from his hotel Milliken said he "would feel a lot better" if the proposed agency were "independent of both life and auto." When he got home he wrote again asking if it would be all right for the agency to represent Co-op Life in rural areas and leave Co-op Life free to establish branches in the cities.

"I consider it of great importance to have all co-operative insurance sales in the province co-ordinated at one point," Harman replied.

The same day he wrote a seven-page letter with a detailed agency proposal, prepared by Hebb, to H. A. Crofford with copies to Milliken, Nicholson and others. The Ontario agency would take over Co-op Life's Ontario staff and cumulative loss, and Co-op Life would pay the agency the $18,000 a year it was spending in Ontario plus the full agent commissions on policies sold in Ontario, commissions paid to the Ontario manager and the two Co-op Life fieldmen, three percent of all premiums for branch office services, and the equivalent of the amounts Hoosier Life (Indiana Farm Bureau) was paying county Farm Bureaus (which would be passed on to county Federations of Agriculture). These various commissions would amount to the following percentages of whole life policy premiums: 63% the first year, 22% the second year, 17% the third, 12% the fourth, fifth and sixth, and six percent for subsequent years.

(At that time an aggressive Canadian company, Crown Life, was offering U.S. general agents who provided branch office services, on whole life, 30-pay-life, 25-pay-life, 20-pay-life and 25-year endowment: first year 70% plus $6 per thousand dollars, second year 20%, third to tenth years 10% and subsequent years three percent. Renewal commissions were vested in the general agent, in the event of termination of the agreement, except for three percent per annum for collection. Nevertheless, the rates proposed to Co-op Life by Ontario were high for a new co-operative life company and were reduced in subsequent negotiations.)

"It would be an essential part of the general agent's agreement that the Ontario agency would have a vested interest in life renewal commissions, so that the Ontario agency would have clear control of the Ontario agents if, for any reason, the agreement should come to an end," Harman wrote. The Ontario agency would assume responsibility for ever increasing sales of life insurance. To solve their sales problems the two companies "must work together in Ontario through the same co-operative insurance agents, these agents must have only one employer, and this one employer must be an Ontario-owned and directed agency."

The objective would be to develop career agents. "Of the about 90 co-operative agents in Ontario who are selling both auto and life insurance, only three are earning as much as $2,000 annually, and out of this amount they must pay automobile and other expenses," Harman said. Part-time farmer agents were making a big contribution, but the Ontario Insurance Agents' Association was asking the superintendent of insurance not to license persons who are engaged in what is commonly accepted as full-time employment.

"This is clearly aimed at our part-time farmer agents - that is, most of our agents," Harman wrote.

Chapter 45

Manager and
Board Disagree

For the special general meeting, to be held later, of Co-op Fidelity shareholders and policyholders, to approve transfer of the business to the new company, there was an audited nine-month financial statement. An underwriting profit of $5,875, which would disappear by the year-end, investment income and a gift of $1,809 from Toronto District Rural Co-operative, reduced the accumulated deficit to just about $1,000.

Meeting on October 30, with the new company director nominees present, Co-op Fidelity board adopted the Ontario "regional development" viewpoint resolution with its "hearty disapproval" of recognition of Wawanesa, and authorized a committee consisting of the president of Co-op Fidelity (Harman), the president of Co-operators Insurance Association (still to be chosen) and the general manager of Co-op Fidelity (Hebb), in consultation with Bailey, to work out a general agent's agreement with Co-op Life, sending a representative or representatives to Regina if necessary, but the agreement was to be subject to ratification by the board of Co-operators Insurance Association.

Hebb recommended that the board authorize a policy fee of $1 on medical payments, but, on motion of Savage and Brown, the board referred this recommendation to the new board. Perhaps as a result of this incident, Hebb reviewed the board's delay earlier in the year - at the instance of Savage then too - in approving his recommendation that Co-op Fidelity staff should deal with some automobile claims rather than refer them to the adjusters, Keddel & Shea. It had been his proposal originally to use a firm of adjusters as a temporary claims department, and he felt that he should have been able to terminate the arrangement, with board approval, when he wished to do so.

"Only rarely should the board turn down management recommendations concerning operational matters," he argued in a subsequent letter of explanation to Brown, who did not agree entirely with Hebb's position. "The directors of an insurance company have to find someone competent to manage their business, and concern themselves primarily with larger questions of policy .... Of course the board should have the last word on anything it wants to have a word on, but unless we do a good job of dividing our responsibilities among board, officers, and management, we are not likely to make the progress we should, nor to compete effectively with private enterprise business."

Chapter 46

UCO as Trustee

Bailey introduced at this October meeting a major statement of the UCO's role in the new insurance company, and asked Harman to read it. During the reorganization discussions Mitchell said he assumed that there would be a written agreement among the sponsors about how the UCO would exercise its voting power, but Harman and Hebb wanted more flexibility and were prepared to put their trust in UCO's "high purposes." They regarded UCO as a trustee for the policyholders. Together with Bailey they agreed on a statement of "Responsibilities of United Co-operatives of Ontario in the Co-operative Insurance Program."

Harman had a fervent belief in the goodness and destiny of UCO - it might make mistakes but it could do no wrong. It wasn't difficult for Hebb to share a good deal of his confidence in a company which had changed its name from United Farmers' Co-operative Company to United Co-operatives of Ontario as an expression of its breadth of outlook and democratic control by local co-operatives.

"United Co-operatives has a long history of service .... is very broadly based and is not permitted to overlook the needs of co-operators in any part of this vast area .... A number of urban organizations are found in its membership .... Though prospects are not bright at present, there should be great expansion in the urban field

eventually .... The wholesale has supported heavily such important
projects as the organization of the Ontario Federation of Agriculture,
securing legislation under which credit unions could operate soundly,
and development of the Co-operative Union of Ontario," Harman
wrote in explanation of UCO's willingness to "assume the main
responsibility for the success of the co-operative insurance program in
the province."

UCO had become "a very large organization," with volume of 50
million dollars (including value of livestock sold on commission),
assets over three million dollars, and annual earnings around three
hundred thousand, most of which was paid to local co-operatives in
patronage dividends. To "stabilize the government of the co-op
insurance program," Harman continued, UCO had accepted "major
responsibility for the success of the co-op insurance program on behalf
of all policyholders and shareholders.

"The co-operative insurance organization will one day be among the
largest and strongest co-operatives in the province," Harman wrote.
"As it grows it should strengthen all organizations with similar
co-operative aims and help them grow. There are far too many
examples of insurance organizations which were initiated by men of
high ideals but which, with the passage of time, have become isolated
from the farm and co-operative movements and have lost their original
purposes. United Co-operatives is determined that this will not
happen to Ontario co-operative insurance."

UCO wished to stress certain objectives implicit in the 12-point
proposal for financing and reorganization, the document continued:

"(1) Strong, continuing and unified direction of business
operations is a necessity. This requires an active and
harmonious board of directors.

"(2) Indirectly, through the sponsoring organizations, the most
effective representation possible must be maintained for
policyholders. This can be achieved partly through
members of the board of directors. In addition, the
management of the business must be sensitive to the day-
to-day suggestions, requests, complaints and criticisms of
policyholders and third-party claimants; there should be a
continuing effort to develop the activities of insurance
committees in the credit unions and the counties; and, as it
becomes financially possible, there should be systematic

policyholder conferences.

"(3) Insurance at cost. A fair but not exorbitant return on capital.

"(4) To strengthen sponsoring co-operative and educational organizations financially and otherwise .... there should be every effort to fulfil this intention, which went beyond remuneration of these organizations for expenditures in promotion of insurance.

"(5) The co-operative insurance program must at all times remain co-operative in spirit and, so far as possible, in fact. This means that, so long as the program is organized as a joint stock company, co-operatives or other democratic organizations, and not individuals, must hold a majority of the common stock and control the company ...."

UCO accepted the 12-point proposal "as a fair and constructive effort to meet today's problems and needs," but "as majority shareholder it can assume such large responsibilities, to the various organizations, and to present and future policyholders, only on the understanding that the co-operative insurance program remain as flexible as possible within the limitations imposed by public regulation. In the event of some now unforeseen problem or crisis arising in the co-operative insurance program, United Co-operatives, after consultation with the other sponsoring organizations, must be considered free to take such decisive and fundamental action as it may be convinced is necessary ...."

Savage and Betzner moved approval of mailing the UCO statement to policyholders and shareholders with the notice of the special general meeting. Milburn and Savage moved approval and mailing of the nine-month audited statement.

As yet no date was set for the special meeting, but Co-operators Insurance Association was taking shape. Ontario letters patent were issued on November 1, 1950. The first minute book of the new company records organization meetings on Monday, November 6, that did not take place or were sparsely attended, but makes no mention of a full board meeting that had taken place a week earlier. To waive "defects and irregularities" the nine board nominees (at their convenience) signed minutes, prepared by Mitchell, of a meeting of provisional directors at 2:15 p.m. on November 6, when each subscribed for one share, a special and general meeting of shareholders at 2:30 p.m., to organize the company and elect directors, a directors' meeting at 3 p.m., when they enacted by-laws and each subscribed for an additional 19 shares, and a resumed shareholders' meeting at 3:30 p.m. to confirm the by-laws. At these meetings Stauffer was chairman and Betzner secretary. Perhaps those attending with Mitchell were Stauffer, Betzner and Savage.

Chapter 47

Impasse

For the unrecorded CIA meeting on Monday, October 30, 1950, UCO president Stauffer was chairman, with the other eight directors of the new insurance company all present, and Hebb sitting beside the chairman. The five new directors from UCO were not particularly aware of the breakdown in Co-op Fidelity's representation plan that had determined Harman to seek reorganization. None of them had attended the annual meeting in February, and only Stauffer was a Co-op Fidelity shareholder. Most of the UCO debate had been whether to invest such a large amount of money in so doubtful an enterprise.

Prior to this meeting the UCO directors had discussed who the officers should be, and perhaps had been influenced by Hebb's plea to the UCO board on August 3 to be fair to the minority directors representing the OFA and the OCUL. But election of Savage as president took Hebb completely by surprise. Savage may have had some earlier intimation that he was to be president, for he said he would accept on the condition that he spend two days a week in the office.

The meeting proceeded to the election of first and second vice-presidents, perhaps Betzner and Rice, but more likely Rice and Betzner, as Stauffer tended to be critical of Betzner because of his association with R. J. Scott's attempt to win control of the United Farmers' Co-operative Company board in 1945. There was then a motion to appoint Hebb general manager, but Hebb said that he could not accept. Why not? he was asked.

Savage's election was Hebb's opportunity to forget that Savage had associated himself with the charges of mismanagement and his contribution to the breakdown of the representation plan at the Co-op Fidelity annual meeting, Savage's subsequent failure to resign as requested by the board, and his tendency to encourage the board not to accept the general manager's recommendations.

The new UCO directors were being generous to one of the minority sponsors, just as Hebb had requested on August 3, and were indicating by a magnanimous gesture that they were not going to dominate the board. However, they had given Hebb no prior warning of their intention and he had no opportunity to discuss this surprising development with Harman, president of the old company and architect of the new, or Milburn, vice-president of the old company and chief promoter of automobile insurance. Neither was present.

Why not accept the appointment as general manager? Because of the election of Savage as president, Hebb replied. "It was Mr. Savage who broke the gentlemen's agreement and forced the reorganization. And, besides, there is no need for the president to spend two days a week in the office."

In the ensuing discussion Hebb asked Savage what he would do in the office. "Answer letters," was the reply. The board decided to adjourn and give Savage and Hebb an opportunity to talk it over. Savage would visit 30 Bloor Street West the next week.

"We didn't know anything about insurance," Stauffer said after the meeting. "We thought Savage was the only board member who knew enough about insurance to be the president."

"I told them that wouldn't work," Bailey said when told of the election of Savage. "Those fellows are entirely different - they couldn't work together."

The following Monday Hebb, at the request of Savage relayed by Bailey, sent out a notice for a Co-operators Insurance Association board meeting on Friday, November 24, at 11 a.m. Co-operators' Fidelity and Guarantee Association would hold its final board meeting the afternoon of the same day, four struggling years and nine contentious months after its organization on February 26, 1946.

On Tuesday, Savage visited Hebb at 30 Bloor Street West. "I won't interfere," he said, but Hebb was adamant. Savage did not offer to serve as president without spending time in the office, and Hebb did not offer to serve as general manager on those terms, missing the chance to let the UCO bind the urban-rural wounds, and make a fresh start. In addition, Savage might have re-established the whole-hearted support of the Ontario Credit Union League, which was beginning to drain away and would not be recaptured until after Donald R. Bell, League president, joined the CIA board in 1963.

Hebb thought, however, that election of Savage as president would be undeserved vindication of his actions at the February annual meeting. Hebb felt strongly, moreover, that to accept appointment as general manager, and thereby seem to approve Savage's election as president, would be desertion of, and disloyalty to, the Ontario Federation of Agriculture and those who had demanded Savage's resignation as a Co-op Fidelity director. Hebb was prepared to lose a job he had grown into but had never sought.

Savage reported the impasse to Bailey, and, putting the interests of the company before personal position, agreed to treat the meeting which elected him president as not having taken place, provided that the League executive agreed. UCO president Stauffer was to visit the League and the OFA to secure their approval of a new board election. Would the League agree or would CIA lose League sponsorship? Or would Hebb lose his job?

When farmer Dan Stauffer met with the League executive at the Royal York in Toronto on Saturday, November 18, 1950, to mend fences, he knew at least five of the credit unionists. They were, like himself, co-operative banking pioneers - OCCS president Savage of course, OCCS vice-president and UCO solicitor Mitchell, OCCS director and League past president Cy Watson, League president J. M. Best, who had become the Credit Society manager during the summer, and OCCS director John Hallinan, who as League manager had been the first manager of the Credit Society. In May Stauffer had replaced N. M. Marshall, his predecessor as UCO president, as an OCCS director. Stauffer met also, perhaps for the first time, three residents of credit union city Hamilton - League vice-president Aubrey Dalgleish, League comptroller Percy Quinton, just elected that very day a Credit Society director, and League director John Homer.

Stauffer presented his case tactfully. Sensing Hebb's lack of

popularity in League circles, Stauffer pluralized the difficult manager:
Some of the personnel of CF&GA stated their refusal to work with the new company, when it is established at the first of the year, if Mr. Savage is president. Mr. Savage was elected president by the provisional board. Those objecting to Mr. Savage as president have agreed they will continue to work if Mr. Savage becomes vice-president, and Mr. Rice of New Liskeard is president.... Harmony is necessary in this situation and, if the present manager leaves, the new company would run the risk of not getting anyone as quickly as needed to run the business, thus making the situation more critical.

Savage endorsed Stauffer's remarks. He was prepared to step down to vice-president or, if necessary, to resign, because "the objectives are greater than any of the individuals." He added that he had told UCO that "whatever he does regarding this situation must be done with the approval of the executive committee of the League."

"We should go along with the proposal," said Mitchell, but Watson disapproved: "How long are we going to compromise?"

In this impasse president Best, who as Credit Society manager had to try to hold credit unions and co-operatives together, left the chair to urge acceptance of the proposal: "We have Mr. Stauffer's assurance that this would be a compromise to end compromises." Mitchell felt that "in the interests of harmony, and with the possibility of the new company being left without a manager, we should go along with this compromise." Mitchell supported Best, and then Dalgleish and Mitchell moved concurrence in the proposal. Watson asked that his dissenting vote be recorded.

Stauffer left happily, and CUNA and CUNA Mutual Canadian manager Gordon Smith was welcomed to the OCUL executive meeting. Smith was no ordinary visitor. First League president, welcome at all board and executive meetings, his suggestions usually enjoyed majority support.

Due to severe losses in Canada, Lumbermen's Mutual Casualty Company would not continue to provide, through CUNA, credit union bonding insurance and CUNA was seeking another "carrier," Smith reported. (This was a setback, but, in Ontario, Co-op Fidelity offered bonding insurance and might be able to fill a gap - an option which he did not discuss.)

Smith's next announcement was "dynamite" - Co-op Fidelity's partner, Co-operative Life, had proposed a move which might cost both companies the goodwill of Ontario's credit unions. Co-operative Life had asked CUNA Mutual to vacate the credit union loan and savings insurance field in Canada; and, at a CUNA meeting in Detroit, Canada's so-called "national directors," Best and Watson, and CUNA Mutual director Mitchell, had pronounced strongly against this step - proposed, it was said later, in a spirit of Canadian nationalism.

Ontario co-operators and credit unionists, however, did not share in anti-Americanism. UCO was linked with USA co-operative wholesales, and Co-op Fidelity and its sponsors, and the Ontario wing of Co-operative Life, were asking and receiving extensive USA help. As a member of the Co-operative Union of Canada (CUC) executive, Savage said that he knew of no occasion when this Co-operative Life proposal had been promoted or considered by the CUC. (In January the League directors had authorized participation in a Co-operative Life pension plan, and had agreed to "contributions on behalf of employees who wish to participate.") On motion of Quinton and Watson, the executive "reaffirmed" its position that loan protection and life savings insurance and group life insurance for credit unions in Ontario should be sold only by CUNA Mutual Insurance Society, and asked that CUNA Mutual be "notified of this motion."

Mitchell informed the executive that CUNA Mutual had decided to invest up to $100,000 in mortgage loans in Canada at four percent (and to pay $50 toward legal fees on each mortgage), and was trying to secure an amendment to Wisconsin law to permit broader investments in Canada.

The League (OCUL) executive turned to another troublesome subject - Ontario Co-operative Credit Society (OCCS). Back in 1946 a League annual meeting had turned down a proposal to develop OCUL's "Central Credit" into an Ontario co-operative savings and loan organization "as a separate entity in the credit union family." Instead, on motion of P. J. Mulrooney and United Farmer William G. Nicholson, the delegates decided to explore with the Ontario Co-operative Union the possibility of establishing a co-operative loan and savings association "which would serve both the credit unions and various other types of co-operatives in Ontario." Citing the example of Saskatchewan, Leonard Harman took a positive part in the discussion then and again at the 1947 annual meeting. When OCCS came into being it did not replace Central Credit, and now in the autumn of 1950 each had its own manager. Although the OCCS manager was OCUL president, and the OCUL (Central Credit) manager was an OCCS director, the two co-operative central banks-to-be were competing for credit union funds.

At this League executive meeting Best reported that office space provided free to OCCS by Co-op Fidelity was not satisfactory, and, perhaps to get OCCS back into the credit union mainstream, asked permission to share the League's own space on another floor of the same building at 30 Bloor St. West. The executive asked general manager Hallinan to report on space available. At the same meeting the executive increased his salary from $3,900 a year to $4,500, possibly to catch up with the Credit Society manager's salary. Central Credit had the inside track. Intended to unite and serve credit unions and co-operatives, "Co-op Credit" was destined to be divisive.

With the earlier election erased, the new insurance directors, meeting the following Friday, November 24, elected one of the UCO nominees, C. Foster Rice, manager of a farm supply co-operative at New Liskeard, president; OCUL nominee A. C. Savage first vice-president; and OFA nominee Kenneth M. Betzner second vice-president. Born in Quebec province, Rice, now 48 years old, grew up on a farm in Temiskaming district of northern Ontario, and graduated from Haileybury School of Mines. He worked as a prospector for mining companies for many years, and during the second world war was a construction superintendent on the Alaska highway.

They appointed Harman secretary, Shea treasurer, and Hebb general manager, effective January 1, 1951, "at a salary of $6,000 a year with authority over all the operations of the company including the distribution of automobile insurance and the appointment and supervision of agents."

The statement that the agents were under the control of the general manager rather than under the independent control of Staples as distribution manager of the "Ontario Co-operative Insurance board" was part of the growing disagreement with Co-operative Life Insurance Company. Savage and Best, of course, knew that Co-operative Life was proposing to replace CUNA Mutual as the source of credit union savings and loan insurance in the English-language provinces.

The Co-operators Insurance Association (CIA) board appointed an executive consisting of the president and two vice-presidents, established its head office in Toronto at 30 Bloor Street West, decided that common shares would be 50 percent paid, agreed to apply for an insurance licence, agreed to purchase from Co-operators' Fidelity and Guarantee Association all its "assets and undertaking," and decided to invite the managers of the four sponsors (including Co-operative Union of Ontario) to all board meetings. Only the directors and probably Mitchell attended the morning meeting.

In the afternoon the directors and Bailey and Hebb were present. On motion of Savage and Anderson, the board instructed the solicitor not to take any action about an agreement among the sponsors about board representation. On motion of Nephew and Anderson, the board appointed the executive and the general manager as a committee to negotiate an agency agreement with Co-operative Life. It was "agreed that it was essential that the Ontario company have control of Ontario agents." In asking Co-operative Life board for an appointment in Regina for an Ontario committee, Harman was to say that "the Ontario board considered it unwise to go on with the present arrangement indefinitely."

Immediately following the board meeting there was a special general meeting of shareholders, who conveniently were only the board members, to confirm the by-law to purchase Co-op Fidelity assets and liabilities. Harman was not present at these meetings or at the final meeting of Co-op Fidelity board which enacted by-laws to sell the business and to make application to surrender the company's charter, and approved the calling of a special general meeting of policyholders and shareholders to confirm these by-laws.

Chapter 48

Co-op Fidelity Turns a Profit

A covering letter over the names of all nine Co-op Fidelity directors, and agreed to by all of them, went out with the notice calling a special general meeting on Monday, December 11, 1950. The meeting would take place at the Royal York Hotel, perhaps to help everyone forget the meeting 10 months earlier at the King Edward. The notice had to go to both policyholders, more than 8,000 of them by this time, and 779 shareholders.

"The purpose of the meeting is to consider a by-law authorizing turning over the business of the present mutual company to a joint stock company in which United Co-operatives of Ontario will have a controlling interest," the directors said. "Policyholders will not have a vote in the new company but [shareholders] will receive one share in the new company for each share they hold in the present company."

The enclosed, audited financial statement, to September 30, taken off before the onset of winter automobile claims, showed a deficit reduced to only $1,042. The gift from Toronto District Rural Co-operative had taken the form of UCO preference shares worth $1,809 (as there was no immediate market for these shares, which were part of the UCO reorganization of 1948, a proposal that this gift would go in cash to FIIA - to provide a market for Co-op Fidelity shares - fell by the wayside).

The directors' letter explained that "because of insurance accounting practices the statement of assets does not show about $8,000 in equipment which the Association has purchased and paid for in the last two years." (Desks, chairs, filing cabinets and typewriters were "unadmitted assets." The directors could have commented that in reality, with this uncounted equipment, the company had a substantial surplus. However, there was another reality - unearned premiums were calculated at 80 percent and, even counting the equipment, the company would have had a deficit on a 100 percent unearned basis. In other words, if the earned premium had been calculated on a true count of expired calendar days, as the chief insurance supervisor had proposed but had not as yet required, it would have been considerably less than the $131,160 shown on the financial statement, causing an underwriting loss instead of a profit.)

"Objectives of the proposed reorganization are to secure additional capital and to provide stable control," the directors continued. The 12-point proposal (enclosed) had been approved by the Co-operative Union, the League and the OFA, "and was recommended by the board of United Co-operatives of Ontario to a meeting of its 140 member co-operatives and was approved by them." Co-op Fidelity board of directors "now recommends this proposed reorganization for your approval."

Chapter 49

Buoyant Sales
Despite Restrictions

Meanwhile company operations went on. Margaret Chambers as accounting manager, Ernest Moores as office manager and Bernard Shea as underwriting manager, and supporting staff, struggled with new situations almost daily. Even more vital were the company's sales activities throughout the province. Credit unionists, particularly in Toronto, like Karl Roche, St. Peter's Parish credit union and a Toronto chapter president, Harold Anthony, Toronto Police Employees credit union, George Scott, Terminal Employees credit union, Earl Babcock, Ontario Telephone Employees credit union, and C. W. Lang, Tech (Toronto) credit union, were directing applicants for automobile insurance to the company. Stellar credit union at the Toronto Star office was an active supporter. In Hamilton, Joseph Bonner was a helpful shareholder. An employee of National Steel Car Corporation, Bonner was a founding member of Nasco Employees' credit union and one of the first directors of Wentworth Co-operative Medical Services. Credit unions were forbidden by the superintendent of insurance to make out applications or quote rates for their fellow members, but in Toronto they sent applicants to the Co-op Fidelity office or provided prospects for Jeff Bradford or Mrs. Violet Davis.

The superintendent's office imposed these restrictions on credit unions at the insistence of the Ontario Insurance Agents' Association, which was a "general insurance" organization. Life insurance agents weren't worried about competition from co-operative companies, and there were no similar restrictions on the use of CUNA Mutual Insurance Society manuals. CUNA Mutual mailed out its manuals freely, and credit union leaders freely helped their fellow members to apply for life insurance.

Part-time non-life agents were not permitted in municipalities of over 10,000 population, except for lawyers and real estate salesmen who had held licences for some years. But the Ontario Insurance Agents' Association was unable to persuade the superintendent of insurance or the government not to license part-time agents in rural areas or to persuade the superintendent not to allow a farmer to qualify as a part-time agent on the ground that he was "engaged in what is commonly accepted as full-time employment".

As a result, and because it was the farm people who had raised the necessary capital for automobile insurance, it was in the rural areas that most automobile policies were written in 1949 and 1950. In 1949 Grey county, with 668 policies, and Huron, with 666 policies, together produced a quarter of all policies issued by Co-op Fidelity. Bruce produced an additional 450. These were the counties where Farm Forum and the county Federations of Agriculture were strongest too. Production in these three counties was about a third lower in 1950, with Lambton county moving up to write almost as many policies as Bruce.

County Federation of Agriculture leaders and county insurance committee members worked side by side with the agents. They were all farmers together, with some of them as agents receiving enough in commissions to pay their automobile transportation costs. With more talent for selling, or in more productive territory, or receiving more committee help, a number of agents earned more than enough to pay travelling expenses. A few were leaving their farms for full-time insurance careers. The committee members discussed the agents' underwriting problems, or remuneration problems, and, if they were more sympathetic, took up the cause with field supervisor, or head office, or maybe with Ontario Federation of Agriculture insurance wing, FIIA. OFA or Co-op Fidelity meetings were favorite forums for agent, county Federation committee and policyholder complaints. The farm people made the insurance company their own and it throve under their green thumbs.

Staples mailed weekly co-operative insurance bulletins, with extra enclosures for life-licensed agents. In a September 1950 bulletin he reported that there were 79 automobile policies issued the previous week (eight from credit unions without commission), which was six more than in the corresponding week of 1949, but recently most agents were "on the inactive list."

"If present trends continue, the future is bright indeed," Staples wrote. "Insurance service for our people can be improved, and the cost controlled. Agents, considering all the difficulties, have discharged their responsibilities remarkably well, but there are 157 agents as compared with 130 a year ago, and most of them are experienced. Furthermore, about four new cars have been sold in Ontario this year for every three that were sold last year."

Two days later he put out an "Extra" to announce "The Race for the Refund" - with $3 cash prizes each week for all members of the most successful agent team. There were four geographical teams. Without regard for the success of his team, each agent could win refund of his $15 (urban $25) annual casualty licence fee due at the end of September. The next "Race for the Refund" bulletin offered help with that frequent question, "Why do I have to pay my premium every six months - it's such a nuisance? Why not just once a year?" Part of the answer was: "Some of the very largest insurance companies in North America - co-operative and otherwise - use the six-month policy .... The directors felt such advice cannot be disregarded."

The first bulletin with the title "Co-op Fideligram" (accent on DEL) seems to have appeared on October 3, 1950. Shea suggested this name, perhaps as a memorial to the company that was soon to go out of existence. The first issue announced that Bernard Shea would organize a claims department, and that Mrs. Olive Bandy would look after claims records. Keddel & Shea would continue to handle bodily injury claims or property damage estimated at over $500. The Fideligram made only occasional appearances at first and dealt principally with underwriting.

Another Staples bulletin at this time was a carefully prepared statement of the responsibilities and duties of county insurance committees, district agents and local agents. A district agent should become a full-time insurance worker within one year from the date of his appointment as a district agent.

"October Opportunity" was a Canada-wide life insurance campaign, with an Ontario quota of $410,000. Graham Froats, with $41,000, was top Ontario salesman, and produced the Dundas-Grenville sales "almost single-handed." District agents were supposed to develop and help local agents, and Wellington county, under Frank Holliday, produced the best all-round county performance. (Later, Holliday complained justly that he had worn out his car, in the service of Co-op insurance, without compensation.)

An October casualty circular offered strict conditions under which an agent with binding authority could provide automobile insurance coverage by telephone ("hold covered"). Eastern Ontario counties, and southwestern Ontario counties (excluding "west" counties) more than doubled their automobile insurance production in 1950, compared with 1949. Eastern Ontario sales were about half southwestern Ontario sales in both years. The so-called "west" counties, which included Huron, Grey, Bruce and five other counties (with Simcoe and Dufferin the low producers), produced 400 fewer policies in 1950 than in 1949, but still were ahead of the 12 southwestern counties from Wentworth to Essex and Lambton, although George Barclay had found, with committee help, appointed, trained and encouraged a surprising number of new agents.

"Many agents moralize they're being the scapegoats of the insurance program," Barclay reported to Staples in early December. "May I suggest that the management executives of CF&GA (other than distribution) consider their giving out thanks to the agents at effective moments?" But farmer insurance agents were tolerant. Many dropped out quietly - some were disappointed with the remuneration and some felt that they had done their bit to help launch the company. A few complained. Others waited patiently for the company to grow stronger and for renewal service fees to build their remuneration. Harve Hallman, Waterloo county agent with State Farm Mutual background, prodded good-naturedly. Through director Kenneth Betzner, Hallman was responsible for Co-op Fidelity's early provision of a medical payments policy. A policy fee of one dollar permitted purchase of either or both fire-and-theft and medical payments. The general manager was trying to get board approval of a separate policy fee of one dollar for medical payments, with a consequent improvement in agent remuneration.

Chapter 50

Special General Meeting

Only a few agents attended the special general meeting of Co-op Fidelity on Monday, December 11, 1950, and they attended as policyholders or shareholders. A person (or corporation) who was both policyholder and shareholder had only one vote. Sixty-three individuals and 24 corporations were registered to vote at the meeting - 87 votes out of a possible total of more than nine thousand. Without controversy the meeting approved the sale of the company's assets to Co-operators Insurance Association, and authorized surrender of the company's charter.

Harman presided over these final steps in his announced determination to put the Ontario co-operative insurance program under stable, co-operative control. Milburn took the chair to introduce the president of the new company, Foster Rice, who introduced the other board members. Milburn then invited Harman to address the meeting.

Fluently and forcefully Harman reviewed the four and a half years of Co-op Fidelity. Providing his hearers with a 20-point outline of his "remarks," Harman began with "our indebtedness to founders," and went on to "guidance from the United States," reinsurance with the CIS, Manchester, relations with sponsors, relations with life insurance, and agency development. He emphasized the "basic points of auto program - six months, cash, policy fee," and explained two viewpoints about eligibility. Ohio Farm Bureau Insurance and Mutual Service, St. Paul, Minnesota, offered automobile insurance to everyone who could qualify for it, whereas CUNA Mutual offered life insurance to credit union members only, and Indiana Farm Bureau Insurance offered life insurance to anyone, but automobile insurance only to Farm Bureau members and associate members.

Livestock transit insurance had proved less favorable than expected, but had "saved farmers tens of thousands of dollars." There had been attacks on co-operative automobile insurance by competitive companies and agents "through derogatory publicity and unfavorable legislation." Turning to the future, Harman concluded with suggestions about safety programs and accident prevention, and avoidance of non-co-operative trends through a persistent adherence to "basic objectives of savings and service" and participation in "development of progressive people's movements."

Chapter 51

New Board
Gets Down to Business

The board of Co-operators Insurance Association (CIA) met the same afternoon, Monday, December 11. All directors were present except Betzner of the OFA. Of the four secretary-managers, Bailey and Milburn attended, but Hallinan and Hughes were absent. Harman, in his new role as secretary, Shea and Hebb were present. The transfer of assets would not take place until January 1, but the new board was in effective control. Not a member of the new board, but a member of Co-operative Life board, Nicholson attended to report discussions in Regina on Ontario agency arrangements. A committee consisting of Rice, Savage, Betzner, Hebb and Harman would negotiate with a committee of Co-operative Life, it was decided.

There was discussion of investment of the additional capital which the new company would have. The president and the general manager were instructed to discuss investments with the department of insurance. The company was to purchase nine more shares (a total of 10) in Ontario Co-operative Credit Society, and, if the department of insurance agreed, deposit up to $10,000 in the Credit Society. Two Co-operators Insurance Association directors, Savage and Stauffer, were "Co-op Credit" directors and another, OCUL president Best, was manager. Best had been pressing Hebb to increase Co-op Fidelity's deposit in Co-op Credit.

Best reported that Lumbermen's Mutual, sponsored by CUNA, was terminating bonding for all credit unions. (A $50,000 loss in a credit union at Winkler, Manitoba, was the "last straw" for Lumbermen's.) This meant many prospects for CIA, Best said, and he raised the question whether the company should write credit union blanket bonds only for members of the Ontario Credit Union League. (CUNA Mutual wrote loan and life savings insurance only for League members but CUNA wrote credit union bonds for members and non-members.)

The general manager distributed copies of a budget or forecast for 1951. The board authorized him to adjust automobile premiums and approved his proposal to establish a policy fee on medical payments. The company would print the signature of the secretary and stamp the signature of the president on all policies.

That same week of the special general meeting, life-licensed agents travelled to Cherry Hill Farm, Unionville, operated by John and Betty Madsen, who had converted a huge barn into an adult education and recreation centre, for a two-day agents' training school. Each agent brought "a sheet, pillow case and not less than two blankets." Agents would receive extra commission of $2 per $1,000 of life insurance written in the next fortnight, up to a maximum of $30 per agent, to help defray travelling expenses. Term insurance would not qualify.

Wilfred H. McLeod, a jovial and warm member of Co-op Life's head office staff, helped with sales discussions. Leonard Mitchell discussed life claim settlements, and death and income taxes. A retired Sun Life Assurance sales manager for Toronto, Walter C. Rean, threw a new and more favorable light on endowment insurance.

Unaware of Co-op Life's proposal to invade the credit unions, Co-op Fidelity staff members left Unionville with renewed enthusiasm for life insurance and for Co-operative Life, but awaiting them at home were two disturbing headlines in red ink across the front page of the Rural Co-operator of December 12, 1950.

CO-OP LIFE DEMANDS CUNA
QUIT CANADIAN INSURANCE

Editor Kingsley Brown was afraid of neither man nor beast. An experienced newspaperman and a bomber pilot during the second world war, Brown had been a general store operator in West Jeddore, Nova Scotia, when he succeeded Andrew Hebb as editor in October 1949. A writer of courageous editorials, he had been in the editor's chair for only about six months when, striking a blow on behalf of a faltering sheep industry, he raised an angry howl throughout rural Ontario with the question: Is the Dog Necessary?

Let's drop all the silly sentimental eyewash about dogs and admit frankly that they have outlived their usefulness and their welcome.

Now, dropping a bomb on the Ontario co-operative scene, he published as the front-page leading story a statement that "the executive committee of the Canadian District of Credit Union National Association", meeting in Detroit, had declared "unqualified opposition to the suggestion that Co-operative Life Insurance Co. enter the credit union insurance field to provide loan protection and life savings insurance." The meeting asked CUNA vice-president J. D. N. MacDonald of Nova Scotia, a United Church clergyman (who later received a St. Francis Xavier honorary degree), to make a "strong protest" to the CUC and Co-op Life. Under the red headlines was the subhead:

CUNA Protests Against Drive for Monopoly

Protests from three Co-op Life partisans filled one and a half tabloid pages of the next issue of the Rural Co-operator. Lloyd Matheson of Maritime Co-operative Services, Moncton, complained that a suggestion was not a demand. Ralph Staples, Ontario manager of Co-op Life, criticized sensationalism in "a medium dedicated to the causes of truth and light." Co-op Life president H. A. Crofford regretted "such an unfair attack on a co-operative company." Requests "from nearly every province in which Co-operative Life does business to provide loan and share insurance for credit unions" and entry into this field by two other companies within the last two years indicated that "the field is not being adequately serviced at the present by CUNA Mutual." Crofford also enclosed and successfully requested publication of his long Canada-for-Canadians letter to CUNA Mutual managing director Doig.

All this fuss in the Rural Co-operator about credit union insurance meant little to most farm readers, but Harman, Bailey and Stauffer at the UCO, who had just made CIA's peace with the Ontario Credit Union League board, were taken aback. If Crofford could step on the toes of CUNA Mutual, and Canadian CUNA leaders, without prior consultation with the Ontario insurance and Co-op Life advisory board, what would he do next?

Chapter 52

A Going Concern
Takes a New Name

As inevitable as winter, automobile claims were heavier in the last three months of the year - policyholders had to relearn each year how to drive on snow and ice - and Co-op Fidelity's audited statement for 12 months was not as favorable as for nine months. Net profit for the year 1950 was down to $4,468, and the deficit stood at $5,133, but it did not matter - for several reasons.

The company had done much, much better than the $10,000 probable loss predicted in the directors' report for 1949, and owned $8,000 in equipment as an offset against the deficit. Unfortunately for the devotees of economic democracy, there would be no annual meeting and no critics to satisfy.

The company had issued about 5,500 new automobile policies during the year, compared with 4,458 in 1949, and had 9,149 policies in force. The expense ratio had dropped from 74.8 (expenses other than claims as a percentage of earned premium) in 1949 to 44.0 in 1950. Gross premium had increased from $93,000 to $258,000. Payments to Ontario Credit Union League, one of the company's parents, for promotion services increased from $299 in 1949 to $432 in 1950, to county Federations from $2,883 to $3,032. The company had paid dues for the first time to the Co-operative Union of Ontario - the other parent - an amount of $200, and had made its first payment to foster-parent FIIA (Ontario Federation of Agriculture) - the sum of $500.

One debt stood out among many unpaid debts - who could measure the value of the help given to the automobile insurance program by Co-operative Life? Well known as former national Farm Radio Forum secretary, manager Ralph Staples had a key to rural Ontario. Co-operative Life had benefitted from the enthusiasm for automobile insurance, but without Co-operative Life's help it is doubtful whether Co-op Fidelity could have survived. Survive it did, however, and now was turning over a going concern to Co-operators Insurance Association.

Chapter 53

"Fresh Woods and Pastures New" - an Epilogue

Meeting just before year-end 1950, Co-operators Insurance Association (CIA) board decided that the company would bond only League member credit unions, although competitor CUNA (which soon found a new and strong "carrier") bonded members and non-members. League president "Joe" Best made the proposal without adequate prior consideration. In subsequent interpretation and practice, League manager Hallinan agreed that the resolution did not apply to caisses populaires, but, handicapped in competition with CUNA, CIA bonding (at year-end 1950 insuring 158 of 358 English-language League member credit unions, five non-member credit unions and 25 caisses populaires) was soon on the way down. After CIA's managers became jittery about writing bonds for credit unions which cashed payroll cheques or operated store-front "banks" with money stashed in shoe-boxes, the League, by resolution of the directors, stopped sending CIA bonding literature to new credit unions at the beginning of February 1952.

Earlier, UCO board had used its influence to curtail Co-op Fidelity's livestock transit insurance. Now, before the UCO nominees had found their sea legs, they and their fellow directors of the new company were yielding, as it turned out, credit union ground slowly won by Co-op Fidelity. Comfortably and confidently "at home" in their own board room, used rent-free by Co-op Fidelity for four years, the UCO nominees had accepted Best's unhappy proposal as a demonstration of good will toward the League. Eventually, CIA turned its declining credit union bonding over to CUNA.

At this year-end 1950 meeting the directors of the new company asked for a report on the cost of paying themselves for time and expense in attending board meetings. Probable cost of 12 one-day meetings, they were told in February, was $3,000. This seemed to be a lot of money for a company, with a deficit, about to report its first profitable year and an earning of less than $5,000. As a safety measure, Stauffer and Brown wanted to ask the sponsors to pay the per diem and expenses of their nominees, and to be repaid at year-end if CIA had adequate earnings, but they were overruled. The decision was to pay the president $15 a day and other directors $10; expenses would include automobile mileage at seven cents.

The committee which had gone to Regina in January, to negotiate a continuance of joint selling with Co-operative Life in Ontario, reported a cordial reception but unsuccessful negotiations. Former Co-op Fidelity president Leonard Harman, now CIA secretary, who had been a member of the committee, prepared two long memoranda for the board, one on company progress, the other on "Alternatives for Co-operative Insurance." He was away ahead of everyone else. He had concluded that an Ontario agency would not reconcile the interests of Co-operative Life and Co-operators Insurance. Of the life company he wrote: "As a mutual, control could be seized by a busload or two of Saskatchewan people."

Anticipating the shape of eventual reconciliation by a quarter-century, Harman proposed a National Co-operators Holding Company, which would own a national life company, a national fire and casualty company and a national insurance agency.

Twenty years from now, or even ten years from now, some such structure might be possible if sufficient experience and strength can be built in the regions.

For the present, however, "we should study very carefully the requirements for operating our own co-op life insurance in Ontario and attempt to move rapidly in that direction ...."

Later in February, Lynn Matteson of Mutual Service Insurance, St. Paul, Minnesota, came to Toronto to spend two days in discussion with CIA directors. His visit encouraged the board to ask Co-operative Life for a new proposal. In March Jack Rosebrough, general manager of Indiana Farm Bureau Insurance, spent a day with CIA directors and a day with Ontario Federation of Agriculture (at the annual meeting of Farmers' Insurance Information Association). Hoosier Farm Bureau Life Insurance Company, he said, offered life insurance to anyone who wasn't too fat or too thin. Farm Bureau Mutual Insurance Company offered automobile insurance only to members of Farm Bureau, including non-voting associate members, resident in communities of up to 2,500 population. He thrilled his Federation listeners when he said that Indiana Farm Bureau included about 90,000 farm families paying an annual membership fee of $10 each. Nine hundred thousand dollars!

The farmers of the Federation had built the insurance company, CIA president Foster Rice said. Following a luncheon provided by Co-operators Insurance Association, FIIA elected K. M. Betzner of Waterloo president, M. J. Brown of Norval first vice-president and Charles Watson of Cayuga second vice-president. Other directors elected were: OFA president J. C. Brodrick, St. Catharines, OFA first vice-president Clarence A. Milligan, Napanee, OFA second vice-president J. A. Ferguson, Port Stanley, Alex Anderson, Guelph, W. W. Dawson, Peterborough, and Ed Timmins, Carleton Place. Betzner and Brown were to be the OFA's nominees as CIA directors and OFA secretary-manager V. S. Milburn was to attend CIA board meetings as a non-voting participant.

Later in March CIA directors welcomed R. H. Milliken, who had become president of Co-operative Life, H. A. Crofford, now general manager, and Ontario director William G. Nicholson. Negotiation resulted in proposals which Milliken wished to discuss with Co-operative Life's actuary.

In January 1951 CIA's younger "sister", Ontario Co-operative Credit Society, launched in 1949 by Ontario Credit Union League and the Ontario Co-operative Union, had 57 credit unions and 27 co-operatives as members but was not yet profitable. The League's "Central Credit" chairman, Leonard W. Mitchell, who was also OCCS vice-president, proposed to recommend to the OCUL annual meeting merger of Central Credit and OCCS, but the League board voted to delete this recommendation from Mitchell's report. At the OCUL annual meeting in Toronto in April, however, Terminal credit union of Toronto offered a resolution supporting merger. The fat was in the fire! A. C. Savage, for, and Cy Watson, against, were the leaders in the warm debate which followed. A majority of delegates sided with Watson, against merger of Central Credit and Co-op Credit, and the two co-operative banks became open competitors for credit union funds and borrowers. Co-op Credit (OCCS) offered chequing accounts to its shareholders; Central Credit didn't offer chequing.

At the OCUL board meeting which followed the annual meeting, Best retired as president, and Aubrey S. Dalgleish of Hamilton defeated Savage to succeed Best. Savage defeated George Scott to become vice-president.

At a Co-operators Insurance Association board meeting on April 27, 1951, Best resigned as a director "because of increasing responsibilities" as manager of the Credit Society, and was succeeded as a CIA director by J. E. O'Dell of Corunna in Lambton county, as a nominee of the League. At this meeting the CIA directors adopted the UCO practice of reading their expense accounts aloud.

· In June, Milliken brought six other persons with him, including Co-operative Union of Canada secretary A. B. MacDonald, to a CIA directors' meeting. Three members of the group, Milliken, H. A. Crofford and Alex. F. Laidlaw, associate director of extension, St. Francis Xavier University, Antigonish, Nova Scotia, were provisional directors of a national fire and casualty company which Milliken was then organizing.

Negotiations between CIA and Co-operative Life were unsuccessful, but the Ontario sales alliance wasn't easy to unravel. In July, by board resolution, CIA asked its four associates to announce that they were no longer sponsoring Co-operative Life, but UCO board - on motion of CIA president Rice himself! and seconded by Co-op Life employee Musgrave - declined to do so. Subsequently and understandably, the Co-operative Union of Ontario did not "see fit to acquiesce in the request." Ontario Credit Union League did not reply, and Ontario Federation of Agriculture found that its county Federation insurance committees, financed by CIA, were inclined to continue to help Co-operative Life.

It was now apparent that 1951 would be a successful year for CIA. Chief inspector Richards had not imposed, or mentioned again, a 100 percent unearned premium reserve. The company auditors had reported in February that claims estimated at the end of 1949 at $15,191 had cost only $8,162 - the real loss in 1949 had been only a little more than one thousand dollars! - and that well offset by furniture and equipment bought and paid for by the company (unadmitted assets). All that fuss and quarrelling about an imagined loss! However, there was a long-term gain - a new start as a joint stock company under a substantial "trustee."

Another joint stock company advantage was more investment freedom. If the board agreed, and the superintendent of insurance didn't object, CIA could invest in common stocks of Canadian tax-paying companies, with typical dividends of four or five percent tax-free in CIA's hands, compared with about three percent interest, fully taxable, on Canadian government bonds. That would be a marvellous help in building the surplus the company must have to permit growth.

The general manager's recommendation at a meeting in June 1951 to invest in common stocks was a departure from "the co-operative way" (narrowly defined). Secretary Harman favored Hebb's proposal, although his personal philosophy would not allow him to invest his own savings in financial common stocks. The UCO nominees looked to veteran co-operator Amos for guidance. Although not about to accept the stock market as "fresh woods and pastures new," he made no objection, and the board adopted a motion by Savage and Stauffer to invest in industrial stocks and/or bonds up to a limit of 10 percent of assets (which the board changed in September to 25 percent).

In July, after a visit to Indiana and Ohio by Shea, Moores, Barclay and Hebb, the board agreed to abandon the district and local agent remuneration scheme in favor of an "active" and "special" agent plan. The directors agreed to continue to reimburse sponsors for expenses incurred in the promotion of automobile insurance. They also decided that membership in a sponsor would not be necessary to qualify an individual for automobile insurance.

Although denied the presidency of the company he and Leonard Mitchell had founded, "Bert" Savage bore no grudges. Of 12 resolutions at a board meeting in April, Savage had initiated eight. He attended his last board meeting in September, when he asked, as a member of parliament might, for a statement of expenses in four categories and "all salaries paid over $3,000 per annum, and the names of the recipients and their positions." (At UCO, salaries over $2,000 required board approval.) The co-founder of "CF&GA," as he and Mitchell had called the original company, died in October, but the answer to his question may have been the beginning of the company practice of providing each director and every employee with an annual list of all salaries.

In November UCO bought, as a 1951-52 business year transaction, 1,000 CIA shares for $50,000, having bought 500 shares earlier in 1951, as part of its 1950-51 year. The CIA general manager offered to deposit $25,000 of this money in Co-op Credit at two percent if Co-op Credit would redeposit it in UCO at three and a half percent. (UCO was not a bank but at that time accepted deposits from friends and its employees.)

At the CIA annual meeting in March 1952, A. H. K. Musgrave, who had excelled as a co-operative insurance sales supervisor (employed by Co-operative Life), succeeded J. E. Nephew as a CIA director nominated by UCO. After the annual meeting Alden McLean of Muirkirk succeeded Irvin Anderson as a UCO nominee on the CIA board, and Arthur Briggs of Customs (Toronto) credit union took the place of George Scott, nominated by the League to succeed Savage. Scott was unable to leave his employment to attend "week day" meetings; Briggs also found it difficult, and often had to leave meetings early.

Born in Yorkshire, England, in 1900, Briggs came to Ontario with his parents at age seven. At age 16 he enlisted in the Canadian army and served overseas during the first world war. An OCUL director, nominated by his fellow directors to be an insurance director, he joined the CIA board in April and was elected to the OCCS (Co-op Credit) board in October.

"Art" Musgrave brought both rural and urban backgrounds to the CIA board. Born near Seaforth, the son of a Presbyterian clergyman, he was nine years old when his father died in 1903 and his mother took him to Toronto. His extensive experience with automobiles began in the summer of 1916, during his Ontario Agricultural College years, when he worked on a farm near Leamington. His farmer employer taught him to drive his 1913 Willys Overland touring-car and his Willys Overland truck. During the last year of the first world war he spent six months in the Royal Air Force but had not advanced to taking off or landing a plane when the war ended. A few months

after his election to the CIA board, he became a director of
Co-operative Life Insurance Company also, nominated by the
Co-operative Union of Ontario.

Musgrave, Briggs and McLean did not participate in a springtime
tour, led by CIA president Rice, of the other directors (without "per
diems"), of Farm Bureau insurance companies in Ohio, Indiana and
Michigan. On their return the six travellers reported unanimously that
CIA needed a life insurance program in order to build a full-time
agency force. The board appointed a committee to make life insurance
"representations." The committee met without Harman or Hebb, and
at the following board meeting president Rice, as a committee
member, reported that "the committee felt it was not possible to
organize our own life insurance company at the present time."

CIA board meetings were first-rate, debate lively, with Bailey
usually "sitting in," Milburn and Hughes sometimes present and
Hallinan, with the League, its "Central Credit" and a contentious
board of directors to manage, absent. The sponsor-picked directors
came from diverse directions and interests, and the company dealt in a
commodity which everyone thought he understood - money! There
were detailed written management reports at a time when the UCO
general manager was reporting orally. Annual meetings were
co-operatively acceptable, if not democratic, because secretary Harman
insisted on worthwhile guest speakers, and, although unable to vote,
policyholders and agents (known later as "field underwriters")
provided criticism based on experience and asked pointed questions.
However, the election of directors was as cut-and-dried as in a 15-
minute annual meeting on or near Bay Street.

In February, 1953, on motion of Betzner and Musgrave, the
directors, unasked, increased the general manager's salary from $6,000
a year to $8,000, effective from January 1. In 1952 the company had
sold 36 fully paid $100 preference shares and at year-end, after income
tax of $13,000, had added $20,000 to surplus of about $7,000 at the
end of 1951.

When Co-operators Insurance Association announced its first share
dividend (five percent) in March, 1953, some shareholders had waited
seven years! After the annual meeting in that month, Harman resigned
as secretary, to give his full time to UCO as locals manager. At the
same time Ralph Staples who had retired from the UCO board in
December 1951, resigned as Co-operative Life manager in Ontario, to

become full-time president of the Co-operative Union of Canada, a position in which he laid a foundation for the eventual coming together of Co-operators Insurance Association and Co-operative Life.

A two-page statement of "Guiding Principles and Objectives," adopted by CIA board of directors in March 1953, said:

> *Our co-operative insurance organization represents co-operative action in the broad field of insurance because it is owned and controlled by democratic co-operative organizations. Our company can have only one basic purpose - "Service to People."*

Corporate Abbreviations

CBC	Canadian Broadcasting Corporation
Central Credit	a department of the Ontario Credit Union League
CF&GA	Co-operators' Fidelity and Guarantee Association
CFA	Canadian Federation of Agriculture
CIA	Co-operators Insurance Association
CIS	Co-operative Insurance Society, Manchester, England
Co-op Credit	Ontario Co-operative Credit Society
Co-op Fidelity	Co-operators' Fidelity and Guarantee Association
Co-op Life	Co-operative Life Insurance Company, Regina, Saskatchewan
COPACO	First Co-operative Packers, Barrie, Ontario
CUC	Co-operative Union of Canada
CUMBA	CUMBA Co-operative Health Services, Toronto
CUMIS	Canadian life and casualty insurance subsidiaries of CUNA Mutual Insurance Society, Madison, Wisconsin, but operating independently
CUNA	Credit Union National Association, Madison, Wisconsin
CUNA Mutual	CUNA Mutual Insurance Society, Madison, Wisconsin
CUO	Co-operative Union of Ontario
FIIA	Farmers' Insurance Information Association, a subsidiary of Ontario Federation of Agriculture
OCCS	Ontario Co-operative Credit Society
OCU	Ontario Co-operative Union, predecessor of Co-operative Union of Ontario
OCUL	Ontario Credit Union League
OFA	Ontario Federation of Agriculture
RCAF	Royal Canadian Air Force
UCO	United Co-operatives of Ontario
U. F. Co-op	United Farmers' Co-operative Company
UFO	United Farmers of Ontario
United Farmers	United Farmers of Ontario or United Farmers of Ontario and United Farmers' Co-operative Company

Index of Persons

Supplementary Notes

Reviewing the completed text, the author and editor decided upon the following final modifications to improve the consistency and accuracy of the text.

Page 78, paragraph 1, line 1 — MISSPELLED WORD
country should read: *county*

Page 85, point (4) at bottom of page — PUNCTUATION
to end of first sentence add period (.): ... *extensively.*

Page 89, paragraph 2, line 11 — TEXT CHANGE
replace
The League then had only about 50 member credit unions ....
with:
The League then had fewer than 300 member credit unions ....

Page 104, paragraph 2, lines 5 and 8; and paragraph 3, line 2
— PUNCTUATION
remove punctuation, period (.), after *Miss.* to read: *Miss Chambers*

Page 183, paragraph 2, line 1 — PUNCTUATION
add square bracket: *[At an annual ....*

Page 183, paragraph 3, line 4 — PUNCTUATION
remove punctuation, period (.), after *Miss.* to read: *Miss Macphail*

Page 213, paragraph 2, line 5; and paragraph 3, line 3 — PUNCTUATION
remove punctuation, period (.), after *Miss.* to read: *Miss Chambers*

Page 257, paragraph 5, line 2 — TEXT CHANGE
replace
seems to have appeared on October 3, 1950. Shea suggested this name, perhaps as a memorial to the company that was soon to go out of existence. The first issue ....
with:
may have first appeared in 1949. Shea suggested this name, which became a memorial to the company which was soon to go out of existence. An October 1950 issue ....

Page 268, paragraph 1, line 6 — MISSPELLED WORD
eventally should read: *eventually*